THE EMPEROR'S GOD

Imperial Misunderstandings of Christianity

D. Michael Rivage-Seul

The Institute for Economic Democracy Press

Copyright © 2008 by D. Michael Rivage-Seul

We believe all ideas should have maximum exposure. Thus for any properly cited individual quotation up to 500 words no permission is necessary. By expanding upon parts of this manuscript, or nesting your work within the framework of this in-depth study, you can present a clearer picture while producing a book in six months as opposed to 6 to 10 years. Permission will be granted (ied@ied.info). The authors, the Institute for Economic Democracy, and their officers and supporters, specifically retain full rights to this and other published research so that others may use it, correct it, expand upon it, and produce an ever-more powerful and workable plan for world development and elimination of poverty. At only the cost of alerting others to this unique research, universities and serious progressive groups within the developing world will be granted the right to expand upon this work, translate, and publish. Please request the latest manuscript.

Published by: the Institute for Economic Democracy Press
313 Seventh Ave., Radford, VA 24141, USA
888.533.1020 / www.ied.info / ied@ied.info

In Cooperation with the Institute on World Problems
www.worldproblems.net

ISBN 978-1-933567-17-4 (pbk) – ISBN 978-1-933567-15-0 (hdbk)
1. Religion. 2. Liberation Theology. 3. Empire. 4. Fundamentalism.
5. Economics. 6. Politics. I. Title
BT83.57.R58 2008
230–dc22

2008020768
The above were provided by The Library of Congress
7. liberation theology 8. Fundamentalism 9. Christianity–Essence, genius, nature

Book cover designed by Linda Kuhlman
This book is printed on acid free paper.

TABLE OF CONTENTS

Introduction. i
Foreword iv

I
MISUNDERSTANDINGS ABOUT FUNDAMENTALISM

1. Once a Fundamentalist, Always a Fundamentalist 3
2. Only Fundamentalists Are Truly Christian 9
3. Christian Fundamentalists Resist the Modern World;
   Liberals Cave In. 17
4. Liberal Christianity Seeks Domination Too 25
5. Fundamentalists Interpret the Bible Literally (Sometimes). 35
6. God Supports Fundamentalist Politics. 43

II
MISUNDERSTANDINGS ABOUT THE BIBLE

7. There Is Only One God 53
8. Eve Sinned First 59
9. Abraham Would Have Killed His Son for God. 69
10. Jesus Is God's Only Son 73
11. Apocalypse Is about the End of the World 85

III
MISUNDERSTANDINGS ABOUT THE CHURCH

12. Christianity Is Compatible with Empire 97
13. Churches Committed to the Rich or to the Poor
    Worship the Same God 105
14. (Left) Politics Has No Place in Church 117

IV
MISUNDERSTANDINGS ABOUT CONTEMPORARY ISSUES

15. Fundamentalists Reject Darwin. 139
16. Abortion Should Be Outlawed 149
17. God Hates Homosexuals. 159
18. Our Violence Is Holy; Not Theirs 167
19. Activism and Spirituality Are Incompatible. 177

APPENDIX

Clarifying Concepts: Economic Systems 189

INTRODUCTION

I am pleased to introduce Mike Rivage-Seul's important new book, *The Emperor's God: Imperial Misunderstandings of Christianity*. I have known Mike for more than 20 years. Here he shares his personal faith journey to address believers and non-believers, and even those in-between – the former believers, and half-believers – who have somehow "lost faith" in what passes for Christianity in our contemporary world.

Mike's faith journey is a remarkable pilgrimage from being a conservative Roman Catholic priest studying in Rome to a very different view of faith: more challenging, more inclusive and more catholic. His fellow graduate students from other countries asked hard questions. Later, in Brazil, Central American and in revolutionary Nicaragua, he listened to the experience of the poor. Mike began to see his faith and his own country from a very different point of view. He began to realize firsthand how politicians and clergy in power used faith and patriotism for their own purposes.

Mike was forced outside his own frame, outside of the narrow box of assumptions with which he was raised. He had too easily believed that America was the "beacon on the hill" for the rest of the world, that "Might in the service of democracy was Right," and that because of our good intentions, we could not, would not do terrible things to others. Christian missionaries, for example, intended to bring "savages" not only salvation but a better way of life. However, in fact, the missionaries undermined, uprooted and destroyed "native" ways of life.

As Mike relates his faith journey, he summons us to wrestle with basic concepts such as empire, orthodox Christianity, and fundamentalism of all sorts. He shows how these have played major roles in Christian history, both for good and for ill. He looks unflinchingly at such current issues as evolution, abortion, violence, and gay marriage. His deep concern is the message of Jesus of Nazareth: the true meaning of the gospels. He summons us to a new and different view of faith.

What is intriguing to me is that my own faith journey, although quite different, has led me to the same conclusions as Mike's. My walk has also been "in the trenches," not inside organized religion - pulpit or classroom - but *listening and learning* from many others. I have spent thirty years, some 45,000 hours, listening to people's problems mainly as a marital therapist, with an interfaith ministry promoting understanding of diverse Wisdom traditions in Central Kentucky. This ministry has included extensive prison ministry and psychological consulting in organizational effectiveness, as well as college teaching. Like Mike, it is the people, their faith journeys - their heart's desire and dimmed hopes - that have changed me.

Vietnam was also a "wake up" call for me. By then, during the Cold War, I had served in or with all four branches of the U. S. Military, both enlisted and commissioned, active duty and reserve, with two commissions in the Naval Reserve, as chaplain and later as psychologist. When Daniel Ellsberg risked condemnation and personal attack to reveal the Pentagon Papers, we knew then in the middle of that war that our leaders had concluded the war could not be won. Still they sent another 25,000 American young men and women to their deaths. I resigned my second commission and became an activist for peace and justice.

What Mike and I, separately, began to grasp was how easily humans could "absolutize" their belief systems. We humans are, in fact, so constructed that we need, desperately need, something to believe in, outside ourselves. When we find this belief, we can easily, too easily, fall on our knees to give this object, this vision, our exclusive devotion. In effect this belief takes on the aspect of being an idol. It must not be questioned.

Idols have one intriguing characteristic. Idols are jealous of other idols. That is, another idol cannot, simply cannot ever be as precious, as unique and necessary as this singular idol that I have found. Human vanity and pride are already at work. We soon begin to measure the caliber and even the spirit of others by whether they hold the same belief that we hold

The persistent question that Mike addresses is whether this way of thinking, which he demonstrates has many hidden consequences, is part of the revelation we have in Christ Jesus, or whether it is something added on - really contrary. He explains these misunderstandings are not only harmful to building human community, but also detrimental to the kind of faith that can change and remake the world for the better. In other words, the consequences of a non-reflective faith are enormous, actually dangerous to our well being and the future of civilization.

Mike challenges us repeatedly to get out of our boxes, our small conceptual bubbles in which we too easily move, and live and have our being. If we have only been listening part-time, only hearing the mainstream media, we have been lulled into a semi-conscious sleep. Few of us have thought much about empire, or orthodox Christianity or fundamentalism, or their consequences for peace and justice. Except maybe to assume that if we are sincere in what we do we cannot be wrong but will only be helpful.

One of the misunderstandings of humans today is the private belief that if I am sincere, I cannot be wrong and will not harm others. We believe that religious belief is a good and holy thing, not only beneficial and helpful for what is wrong with society. We assume that what we believe is good also for others. Yet, right belief, or orthodoxy, has been employed as justification for burnings at the stake, persecution, torture and killing of countless persons. Even today.

History shows repeatedly that true believers too easily believe God is on their side, - that others should hold the same beliefs as we hold. We too quickly come to the conclusion that others, even maybe most others, are farther from this mystery we call God than we are. We have become the privileged believers, the only ones entitled to speak about God to others.

In this book, Mike repeatedly illustrates that this making of our own belief system an "absolute" is not only harmful to humans and our many projects, but is not a conscious, reflective spirituality. This is not the message of Jesus nor is it the message of other religious founders, either of the Hebrew faith or Islam or Buddhism.

Mike has thought deeply about the consequences of faith, religious faith, nationalism, patriotic faith, orthodox faith and uses of the Bible. More importantly, he has moved outside his own comfortable context to observe and study the consequences overseas of practices and policies that flow from unexamined belief systems. He demonstrates much misdirection and misunderstanding in the Christian endeavor

The tough part of this book is that Mike asks us to examine most everything we hold dear and sacred: our faith, our country, and the Bible. He summons us to a conversation that few of us have ever dared to undertake, much less, to imagine. He wants us to recapture the original view of God's mystery and revelation to us. He believes that this central message is to be found in all the Wisdom traditions.

I guarantee this book will be a challenging journey. However, if the reader is not ready to question the status quo, even religious belief and how it plays out and tends to alienate us-one from another, then please give this book to someone else. This is not a book for those whose strong attachment to the hidden Sacred Cows of our society allows no questioning. Like the Old Testament prophets, Mike asks us to go beyond what most today assume. I have found his writing rich with brilliant insights into the Christian message. Enjoy!

> Here is an anecdote that haunts me still and seems relevant. It came to me once in a dream.
> Satan was walking around with another devil, chatting. They saw a human down the road reach down to pick up something and then put it in his pocket.
> *"What did that man pick up?"* Said the devil to Satan.
> *"Only a piece of truth."* said Satan.
> *"Doesn't that bother you?"* asked the devil.
> Satan laughed. *"Not at all. I will simply turn it into a belief for him. Then in the vanity of his discovery, he will*

believe it belongs to him, that it is uniquely his own."
"What good will that do? Asked the devil.

Satan laughed again. *"Don't you see, stupid? He will be ready to judge all other belief as not as good as his own! Then he belongs to me. He is in our camp and never even knows it,"* and Satan laughed with a loud and long roar.

And he keeps on laughing down through the ages.

"Take care, lest the Light in you become darkness." - Luke 11:35

Rev. Paschal Baute, Ed. D.
Minister of the Gospel and Pastoral Psychologist
Coordinator, Human Resource Management program,
School for Career Development, Midway College, Midway Ky
Author, two books, 14 blogs and some 300 articles,
mostly dealing with a healthy spirituality.
www.paschalbaute.com

FOREWORD

At the beginning of the summer of 2006, a dozen Berea College faculty members spent three weeks traveling in the Middle East. We visited Palestine-Israel, Jordan and Egypt. It was a faculty development seminar to prepare participants for teaching a new required course in Berea's Core Curriculum, "Understandings of Christianity." The trip represented a kind of psychological "dig" excavating strata of Christian belief far below the normal consciousness that support the faith of most believers—including versions adopted by the professor-pilgrims directly involved.

The group explored pre-Biblical sites such as the Egyptian pyramids, the ruins of ancient cities like Jerash, Petra, Megido, Jericho, and Beth Shemesh. We spent a week in Jerusalem, visiting holy places there—the ruins of Herod's Second Temple, the Dome of the Rock, the al Aqsa Mosque, and Christian sites such as the Church of the Holy Sepulcher, the Mt. of Olives, and the Via Dolorosa.

Realities of more contemporary significance were investigated as well—an ultra-conservative Jewish neighborhood where residents, still understandably focused on the terror of the Holocaust, observe a manner of dressing and way of life reminiscent of 19th century European ghettos.

We also stopped in a Palestinian refugee camp where residents reported frequent shootings by Israeli soldiers manning the numerous watchtowers that loomed menacingly over the settlement. At every point we were searched by Jewish security—a sad reminder of continuous and ubiquitous threats from terrifying suicide bombers.

Most appalling were the Palestinian homes and villages destroyed by the Israelis in 1948 during what the Arab world calls the "Catastrophe" (the Jewish invasion of Palestine). That landmark event, we were reminded, represents for Arabs and Muslims their own "9/11." Its continuation is congealed monumentally in a huge stone wall that snakes its way throughout Palestine-Israel. The wall's presence and the Palestinian graffiti that deface it, proclaim irrefutably Israel's ever-expanding system that daily swallows up Palestinian territory, and increasingly confines Arab non-persons to Bantustans reminiscent of South Africa before the end of its detestable apartheid system.

Beyond Jerusalem's inspirational beauty and Palestine-Israel's contemporary horrors, our group visited Mt. Nebo where Moses got his first vision of the Promised Land. We rode camels up Mt. Sinai to witness sunrise there. Cable cars took us to the summit of Masada, where in the first century C.E. Jewish patriots committed mass suicide rather than submit to torture by Roman imperial assailants. Afterwards we swam in the Dead Sea and visited Qumran, where in 1948 ancient Christian texts were discovered that changed scripture scholarship forever. Of course, our trip included New Testament locales outside of Jerusalem—Bethlehem, Nazareth, Capernaum, the Sea of Galilee. . .

We also journeyed across the Red Sea, and poured over manuscripts, artifacts, coins, statues, sarcophagi, and inscriptions in the Museum of Egyptian Antiquity. Such experiences were followed by unforgettable explorations of Coptic (Egyptian) monasteries and churches, filled with exquisite icons and relics dating back to the 4th century of our era, and even before. We were awed by Islamic mosques, Ibn Talun, Sultan Hasan and Rifai'I— and even more by the insightful explanations and deep faith of our Muslim guides. We spent a night in a desert Bedouin camp, beneath a blanket of stars that few of us had ever previously seen.

All of this was prepared for by a series of well-chosen readings, and punctuated by lectures and discussions with experts along the way. We dialoged with historians, archeologists, academicians, bishops, monks, sheiks, professional guides, and practitioners of Islam. We met Coptic, Armenian, and Greek Orthodox hierarchs and priests, along with ultra-conservative Jews on the one hand and Palestinian liberation theologians on the other.

Formal debriefings and less formal conversations over meals and on busses between sites demonstrated the benefit of such unforgettable experience in terms of equipping instructors for our planned course. Not only did we get a better handle on the current situation in the Middle East, we were grasping as never before the incredible variety that currently characterizes (and has always characterized) understandings of Christianity.

As church historian, Dr. Petra Heldt, pointed out in our very first Jerusalem conference, the four basic Christian families [Eastern Orthodox, Byzantine Orthodox, Catholic (and Uniat), and Protestant] not only differ importantly in relation to one another; they have themselves been subdivided many times.

Such divisions, however, find their roots in much earlier varieties of faith that characterized the Christian church's first four centuries. Even the canonical gospels themselves give expression to such variation (concerning, for instance, the identity of Jesus, the Christ) – not to mention the texts found in the mid-1940s in Qumran and Nag Hammadi. Well into the 5th century, Arians (who questioned Jesus' divinity) contended with Gnostics (who understood Jesus as the prototype of the divinity available to all humans), and with Nestorians (who understood Jesus as a human who uniquely became God). Each of these beliefs flew in the face of what portrayed itself as official church teaching for the first time at the Council of Nicea in 325 and of Constantinople in 381. That "orthodoxy" declared Jesus to be a single and unique divine person possessing two natures, one fully divine, the other fully human.

In other words, the most prominent misunderstanding of Christianity is that there is and has been only a single way of understanding Christianity, its foundational narratives, and the conduct inspired by Christian faith. Yet, as Dr. Heldt reminded us, there has always been basic agreement about the uniqueness of Jesus' identity whatever the technicalities of specific explanations. Even Arians did not consider Jesus an ordinary mortal. Jesus and the Father, Arius claimed, were 'like' but not of the 'same' substance (Kamil, *Christianity in the Land* . . . 168).

Such basic agreement, however, did not prevent wars and other acts of extreme violence from being waged and perpetrated at least from the 4th century on in the name of a fictitious orthodoxy. The mayhem attempted to force a single understanding of Christianity on those who would follow Jesus the Christ. Ostensibly, disagreements centered on doctrinal fine points like those just referenced. Did Jesus have two separate natures, or a single nature (a mono-physis, as the Greeks expressed it)? Again, it was Dr. Heldt who put all of this in perspective. The conflicts were not really theological, she said; they were political at root. Claiming otherwise is simply "rubbish."

No, there was a clear political agenda masked by the esoteric theological labels. The project was the Roman Empire's desire to establish control of West Asia (Byzantium). Such raw political ambition on the part of Rome's elite could never mobilize ordinary people to fight and die. Only God could do that. So basically bogus theological reasons were manufactured. (The "rubbish" Dr. Heldt referred to.) The annexation of the East was justified as a defense of a correct concept of God and orthodoxy threatened by a non-existent (or relatively meaningless) "heresy" disputing the divinity of Jesus.

This Book

It is the unmasking of bogus theology advanced in the service of empire past and present that is the focus of this book. The theme is timely in an era when understandings of Christianity in the North American context have been co-opted by imperial forces. Like their Roman antecedents, contemporary colonists understand the necessity of covering naked aggression with a fig leaf of abstract ideological justification.

Obviously, one cannot invade another country with the express purpose of appropriating its resources however valuable and necessary they might be – oil included. Invasion can, however, be justified to defend or spread "democracy," or (more accurately) a particular highly restricted interpretation of the same. Even more so, at least among religious fundamentalists, shrouded imperialism can be advanced to protect freedom of religion or to fulfill biblical entitlements or prophecies like those discovered by ultraorthodox Jews or by Christian fundamentalists in their respective readings of the Old and New Testaments.

Manipulating belief in this way necessitates reducing the great varieties of Christian faith to a single set of convictions about a God that can be understood in one way only. This reduction and accompanying intolerance of diversity is what in the past facilitated the persecution of heretics, the Crusades, the Holy Inquisition, the religious wars which followed the Reformation, the Women's Holocaust, and the persecution of liberation theology with its countless martyrs.

Today reductionist beliefs include narrow interpretations of biblical inspiration, along with readings of Genesis that centralize "original sin" and the subordination of women. Imperial manipulation fosters a willingness to sacrifice children to the whims of a blood-thirsty God – or of those who claim to represent him. It involves identifying the biblical God with the rich elite, and transforming Jesus of Nazareth from a quintessential opponent of empire and champion of the poor, into empire's unequivocal patron and backer of wealth and power. The interests of empire demand a Christianity that understands the end of the world as supporting Israel's "reclamation" of the Holy Land, and the welcoming of the prospect of nuclear war as somehow predicted in the Book of Revelation. Finally, the contemporary demands of empire require spurious wedge issues that for Christians trump every other consideration. Today, these issues include most prominently abortion, evolution, gay marriage and unquestioning patriotism – as well as the rejection of interpretations of the Bible that issue from the poor and oppressed.

Each of these issues will be taken up in the chapters which follow. They are organized categorically according to common misunderstandings fostered by contemporary imperial interests. The theme of "misunderstandings" was originally chosen to complement the title of the new course for which our middle-eastern seminar prepared teaching faculty—"Understandings of Christianity." Complementary too is the centralization of Third World (especially Latin American) experiences of Christianity—particularly in the book's third part. This seems altogether fitting, since the majority of Christians today are found not in Europe and the United States, but in the former colonies. For the sake of coherence, most chapters begin with a reference to *Introduction to Christianity* by Mary Jo Weaver— a splendid textbook used in all sections of the "Understandings" course.

Chapters are divided under four separate headings. The first addresses misunderstandings about fundamentalism. It argues that Christian fundamentalists end up embracing a rather new version of

Christian faith, rather than an "old time religion." The book's second section deals with the Bible. It reflects on inspiration and literal interpretation, on biblical politics, monotheism, the subordination of women, God's apparent approval of child sacrifice, biblical approaches to the divinity of Jesus, and the nature of apocalypse.

The third heading takes up imperially-fostered misunderstandings about the church. These include claims that Christianity is compatible with empire, that God and his church favor the rich, or are, at the very least neutral relative to rich and poor, and that there is only one valid interpretation of Christianity.

The fourth section attends to the spurious issues today's empire has chosen to secure Christian support for its projects. Highlighted here are abortion, evolution, gay marriage, the approval of violence in empire's service, the rejection of liberation theology, and the endorsement of U.S. patriotism. The approach adopted here is in part autobiographical – not only relative to the recently concluded faculty development trip, but to what my own life's experiences have taught me from the beginning about God, the Bible, church and contemporary politics. The distortions alleged here are those purveyed especially by Christian fundamentalism – the U.S. Empire's most important contemporary ally. That allegation, I feel, can be asserted without malice or cant, since I think of myself as a recovering fundamentalist (Roman Catholic version), have taught fundamentalist students throughout my teaching career, and have loved and respected them dearly.[1] My fundamentalist students are among the best-intentioned people I have met. Their sincerity, high moral standards and zeal to understand and spread the Gospel message have consistently challenged and inspired me. It is to those students past and future that I gratefully dedicate this book.

Mike Rivage-Seul
San Miguel de Allende, Mexico
July, 2008

---

[1] The Roman Catholic church has been traditionally perhaps the most conservative force in the world. As indicated in the following chapter, I grew up and was educated in that church from kindergarten through my doctoral studies. During the entire process, all of my teachers, except perhaps one or two, were either nuns (through 8th grade) or priests. The orientation was virulently anti-Protestant. Catholic church teaching during that time was shaped by the Council of Trent (1543-'63), and more immediately by Pope Pius IX's *Syllabus of Errors* (1864). Of the Latter, Mary Jo Weaver writes that it "summarized eight modern errors and enjoined Catholics to avoid naturalism, socialism, communism, the conclusions of modern biblical scholarship, modern political arrangements like the separation of church and state, freedom of religion, ethical theories, and even the idea that the Roman Catholic church should reconcile itself with the modern world" (146-47). Until my early twenties, I whole-heartedly

embraced such rejectionism. Only in 1942 did Pope Pius XII give Catholic scholars permission to access the benefits of modern biblical scholarship. But that change did not filter down to me personally, till my early twenties, and has still left most Catholics unaffected. It wasn't until the Second Vatican Council (1962- '65) that the Church began to open itself more fully to the modern world. That precarious process of aggiornamento (as Pope John XXIII called it) is very much in process, and under fire by two consecutive reactionary popes, John Paul II and Benedict XVI (147).

Part I

MISUNDERSTANDINGS ABOUT FUNDAMENTALISM

Misunderstanding One:

Once a Fundamentalist, Always a Fundamentalist

Jesus says, "No one lights a lamp to put it under a tub; they put it on the Lamp-stand where it shines for everyone in the house" (Matthew 5:14-15). The most inner light is a light for the world. Let's not have "double lives"; Let us allow what we live in private to be known in public. (Henri Nouwen)

At one point, I taught for several semesters in a Latin American Studies Program (LASP) in Costa Rica. It was a "term abroad" for students whose universities and colleges belong to the Council for Christian Colleges and Universities. They came from Evangelical schools like Wheaton, Calvin, Dordt, Taylor, Seattle Pacific, and BIOLA (Bible Institute of Los Angeles). All of my students considered themselves fundamentalists and biblical literalists. As Christian fundamentalists, they had internalized the political tendencies which the Republican Party has so successfully co-opted into its platforms over the last quarter century. In fact, nearly all my LASP students thought it a matter of faith and a sacred duty to vote Republican.

My heart always went out to those students. They were earnest and sincere, bright and talented. Above all, they wanted to be good, in right relationship with God, and to save their souls. I remember endless conversations with them, about the Bible, revelation, inspiration, and inerrancy. They were intrigued by exposure to Latin American Liberation Theology, but wondered constantly if it was too political, and not spiritual enough. After all, the spiritual life was about praising God, staying pure, and getting to heaven.

I recognized myself in my LASP students. When I was their age, I too had been conservative, Republican, fundamentalist and a biblical literalist – but within the Catholic Church. What kept me that way was my attitude toward the Bible. I accepted it unquestioningly as inspired. The irony I eventually discovered was that as long as I did that, I had no hope of ever becoming a follower of Jesus. After all, he had felt free to reinterpret the "sacred" texts even in ways that contradicted them entirely. Jesus was the one who taught, "You have heard that it was said, 'You shall love our neighbor and hate your enemy. But I say to you, Love your enemies and pray for those who persecute you, so that you may be children of your Father in heaven; for he makes his sun rise on the evil and on the good, and sends rain on the righteous and on the unrighteous" (Mt. 5:43-45).

However it took me nearly a third of my life to draw the liberating conclusion that the Bible was not inspired – at least not the way my pastors told me it was. Allow me to tell my story. At St. Viator's School on Chicago's Northwest side, the good Sisters of St. Joseph (whom I remember fondly in my prayers every day) had taught me that there was no salvation outside the Catholic Church. We were forbidden even to enter the Lutheran Church just down the street from our apartment building on Harding Avenue. I found myself in crisis using the gymnasium at that church to play basketball and box. Was that equivalent to entering the forbidden church? Was I committing mortal sin?

Later, when I entered the Catholic seminary to prepare for the priesthood, my fundamentalism was reinforced. This time it was my professors, all members of the missionary Society of St. Columban, who did the job. The context was my high school years and the early days of the Cold War, just after Columbans had been expelled from China by the new Communist regime there. The McCarthy Hearings were in the news. Returning missionaries regaled us with stories of persecution under the Maoist regime. Communism was the worst category imaginable. I remember the day of Joe McCarthy's death. One of my most admired professors whispered to me during study hall, "A great man died today."

By the time I reached my 20s and was ready to vote for the first time, I was rabidly Republican – though in retrospect, I see that I knew very little of the world or of what "Republican" meant. I cast my first ballot for Barry Goldwater.

Things began changing for me when I entered the major seminary, and started studying the Bible in earnest. It was the era of the Second Vatican Council. As a conservative and fundamentalist, I found myself in full resistance mode – against both modern biblical scholarship and Vatican II reforms. The approach to Scripture study in the seminary was contextual. It took account of the many literary forms the Bible contains. It wasn't all history, I found. There was myth there, and poetry, legend, fiction, law, debate, letters, parable, allegory, miracle stories, apocalypse. . . Besides that, biblical contents were products of different historical periods, and reflected changing understandings of God and the meaning of life. Over the years texts had undergone severe editing, as each generation changed them in order to address new circumstances. Even more shocking, I found that biblical authors were not above inventing events and sayings – even those attributed to Jesus. They had little concern for what we call historical accuracy, which is a modern expectation.

Of course, I resisted all of that. Why not? For me what I was learning represented the thin end of a wedge. Once I would admit that the story of the Wise Men was "midrash," what would stop me from drawing similar conclusions about the resurrection, or about the divinity of Jesus?[2]

With time, however, I saw my resistance was futile. Evidence presented by my professors, the reading I was doing, and my own reflection convinced me that the Bible was historically conditioned and could not be accepted at face value. At first I was devastated. Gradually however I made an astonishing discovery. I found that my faith had actually grown as my contextual understanding of the Bible deepened. I was no longer threatened by the new discoveries and theories of the experts. I concluded that even if they found the body of Jesus moldering in some grave outside Jerusalem, it would make no difference to my faith. I would still believe in his resurrection. After all, it wasn't about the resuscitation of a corpse. It was about the survival of an indomitable spirit.

I was still Republican though. And I stayed that way till, after ordination in 1966, I was sent to Rome for graduate studies. Ironically, that gave me invaluable new perspective on events taking place back home. John Kennedy had been shot. Medgar Evers and Malcolm too. Then King. Then Bobby Kennedy. The Vietnam War was raging. Mai Lai. The Tet Offensive.

All of this put me on the defensive with the young student-priests I was living with on Corso Trieste in Rome. What was happening in the U.S.? What kind of country was it? They questioned me mercilessly. I was at a loss. Worse still, I found that my Irish, Australian and British friends – not to mention the Italians, Spaniards, Africans and Latin Americans at my university – all knew more history, and more about current events than I did. They even knew more about United States history than I did. Besides that, I was getting my first exposure to Liberation Theology. And that demanded I fill in my historical, economic and political blanks that were becoming painfully apparent to me every day. Under all these pressures, I did so with a vengeance. I devoured *Newsweek* and *Time* every week. I read Howard Zinn's *A People's History of the United States*, along with everything by Noam Chomsky I could get my hands on. Above all, I read "outside the culture" as Dan Berrigan had urged somewhere. That put me in touch with Third World thinkers like historian Eduardo Galeano and his *Open Veins of Latin America*, with Walter Rodney's *How Europe Underdeveloped Africa*, and again with liberation theologians like Gustavo Gutierrez, Pablo Richard, and Franz Hinkelammert.

Once more, what I found out was astonishing. The United States was not at all the force for good in the world I had always thought. On the

---

[2] Midrash is one of the many forms of Jewish interpretation of scripture. It is often a highly metaphorical interpretation not intended to be definitive or literal.

contrary, having won the Second Inter-Capitalist War (World War II), the U.S. had decided to exercise Hitler-like control over the entire world. To do so, it imposed and/or supported Hitler-like regimes everywhere. The Hitler stand-ins included D'Aubisson (El Salvador), Banzer (Bolivia), Diem (Vietnam), the Duvaliers (Haiti), Franco (Spain), Fujimori (Peru), Mobutu (Zaire), Montt (Guatemala), Noriega (Panama), Park (Korea), Pinochet (Chile), Resa Palavi (Iran), Saddam Hussein (Iraq), Sharon (Israel), the Somozas (Nicaragua), Strossner (Paraguay), Suharto (Indonesia). . . . And that was the short list. Beginning in the 1960s, the United States was responsible for installing fascist dictatorships in every country in Latin America, with the exceptions of Colombia, Mexico, Venezuela and Costa Rica.

All of this was in accord, I found, with policy guidelines articulated in 1947 by George Kennan, the architect of Cold War policy for the United States. As Director of the State Department's Policy Planning Staff under Secretary of State George C. Marshall, Kennan had written:

> We have about 50 percent of the world's wealth, but only 6.3 percent of its population. In this situation, we cannot fail to be the object of envy and resentment.
>
> Our real task in the coming period is to devise a pattern of relationships which will permit us to maintain this position of disparity without positive detriment to our national security. To do so we will have to dispense with all sentimentality and day-dreaming and our attention will have to be concentrated everywhere on our immediate national objectives. We need not deceive ourselves that we can afford today the luxury of altruism and world benefaction. We should cease to talk about vague and unreal objectives such as human rights, the raising of living standards and democratization. The day is not far off when we are going to have to deal in straight power concepts. The less we are then hampered by idealistic slogans the better. *(Policy Planning 48)*

I could hardly believe what I was reading. Here was an extremely honored, influential, and high ranking U.S. official. Kennan was considered liberal and humanitarian. He was laying out the overall purpose of his government's policy. Yet for him that was not to alleviate poverty, but to keep it in place. It was about establishing international relationships based on pure power – on the law of the strongest. U.S. policy did not prioritize the spread democracy, human rights or high living standards;

rather it considered those objectives "vague" and "unreal." Altruism and world benefaction were "luxuries," not at all the hallmarks of United States policy.

Here was a smoking gun. I had been deceived. I felt let down by my parents, by my teachers, by my church, by my political leaders. Why hadn't they told me? At least that was my question after reviewing "American" history since 1947, in the light of Kennan's words. Subsequently, I came across other official statements like the one just quoted. Tell-all books by ex-CIA agents contained stories that confirmed my worst suspicions. Now I understood why the U.S. had supported all those dictators, why it sent in the Marines so often, why it fought so many wars. It all checked out. The U.S. was a brutal empire, and the churches were its handmaid. (My knowledge of church history reinforced that latter point, as will become clear in Chapter 2.)

By now I was teaching at Berea College in Kentucky. Students there were largely conservative and fundamentalist too, though they all came from working class backgrounds and qualified for the tuition-free education Berea offers to its students. We were studying Dietrich Bonhoeffer together – the Lutheran pastor-theologian who had resisted Nazism in Hitler's Germany. During the Third Reich, he had taken his students underground to help them rethink theological categories that had so lost their punch and meaning that churches in the very heartland of the Reformation had stood by applauding while Hitler spread his evil empire. Precisely as a pastor, theologian and person of faith, Bonhoeffer found himself repelled by "religion" – the pious language, the bowing and scraping before civil and military might, the theology that had lost its meaning for ordinary people. He wondered if Christianity might be liberated from its clutches and saved from fascism.

I identified with Bonhoeffer. I wondered how my own and my students' faith might be saved from U.S. empire. I had now left the priesthood, married, and was raising a family. I continued to love the church; but found that I had become a member of its "loyal opposition." Virtually nothing the Catholic hierarchy did inspired me. Like the church in Bonhoeffer's Germany, its members were cozily in bed with *der Fuhrer's* American successors. That was doubly true for many U.S. non-Catholic Christians. Under the leadership of Jerry Fallwell, Pat Robertson and others, they had become the backbone of the Republican Party. They were caught up with issues of abortion, evolution and homosexuality. Nothing their Presidents might do could possibly disabuse them of their conviction that the Nixons, Reagans and Bushes were extraordinary messengers of God.

I asked myself, what prevented fundamentalists (Catholic and Protestant) from seeing what was unfolding before their eyes? The ghost of

Bonhoeffer reappeared. "Religion itself," he said. It was the saccharine personal piety; focus on the afterlife; surrender of social justice concerns before legislators eager to embrace "cheap grace" issues like abortion, evolution, and homosexuality. Invoking religious principle about abortion and homosexuality cost politicians absolutely nothing but hot air. Neither were fundamentalist taxpayers inconvenienced by their "pro-life" or "promarriage" stands. Instead the issues of focus represented burdens for "those others" – the queers, and young women too poor to afford illegal abortions not administered in some back alley.

Above all, I concluded, the idolatrous treatment of the Bible was behind fundamentalist Christianity's surrender to empire. I continued to love the Bible, but had come to realize that it was a product more human than divine, full of misleading teachings which if accepted as "inspired," "inerrant," or "revealed" inevitably brought war, and would surely lead to the world's destruction.

So the Bible had to go – at least the Bible accepted as an "inspired" book. It simply wasn't. It was a human product of a primitive tribal group committed to its own self-preservation. Its main idea of God was overwhelmingly blood thirsty and cruel. True, religious geniuses appeared now and then among the "People of The Book." Called "prophets" by their admirers, and "subversives" by their enemies, these were the social critics of their day. They genuinely struggled to discern and describe the nature of the intersection between the transcendent and the human, and to answer the question, "What then must we do?" They often described God in less than violent terms. Naturally, these disturbers of Orwellian peace were treated by the guardians of religion the same way social critics are treated today, and wherever they appear. They were marginalized or killed in the name of God.

Conclusion

My conclusion was that following Christ meant following the prophets by engaging in critical thought even about the "sacred" texts. My studies and my own experience told me the biblical tradition was worthy of great respect. It was, after all, as close as we could get to the words and deeds of Jesus of Nazareth and to the religious tradition that played a central role in his life's work. Yet the tradition was not worth following blindly. Doing so, I could see, had repeatedly led to disaster in the form of Crusades, witch hunts, slavery, and wars too numerous to mention. The realization was liberating to say the least.

Misunderstanding Two:
Only Fundamentalists Are Truly Christian

> In broad outline, if one wants to sum up what elements relating to the concept "People of God" were important for the Council, one could say that . . . it expresses the ecumenical dimension, that is the variety of ways in which communion and ordering to the Church can and do exist, even beyond the boundaries of the Catholic Church. ["The Ecclesiology of Vatican II." Cardinal Joseph Ratzinger (now Pope Benedict VI), Prefect of the Congregation for the Doctrine of the Faith. Presented to the Pastoral Congress of the Diocese of Aversa 15 September 2001.]

Given my personal experience just recounted, it should be clear that this book, like most of us personally, has a viewpoint. In this it is unlike, for instance, Mary Jo Weaver's *Introduction to Christianity*, used in Berea's "Understandings of Christianity" course. Weaver's approach attempts to maintain a purely descriptive attitude towards Christianity. This book is different. It is written in defense of a particular position. It holds that some versions of Christianity have been co-opted by forces inimical to the Spirit of Jesus. Those versions should be seen for what they are and jettisoned, because they lead to idolatry of the worst kind. In turn, that idolatry, because of the violence it espouses, is threatening to destroy us all.

As we shall see, cooptation happened in the Catholic Church way back in the 4th century. It was then that the emperor, Constantine, converted to Christianity. By the Edict of Milan, Constantine made the Christian faith legal within Rome's empire for the first time. Christianity thus became "the emperor's faith." Its God became the emperor's God. As Jackson Spielvogel points out in his review of Western Civilization, Constantine's faith was not highly dissimilar from faith in Jupiter:

> Though effective in producing quick conversions, it is an open question how much people actually understood of Christian theology. Popular belief tended to focus on God as a judge who needed to be appeased to avert disasters in daily life and gain salvation. Except for the promise of salvation, such an image was not all that different from Roman religious practices. (Spielvogel 221)

In other words, under Constantine, Christianity became completely supportive of empire - which is, simply put, a system of robbery. Empire results when militarily strong nations invade weaker ones and carry off the latter's natural resources, people (often as slaves), and money (through systems of outright looting and taxation). Those who resist imperial mandates are most often simply killed. Again, as we shall see, Jesus expressly rejected empire at the outset of his public life.

As for Protestant fundamentalism, it too has been largely co-opted by empire. Subsequent chapters will make this argument too. As a peculiarly "American" form of Christianity, the tendency of Protestant fundamentalism, especially since the 1980s has been uncritically to endorse the U.S. system of government, global reach, and attendant militarism, which has increasingly been identified even by our national leaders as expressly "imperial." Of course, the leaders who make such identification do not consider *their* empire as larcenous. Rather, it is for them a system of universal benefaction for all concerned. The problem is that empires from Rome's to Great Britain's have always seen themselves as unqualified benefactors. Invariably, however, those they imperialize beg to differ - often quite emphatically.

Does this mean that fundamentalists (Catholic and/or Protestant) are somehow "*extra ecclesiam*" (outside the true church)? It does not. For too long Christians have been pointing their fingers at other Christians reading those others out of the Church. Again, the Catholic Church with its *extra ecclesiam nulla salus* [outside the (Catholic) church there is no salvation] has been disgraceful on this score. But today many Protestant fundamentalists have tended to follow the bad example set by their Catholic forebears. For instance, the students I taught in Central America took it as axiomatic that Catholics are not Christian. It's time to get away from such exclusion.

The argument here is that the "tent" of the Christian Church is very broad. It covers Christians who are conservative, liberal, and radical, and many others who fall in between or outside those categories. Most (but of course, not all) are sincerely attempting to know and follow Jesus of Nazareth, the Christ, and risen Lord. Over our life spans, our understandings almost inevitably change and develop. At least that has been my own experience.

At the same time, however, such inclusiveness does not mean that all understandings God and modes of being Christian are equal. It must be admitted that some would not be recognizable or acceptable to Jesus of Nazareth. In fact, several of those understandings and ways of acting in the world might well be diametrically opposed to those embraced by the Nazarene. The way to deal with such deviations, however, is not to declare such positions as "heretical," but rather to engage in dialog informed by history and critical thought. It's that latter approach that this book is attempting to express and elicit.

Caravan Vision

To advance that agenda, it might well be useful to switch from the "big tent" metaphor just mentioned to one suggested by my own church's Second Vatican Council. Between 1962 and '65, the Council Fathers elaborated the image of the church as "the Pilgrim People of God." The Council's imagery refers to the core of the Jewish Testament, the Exodus experience. Following liberation, the escaped Hebrew slaves were a people journeying in caravan to the Promised Land. For today's People of God (the inclusive church), there is also a Promised Land—the Kingdom of God that Jesus proclaimed.

The Caravan image helps to explain the various understandings of Christian faith—even those wedded to understandings of God that Jesus might find unacceptable, and which might even be termed idolatrous. The fact is that throughout the biblical tradition, false Gods and idolatry within the community of faith have been the major problems confronted by the prophets. So the flourishing of idolatries within the contemporary People of God should come as no surprise. It is absolutely normal.

So, let's think for a moment of the Christian Church as a Pilgrim People - as a caravan, a group of freed slaves traveling towards the New Jerusalem. Individuals and groups are in various physical locations in the long line of pilgrims encompassing millions of people. Some are in the rear guard, some in the main body, others in the vanguard; still others are "scouts" far out in front of the huge, slowly moving assembly.

In such a long line of people, not everyone's context is the same, so not all see things the same way. Those in the Rear Guard have little idea of what's happening in the Main Body, miles ahead. Similarly, the problems faced by the Main Body have long since been dealt with by the Vanguard.

The Scouts experience a different level of reality altogether - dangers, problems and challenges which those far behind have no way of anticipating.

The Scouts would consider the problems of the Rear Guard as tame by comparison to what they face. In many cases, Scouts would have forgotten the urgency the Rear Guard's problems once had even for them.

Similarly, the predicaments and solutions of the Scouts and Vanguard would seem incomprehensible to those far behind, if indeed, they ever heard of them.

The Rear Guard

To be more concrete, the Rear Guard, i.e. Christian Fundamentalists, whether Catholic or Protestant, are still passing through the 16th century.

	Rear Guard	**Main Body**
Historical Focus	Reformation	Vatican II ('62-'65)
Defining Issues:	Protestants vs. Catholics	Ecumenical Movement Liturgical Renewal Biblical Study
Spiritual Vision	Church & After life	Church After life This World
Representative	Luther Calvin Aquinas Augustine	John XXIII Hans Kung Karl Barth Rudolf Bultmann

They are wrestling with the problems of the Reformation and Counter-Reformation. Catholics in this location still embrace the belief, *extra ecclesiam nulla salus*. They are concerned about such matters as defending papal authority, the use of Latin in the Mass, and the "rhythm" method of birth control. For their part, Protestants in the Rear are busy (especially in places such as Latin America) trying to convert Catholics. "Missionaries" there deny that Catholics are Christians. They accuse them of "Mariolatry," and of worshipping statues. Protestants keep accurate records of the numbers of Catholics converted, and triumphantly send home accounts of their successes to sponsors at home.

The salvation concerns of both Rear Guard Catholics and Protestants focus on life-after-death. They believe God is located "up there," beyond the furthest galaxies, that hell is located "down there", and consists literally in the eternal fires described by Dante. In heaven, the saved will find the "streets of gold," harps and angels which appear in the imagery of the Book

VanGuard	Scouts
Post-Modern World	The Future
Peace Movement Third World Justice Ecology Women's Movement Racism Etc.	Christianity without Religion
This World	Unity of All Creation
Dorothy Day Phil & Dan Berrigan Dag Hammarskjöld	Dietrich Bonhoeffer Teilhard de Chardin F. J. Hinkelammert

of Revelation. Catholics believe they get to heaven by being baptized, receiving the Seven Sacraments, obeying the Ten Commandments and the Precepts of the Church. Protestants get there by "accepting Jesus as your personal Savior." That is, the theological models for both Protestants and Catholics in the rear stem from Luther and Calvin for the former, Thomas Aquinas for the latter, and Augustine for both.

The Main Body

The main body of Christians is ecumenical. Catholics here have embraced the teachings of the Second Vatican Council (1962-'65). Accordingly, they believe that not only Catholics, but also Protestants (as their "separated brethren"), and Hindus, Buddhists, Muslims, and other people of good faith will gain admittance to the heavenly after-life - which, for this group, still tends to be understood in terms familiar to the Rear Guard.³ The faith concerns of Catholics in the Main Body tend to center around Vatican II interests such as liturgical renewal and Bible study that incorporates modern scholarly methods like those endorsed by Pope Pius XII, in his landmark encyclical, *Divino Aflante Spiritu*, published in 1942.⁴ Protestants in the Main Body had embraced both that modern approach to scriptural interpretation and the ecumenical vision long before Catholics joined them in what became the Main Body, having formed the World Council of Churches around the middle of the 20th century. Theological guides for Catholics in the main body include Pope John XXIII, Hans Kung, Edward Schillebeeckx, and Karl Rahner. All of these figures accomplished their most important work during the 1960s. Protestants of that era came to be inspired by the work of Rudolf Bultmann, Karl Barth, Dietrich Bonhoeffer and Harvey Cox.

The Vanguard

Christians in the Vanguard of the Church as Caravan have moved beyond the "churchy" concerns of both the Rear Guard and Main Body. Catholics in this location have taken their cue from the Second Vatican Council's document *Gaudium et Spes*—"The Church in the Modern World," and have applied it to the "post-modern" reality of the 21st century. Neither Protestants nor Catholics in this part of the caravan spend much time talking about their specific church tradition—at least not as "the truth." Rather, such beliefs tend to be referenced in the spirit of dialog

---

³ It should be noted, however, that even the late Pope John Paul II called into question the nature of the after life. In late July and early August of 1999, he gave a series of three talks in which he affirmed the existence of both heaven and hell. However, he referred to them as "states," rather than "physical locations." "Heaven," he said, "is neither an abstraction nor a place in the clouds, but a living, personal relationship with the Trinity." He acknowledged that concepts of hellfire, the fiery furnace and the "unquenchable fire" of Gehenna are all from the New Testament. However all of them need to be understood in terms of symbolic language. Hell is a self-imposed exile by people who have used their freedom to say "no" to God. It is not the punishment of an angry God. The suffering caused by sin, he said, "make life 'hell'." The pope further said that hell might even be empty of human souls. His actual language was that perhaps no one has been "involved" in eternal damnation.
⁴ Here the Bible is seen not as a single book with chapters, written by a single author, but as a library of books written by different authors, at different times, in a wide variety of circumstances. Those authors used various literary forms to express their highly contextualized interpretations of what they understood as God's revelation. The forms include myth, legend, debate, fiction, law, poetry, gospel, parable, allegory, letter, miracle story, apocalypse, and many others. All of these must be understood on their own terms. That is, to mistake the literary form will lead to mistaken meaning. For example, to read poetry or myth as if it were history will lead to misplaced interpretations and meaningless debates—for example to arguments between evolutionists and creationists.

in terms of "what our faith community believes," and how those articles of faith help address pressing world problems. These are attended to by Catholics in concert with Protestants, other people of other faiths, and people of no religious faith at all. High on the agenda of these Christians are problems of war and peace, justice for former colonies (the "Third World"), anti-imperialism, capital punishment, ecology, gay liberation, the Women's Movement, and racism. For the Vanguard, the Reign of God tends to be understood as a this-worldly reality - the "other world" that is possible within the boundaries of history, where there is room for everyone. Questions of life after death are left in God's hands. Models for living this Christian vision include Dorothy Day (the co-founder, with Peter Maurin, of the Catholic Worker Movement); Phil and Dan Berrigan, both Catholic priests legendary for their opposition to war and the arms race; Dag Hammarskjöld (the spiritually insightful former Secretary General of the United Nations), and Martin Luther King, Jr.

Scouts

Scouts in the Caravan of God's Pilgrim People have their eyes intently focused on the other world that is possible within the boundaries of history. The martyred Lutheran theologian and pastor, Dietrich Bonhoeffer, perhaps best summarized this group's guiding approach to Christian faith. As he wrote from the Nazi prison where he was interned (and eventually hanged) in 1945, he was searching for Christianity without religion - for faith in Jesus without all the baggage of outmoded world vision, complicated doctrine, language, ritual, iconography, and creeds. He called believers to leave the childhood of half-understood dogmas from another era, to "come of age," and accept full responsibility for themselves, one another, and all of creation - living as if there were no God, but always consciously in the presence of God. For Bonhoeffer himself, living in this way called him to oppose the Nazi imperialists, whose project of world domination was very similar to the one pursued by the United States today. He urged his fellow Christians to pray each day for the defeat of the troops his government and the mainline churches of his day told him to support. Precisely as a Christian, he participated in a plot to assassinate Adolph Hitler.

Teilhard de Chardin, the Jesuit biologist and theologian, was another scout. Like Bonhoeffer, he embraced the west's basic scientific advances since the 17th century, not as developments to be resisted, but as signs of human maturity and development. Chardin saw the entire 15 billion year process of evolution culminating in the emergence of human beings

2½ million years ago. For Chardin, humans represented the entire process at last becoming aware of itself. And Jesus the Christ represented the full flowering of human beings, who appropriated at last the God essence that resides at the heart of all creation. For his efforts, Chardin unsurprisingly found himself under constant investigation by the Catholic hierarchy, and was eventually silenced altogether.

Franz Hinkelammert, economist and theologian, and co-founder of Costa Rica's Departamento Ecuménico de Investigaciones (DEI, the Ecumenical Research Institute) is another of the scouts alerting the Church as Caravan to the problems it must address. Born in Hitler's Germany, Hinkelammert came to Latin America as a teenager. He settled in Chile, but because of his radical publications and activism, he was pursued by the U.S.-supported dictatorship of Agosto Pinochet. Hinkelammert fled to Costa Rica, where he has been publishing voluminously since the founding of the DEI in 1977. Hinkelammert is a leading proponent of the Theology of Liberation and throughout Latin America is recognized as a cutting-edge scholar of the highest order.[5] A relentless critic of capitalist totalitarianism, Franz Hinkelammert describes the faith-inspired imperative for Christians to work for a this-worldly "other world," where there is room for everyone. He is a relentless critic of versions of Christianity that cooperate with empire and Darwinian capitalism.

Conclusion

What is especially important to note in this chapter is that the Christian Caravan is a long one. It embraces a wide range of historical orientations, defining issues, spiritual visions and heroes. However, it helps to reiterate that all of those in the Caravan are Christian. There is, in fact, no single way of claiming that designation. Once again, this is not to say that all visions within all groups of Christians are equally defensible, biblically speaking. Golden Calves and other idols have never been absent from what Vatican II referred to as the Pilgrim People of God.

The argument here will be that when Christians endorse the emperor's faith, they are (unwittingly) turning their backs on the God of the Bible. In the end, you might perhaps agree.

---

[5] As we shall see, a simple definition of liberation theology is reflection on the following of Christ from the viewpoint of those committed to the liberation of the poor and oppressed.

Misunderstanding Three:

Christian Fundamentalists Resist the Modern World; Liberals Cave In

> Christians have shown themselves to be creatively adaptive to the modern world in some cases and stubbornly resistant to it in others. (Weaver 198)

So far I've indicated that as a recovering Catholic and as a member of that church's loyal opposition from within, I also consider myself a recovering fundamentalist. As a young person the age of the students I teach in college, I needed a long time to accept modern scholarship's insights about biblical inspiration, authorship and inerrancy. I required as well a good deal of time to revise my political understandings of the role the United States actually plays in the world, and to grasp how Christianity has been deformed to serve the economic and political interests of the U.S.

Empire and the elite that run it

My students in Costa Rica had the same need, as do many I currently teach. Like me, they've inherited their attitudes from their parents, ministers and teachers, all of whom, as we shall see, are selectively suspicious of the modern world. My students often find the insights uncovered by archeology, history, language study, comparative religion, modern science, and the sociology of knowledge just so many stumbling blocks threatening their faith. So they reject the perceived menace, usually on the simple argument that such pseudo-knowledge contradicts the Bible, which always has the final word. It is the only unquestionable written source of knowledge available to human beings. As such its authority trumps every other source of knowledge, whether personal, academic, or scientifically experimental.

With such affirmation of biblical authority, the argument ends. Similarly ended, or at least diminished, is the modern world's threat, which at least since the 17th century has presented challenge after challenge to faith of this kind. Otherwise, as suggested by the quotation beginning this chapter, to fundamentalists modernity could be extremely frightening (Weaver 175, 207, 209, 247). In this fundamentalists are apparently distinguished from Christian liberals. Liberals seem more at home in the modern world. This, at least, is the received wisdom.

This Chapter

The argument here is that it's not as simple as that. In fact, it might well be argued that fundamentalists themselves have actually been quite "creatively adaptive to the modern world" - at least to the aspects of that world that have most definitively shaped it, such as capitalism, social Darwinism, and empire. Their adaptation has allowed their understanding of Christianity to be co-opted by those aspects. Meanwhile, it is Christians on the left, especially radicals, who have proved most "stubbornly resistant" to those elements.

This argument is central to understanding the thesis of this book. It is important to discerning *religious fundamentalism as a key misunderstanding of Christianity and as the root of religious support for empire, violence, sexism, homophobia and the neo-conservative politics that champions those elements.*

Such discernment cannot take place without clarifying some key terms at the outset. Mary Jo Weaver's *Introduction to Christianity*—the text used in all sections of the "Understandings of Christianity" course at Berea College—is useful here. Weaver helps her readers understand fundamentalism and evangelicalism, as well as Christian conservativism and their differences from Christian liberalism and radicalism.

Weaver reminds us that fundamentalists are types of Evangelicals within the Protestant Movement which grew out of earlier attempts to reform the Roman Catholic Church. In the contemporary context, especially in the United States, Evangelicals are proponents of conservative politics. In this as well as in doctrinal matters, they distinguish themselves from Christian liberals and radicals.

In what follows, each of these terms - Reform Movement, Protestant Reformation, Evangelicals and Conservatives - will be briefly clarified and distinguished from one another. With that task accomplished, conservative evangelical fundamentalists can be differentiated from religious liberals and radicals. All these categories, it will be seen, have been shaped by their attitude towards the fundamental political and especially towards the economic questions that have divided the world over the last century and a half. Those questions revolve around economic systems—market, capitalism, socialism and communism. With that argument made, the stage will then be set to explain more articulately in subsequent chapters how misunderstandings of faith purveyed by Christian fundamentalism end up misinterpreting the Bible and supporting elements seen here as incompatible with the teachings of Jesus the Christ.

Reformists, Protestants, Evangelicals, Fundamentalists, Conservatives, Liberals and Radicals

As Weaver recalls, the Reform Movement took place within the Catholic Church. It began in the 14th century with the work of John Wycliffe (1330-84) in England, and John Hus (1372-1415) in Bohemia. The Protestant Reformation emerged within the Catholic Church, but eventually broke away. It took definitive shape beginning in the 16th century. The Protestant Reformation is primarily associated with the thought and accomplishments of Martin Luther (1483-1546) in Germany, Ulrich Zwingli (1484-1531) in Switzerland and Jean Calvin (1509-64) in France. All of these reformers and many other 16th century Catholics rebelled against the evident corruption of the Roman Church, which had dominated the medieval period in a way that forcefully eliminated all rival interpretations of the Christian Faith.

Evangelicals emerged from the Protestant Movement in the 19th century, after it had fragmented into hundreds of separate denominations (179).[6] Evangelicalism was largely a product of the so-called "Great Awakening" which took place in the United States between 1725 and 1770 (127). The Awakening was an outgrowth of heightened concern among Christians of the period about the end of the world (180). The resulting revivalist movement was responsible for bringing together many of the fragmented denominations on the basis of agreement on the fundamentals of Christian faith. In other words, Evangelicalism was an expression of a nascent fundamentalism. As such it represented a quest by Protestants seeking greater unity and cooperation among themselves, to nail down the basic elements of faith to which, they thought, any Christian claiming the name must adhere. These elements included belief in biblical inerrancy, the face value of miracles as described in the Bible, substitutionary atonement for sinners by Jesus, the future Second Coming of Christ as the goal of history, the divinity of Jesus Christ, and the Lord's physical resurrection (180).

According to Weaver, besides identifying themselves by these beliefs, Evangelicals over the years increasingly distinguished themselves by their adoption of conservative attitudes towards the modern world. They found themselves especially threatened by the so-called "advances" of science and its apparent contradictions of the Bible in general and of biblical inerrancy,

---

[6] The name "Church of God," for instance is claimed by more than 200 separate denominations (Weaver 179).

miracles, and the physical resurrection of Jesus in particular. So, in counter-distinction to Christian Liberals, says Weaver, Christian conservatives have tended to shun the modern world in order to preserve an "old-time religion" (173).

> . . . (L)et us make a broad generalization and divide Christians into two main groups: those who have welcomed the discoveries of the age and sought to use scientific insights and methods within Christianity, and those who have scorned or shunned new ideas in order to stay deeply in touch with the "old-time religion." Neither of these groups can be adequately described, but they stand at the limits of the argument, fundamentalists on the one hand and liberals on the other. (173)

Here Weaver contrasts fundamentalists with liberals at the far ends of the spectrum of Christian faith. In this instance, however, she ignores the distinction between contemporary Christian liberals and radicals. In distinction from Weaver, the position adopted here is that fundamentalists do in fact belong at one end of the spectrum she describes. However, radicals belong at the other end, with liberals somewhere in between, perhaps in the very center. In the discussion which follows, unless otherwise indicated, "radical" will be substituted for Weaver's "liberal" whenever the left extreme of her religious continuum is referenced.

As Weaver points out, the term "radical" comes from the Latin word meaning "root" (106). Radical Christians in fact claim interest in getting to the root of their faith and of world problems. For example, relative to faith, radicals show great concern for understanding the original contexts and the authors' intentions behind biblical texts. As believers, liberals exhibit similar interests. Politically and economically, however, radicals seek basic change, while liberals tend to be reformers. Radicals typically identify the root of the world's problems in the system of capitalism, and (in today's world) in U.S. imperialism.[7] They are consequently critical of the basic direction of U.S. policy over the years, and would seek to change fundamentally its underlying economic system. Liberals, on the other hand, tend to accept the capitalist system as basically functional. Their inclination is to explain injustices in terms of dishonest and deviant individuals, rather than systemically. Similarly, what radicals see as

---

[7] See Appendix One for key distinctions between capitalism, Marxism, socialism, communism, and mixed economy.

atrocious display of American imperialism, liberals explain, for instance, as "mistakes" by well-meaning or misinformed Presidents, or as crimes by dishonest corporate leaders. Thus the political agendas of radical Christians tends to be more revolutionary and less reformist than those of Christian liberals.

Rejection of Public Schooling

Conservative fundamentalists, Weaver says, have largely rejected the modern worldview that liberals and radicals have sympathetically engaged. Fundamentalists reveal the nature of their principled intransigence and their general suspicion of the modern world particularly where it affects the lives of their children, viz., in the public education system of the United States. In U.S. classrooms, their children are inevitably exposed to what conservative fundamentalists see as the "religion" of secular humanism. It preaches religious and cultural "diversity" which amounts to an objectionable moral relativism. It offers instruction in sexual promiscuity in the form of "sex education." It discredits the Bible by advocating Darwinian evolution, which in the end is only a theory. At the same time U.S. public schooling refuses to complement such instruction with more biblically certain explanations of the natural world provided directly in the first two chapters of Genesis, and in terms of "scientific creationism" or "intelligent design." Meanwhile, the schools forbid students to pray publicly during the school day, and find display of God's Ten Commandments unconstitutional. No wonder then, so many believers show their resistance to modernism by removing their children from public schools, preferring to instruct them at home (247).

In home schools, conservative fundamentalists can also make sure their children are shielded from revisionist American history. This often amounts to little more than America-bashing on the part of self-hating U.S. liberals. These often take the United States to task for supposed crimes, for example around treatment of Native Americans and African slaves, and for "government welfare" given to Robber Barons who allegedly exploited workers and the natural environment. Such pseudo-history uses modern standards to criticize leaders who were doing their best given the insights available to them at the time.

"Political Correctness" masquerading as history is meant to blind children to the fact that the United States has been and remains a moral beacon to the world, a shining exception to character exhibited by the world's other nations whose leaders and people more easily succumb to venality, corruption, self-interest, and to the politics of terror and unvarnished evil. American exceptionality has been evident from the beginning, and is traceable to the country's origin in faith and dependence on God, rather than to any claim of inherent moral superiority somehow belonging to Americans as such. Contemporary Americans are not exceptional, but their national ancestors were. After all, the Pilgrims came to the New World fleeing religious persecution, finding a new Promised Land, and agreeing to live by religious covenant. In this way, they mirrored the ancient Israelites and their land flowing with milk and honey. Weaver writes,

> American conservative Christians may adopt the rhetoric of America as the new promised land, the new Eden where God has given humanity a chance to gather everyone into the kingdom. America is the home of God's chosen people and God's preferred way of life; the task set for the country is the evangelization of the world, an event that will hasten the Second Coming of Christ at the end of the world. . . . When they stress goals of individual salvation and preservation of the American way of life, they are moved by God's covenant with them and their belief in America as a new promised land. . . . (248-49)

In these words, a fundamentalist tendency to identify the old and the new is evident. Here one finds writ large the "creative adaptation" referenced in this chapter's opening Weaver quotation. "America's" project and Christian faith are identified—God and ancient faith on the one hand and the U.S. government and the even newer contemporary "American way of life" on the other.

After the pilgrims, the roots of such identification are often traced to the Founding Fathers. As understood by religious conservatives, the Founders were basically men of deep Christian faith. They set up a Constitution whose very first amendment guaranteed freedom of religion. This addition was intended to protect Christians like them from threats originating from other religions that would limit the practice of Christian faith which is privileged in the United States as a result of the faith commitments of the country's originators. Once again, the religion presenting such threat most prominently today is "secular humanism" (247). It must be overcome to restore the Christian theocracy originally intended by the Nation's founders, governed by God's law enshrined in the Ten Commandments and echoed in the Declaration of Independence and Constitution.

Embrace of Capitalism

For fundamentalists, all of these insights are honored by political conservatives, and especially in the contemporary Republican Party. Both insure that the country will remain true to its founding ideals, and to protecting the elements that have made America great—capitalism, anti-Communism, and strong defense. In Weaver's words,

> In terms of their political agendas, religious conservatives often sound like political conservatives: they appeal to capitalism, strong defense initiatives, and anti-Communist rhetoric. . . . Conservative Christians distinguish themselves from conservative secular politics primarily by virtue of their religious belief. Their Christian faith, they say, inspires them to act and gives them the strength and wisdom to oppose the directions of the modern world. . . . As activists, they tend to gather around issues of American military superiority, anti-Communism, and a general contempt for the goals of the World Council of Churches. (248-49)

Here again the elements expressed indicate Christian fundamentalist endorsement, rather than rejection, of the most influential elements shaping the modern world. Capitalism is nothing if not a modern development. More than any other, it has actually shaped the modern world technologically, militarily and spiritually.[8]

---

[8] Normally, of course, it is not faith considerations that guide business decisions even for Christian entrepreneurs. Rather business choices are made according to laws of supply and demand, and are shaped by factors of competition, profit and loss. In fact, moral considerations very often run counter to these latter concerns. For instance, if an employer, moved by Christian conviction, wished to improve the lot of his employees by paying them a living wage rather than a much lower and inadequate market-determined sum, that employer would soon be run out of business by those paying their workers slave wages. That is, competitors' final products could undersell the Christian business person's, because the competitors' production costs would be lower. Similarly, a Christian moved to protect the environment by putting scrubbers on factory smokestacks or filters to purify effluents would soon be undersold by producers lacking such moral scruples. In other words, the market system rewards lack of Christian concern and penalizes the presence of conscience. Does this mean that capitalism is inherently immoral or amoral? Christian conservatives evidently answer "no." As we will see, Christian radicals, and to a lesser extent, liberals give the opposite answer. Radicals find unbridled capitalism inherently immoral, and so resist this modern development that has shaped the contemporary world more than any other.

Capitalism's theory was first articulated during the Enlightenment. It received its fullest expression from Adam Smith in *The Wealth of Nations*, published the very same year as the founding of the U.S. Republic. Anticommunism, of course, represents the other side of the coin, the rejection, the antithesis of capitalism. American military superiority is even more modern, having emerged following World War II, and reaching its high point after the fall of the Soviet Union in the final decade of the 20th century. That superiority, expressed most unmistakably in the vast U.S. nuclear arsenal, and in "America's" alleged right to determine who else might possess such weapons, is the precondition to the establishment and maintenance of U.S. Empire. Military superiority keeps the world as it is in order to protect the American Way of Life based (as we saw in the words of George Kennan) on an extremely disproportionate consumption of wealth and resources by the United States.

Conclusion

Thus Christian fundamentalists, at the very least, offer the shaping of the modern world by U.S. Empire their implicit support. At most, fundamentalist Christians give their unconditional and clearly expressed support to U.S. Empire. To reiterate: this represents "creative adaptation" to the modern world, rather than "stubborn resistance."

Misunderstanding Four:
Liberal Christianity Seeks Domination Too

> U.S. foreign policy must begin to counter (not react against) liberation theology as it is utilized in Latin America by the 'liberation theology' clergy... The role of the church in Latin America is vital to the concept of political freedom. Unfortunately, Marxist-Leninist forces have utilized the church as a political weapon against private property and productive capitalism by infiltrating the religious community with ideas that are less Christian than Communist. [Roger Fontaine, Lewis Tambs et. al.(advisors to the incoming Reagan administration)]

As we have just seen, conservative fundamentalist resistance is often contrasted with liberal and radical adaptation and accommodation to the modern world. Liberals and radicals do not seek absolute certainty of belief; they are more at home with ambiguity than fundamentalists. Ambiguity, leftists typically argue, is part of the human condition. Being human inevitably involves an oftentimes uncomfortable quest for truth, rather than a challenge to suspend one's critical faculties in the face of divinely revealed certainties.

Thus liberals have, in Weaver's words, "welcomed the discoveries of the age and sought to use scientific insights and methods within Christianity" (173). As a result, they are not worried about the findings of modern science, whether biblical or biological. They embrace discoveries that Moses did not author the Pentateuch, that Jewish belief in the afterlife was a late development, that the Gospels offer discordant understandings of Jesus' identity, that the Book of Revelation does not really offer details about the contemporary Middle East, and that diversity of belief among Christians rather than rigid orthodoxy characterized the first four centuries of the church. All such developments, they argue, are what any adult would expect. As one grows up, the truths accepted in childhood change and grow more complex. In no other area of life except religion, could anyone successfully contend that one's understanding of facts (historical, literary, mathematical, scientific...) at the age of 7 or 12 should not undergo basic change and adjustment.

For most U.S. radicals, key "grown up" learnings involve not only (or even principally) the inerrancy or inspiration of the Bible. They instead address the way the world works, and the roles that the United States and religion have played in that process. In radical analysis, capitalism emerges as the most powerful factor that has shaped the modern world. In its unbridled form, the system necessarily exploits workers and the environment. It concentrates wealth in the hands of the powerful few. And to protect that concentration, it resorts to wholesale terrorism, obscene violence and war against the world's poor.

It is this system in its unmodified, uncontrolled form that radical Christians (and to a lesser extent, liberals) "stubbornly resist." Recent resisters indicated by Weaver include Mother Jones (152), Reinhold Neibuhr (177), Dorothy Day and Peter Maurin (230, 233, 241), Dan and Phil Berrigan (214, 241), Elizabeth McAlister (231), Martin Luther King, Jr. (214, 227, 236-237, 246), Thomas Merton (180, 242), James Cone (189, 262), Clarence Jordan (237), Gary MacEoin (180), Mary Daly (261), Jim Wallis (214-215), Ita Ford, Dorothy Kazel, Maura Clarke, and Jean Donovan (192-193), and the practitioners of liberation theology.

In contrast to such rejection, the fundamentally unjust capitalist system finds its principal proponent and defender in the United States of America. The U.S. task is facilitated by members of conservative, fundamentalist Christian churches which recommend uncritical acceptance of capitalism and the Empire it serves. In radical eyes, fundamentalist Christianity has in this way run the risk of becoming the ideological servant of structured injustice. Among fundamentalism's principal proponents, Weaver identifies Ralph Reed (248-9), Charles Fuller (254), Oral Roberts, Rex Humbard, Billy Graham, Richard Vigeurie, Tim Le Haye, Morton Blackwell, Ronald Reagan, Jerry Falwell, Pat Robertson, Jimmy Swaggart (255), and W.A. Criswell (259).

Domination

Weaver goes on to show where fundamentalist and radical Christians come together. Despite their differences, both are expressions of what she terms "domination systems" (211-21). That is, they seek to obliterate their opponents, and to impose their understanding of Christianity on others in the form of public policy despite the fact that they exist in a culture (at least in the United States context) where not all are Christians, and certainly not liberal or conservative Christians (211). Weaver finds advocates of the domination system on both the left and right wings of Christianity. She writes,

> Some right-wing Christians – for example, members of the Moral Majority in the 1980s – identified their religious beliefs with conservative

political views and linked Christianity itself with a specifically conservative political agenda. These Christians take political positions – against communism, against welfare, in support of capital punishment and conservative fiscal policy – and tie them up with God's will or the gospel. Their reading of the Old Testament and the words of Jesus leads them to a political-religious viewpoint that is essentially right-wing. On the other end of the spectrum, some large church organizations – the World Council of Churches, for example – have sometimes supported left-wing political viewpoints. In certain circumstances, they have identified their religious beliefs with select revolutionary movements and have given financial support to aid victims of "liberation movements" (like the revolution in Zimbabwe). Their reading of the Old Testament and the Gospels leads them to a political posture that is left-wing. In both cases – from the right and from the left – churches and church members have been asked to endorse political viewpoints as if they were both the clearest readings of the gospel and the best course for worldly governments (213-4).

Key words in this analysis enable Weaver to classify both left religious viewpoints and their right-wing counterparts as sharing a "domination" mentality. In relation to right-wing Christians, the words are "Their reading of the Old Testament and the words of Jesus leads them to a political-religious viewpoint that is essentially right-wing." In relation to left-wing Christians, and especially to adherents of liberation theology whom Weaver singles out (212-3), the key words are "Their reading of the Old Testament and the Gospels leads them to a political posture that is left-wing."

The parallelism Weaver advances obscures a key difference between right and left versions of Christianity, especially as found in liberation theology. That is, right-wing versions do in reality tend to take their positions *expressly because those postures are endorsed specifically in the Bible.* This becomes most clear in arguments favoring support of Israel in the Middle East. Support is given because of Jewish Israelis' privileged position as God's "chosen people." Support of Israel is also required by right-wing readings of the Book of Revelation. Those readings indicate that the Second Coming of Jesus is premised upon the re-establishment of the kingdom of Israel.

Similarly, the environmentalist movement tends to be viewed with suspicion by right-wing Christians, because their reading of the Book of Revelation leads to the belief that the world is doomed to imminent destruction. So what's the point of environmental conservation? Even, what's the point of opposing the use of nuclear weapons, since they are very likely the instruments chosen by God to end the world?

Put succinctly, according to right-wing versions, the Bible is the privileged and ultimate tool of analysis. As previously indicated, its statements trump all other sources of knowledge, including history, science, and reason. For the right-wing, it is indeed true, as Weaver says, that reading the Old Testament and the words of Jesus lead them to a political-religious viewpoint that is essentially right-wing. Consequently, Weaver is correct in saying that the right-wing political program is to impose a specifically right-wing *religious* program even on the unwilling. It merits classification as a "domination system."

Despite Weaver's parallelism, this tends not to be the case with left-wing versions of Christianity, especially in liberation theology. There positions are not primarily adopted because they are found in the Bible. In fact, history shows that left politics emerged in the modern world exactly in opposition to orthodox strains of Christianity. So when Christians (very infrequently) found themselves adopting left positions, they were typically not leading movements "to create a Christian society" (213). Rather, they were following those whose conclusions had been reached independently of and in opposition to received understandings of Christian faith. Thus when the Social Gospel emerged at the beginning of the 20th century, its advocates were rejected by the mainstream as dupes of socialists and communists. In 1984 when the Vatican officially distanced itself from liberation theology, it did so because of liberation theology's use of Marxist analysis. Marxists and communists, of course, had no interest in creating a Christian society.

The point here is that the social movements associated with left-wing Christianity had a flourishing life independent of Christians and their readings of the Bible. Moreover, the struggle for left-wing Christians was precisely to justify their joining those whose social, political and economic conclusions were drawn exactly in opposition to Christianity itself.

In fact, the methodology of liberation theology specifically downplays the role of theology in determining the political positions it suggests. Its methodology specifically locates theological reasoning as a tertiary act – subordinate to everyday experience, assumed only at the end of the day, "after the sun goes down." Experience comes first. Then (for some) comes historical, economic, political and social analysis. Both steps precede Bible reading which in liberation theology is a third-stage act. For

Christians, this third step may provide further incentive (i.e. beyond that provided by life and antecedent analysis) for praxis or world-changing action. For instance, Christians might find that the cooperative and community values of socialism seem much more compatible with Christian faith and the practice of Jesus and the early church than the competition and individualism of capitalism.

All of this is to say that left Christianity's advocacy of particular political programs is misclassified as an attempt at "domination" in the sense of imposing a particular religious view on the unwilling. Its political position is neither primarily derived from nor dependent upon particular readings of the biblical tradition. Rather it stands or falls on the basis of its protagonists' (the poor mainly) experience of life, and of analysis whose tools are provided by disciplines such as history, economics, political science and sociology. Consequently, any "domination" or "imposition" involved is not of a specifically religious program. If domination is involved, it is the domination or imposition inherent in any political process whatever.

Fundamentalism and the Third Great Awakening

The domination thrust of Christian fundamentalism becomes apparent when fundamentalism is viewed in relation to Liberation Theology, and in terms of a Third Great Awakening in the final quarter of the 20th century. Here the implied comparison is with the First and Second Great Awakenings that played important roles in the 18th and 19th "American" Christianity. Both earlier stirrings of religious fervor and return to God and religious faith took place after extended periods when religion itself was discredited and had become decidedly less important in people's lives (126). Understanding contemporary fundamentalism as a Third Awakening will perhaps assist in appreciating the overall thesis presented in this book—that fundamentalist misunderstandings of Christianity end up supporting war, empire and associated phenomena generated by the capitalist system.

More specifically, if we understand the First Awakening (1725-1770) as an 18th century phenomenon coinciding with the political turbulence leading up to the American Revolution, we can recognize the Second Great Awakening as contemporaneous with similar disturbance surrounding the spread of bourgeois rebellions throughout the world in the middle of the 19th century, and with the disorder leading up to the Civil War in the United States.

The turbulence of the First Great Awakening had important economic and intellectual dimensions. Economically, religious revivalists were worried about a pervasive fascination with mercantilism, commercialism, and the drama of making money (126). That allure eventually came to a head with Adam Smith's publication of *The Wealth of Nations* in 1776. Intellectually, the spirit of the Enlightenment had spread from the drawing rooms of Europe to infect the emerging political class in the New World. Thomas Jefferson, Benjamin Franklin, Thomas Paine and many other political leaders of the day were all Deists. They opposed the irrationality of traditional religion, and the blind obedience it required (128). In response, preachers such as Jonathan Edwards sought not only to revive religious faith, but to give it intellectual respectability, while regrounding it in life-changing experience and in a resulting emotional conviction.

Similarly, the Second Great Awakening coincided with economic changes and moral controversies surrounding the U.S. Civil War. Economically, the burgeoning industrial and mercantile classes of the North were challenging the hegemony of the South's landed aristocracy. The question was which class would shape the nation's economic and political destiny. That matter was intimately connected with slavery, which became the great moral question of the day. Some religious figures like John G. Fee, the founder of Berea College in Kentucky, took advantage of religion's renewed popularity to push an abolitionist agenda – an implied criticism of the very basis of U.S. economic life (234-5). However, the vast majority of Christians, particularly in the South, used the Bible to defend their "traditional values," pointing to key passages in the Bible to uphold slavery (235-6). It was in the post-Civil War context characterized by the emancipation of slaves and postwar reconstruction that Christian Fundamentalism was born (179). In effect most fundamentalists identified with the economic interests of the southern aristocracy, and with white supremacists in opposition to emancipation. They insisted on readings of the Bible whose plain meaning supported those positions, especially slavery, and eventually Jim Crow laws and segregation.

Third Great Awakening

Although the designation is not commonly used, we can say that the revival of fundamentalism in the final quarter of the 20th century constituted a Third Great Awakening. Like the first two, this one was associated with the discrediting of religion. Both worldwide and in the United States, that had happened in the 1960s and '70s. That same period had seen the advance of communism throughout the world. One of the main reasons for Pope John XXIII's convoking of the Second Vatican Council was that the Catholic Church was losing Europe's working class to

Marxism and Communism. Communists, of course, classified religion as a narcotic desensitizing poor people and workers to their exploitation at the hands of their employers and the politically powerful.

In the '60s Communism also made advances in the Third World. Increasingly, Christian theologians were opening themselves to dialog with Marxists. That conversation eventually led to the development of liberation theology. Its rise in the 1960s caused panic in centers of imperial power, i.e., in the United States and its client regimes in the Third World. The Santa Fe Document, published for the benefit of the incoming Reagan administration warned that liberation theology represented a threat to U.S. interests, especially in Latin America. It advised strong measures to counteract its influence.

The result was massive C.I.A. funding for right wing evangelicals who on the one hand drew Third World congregations away from left politics, and on the other urged North American worshippers to politicize by voting for conservative politicians at home, and opposing movements described as "communist" abroad. In particular U.S. evangelicals were urged to support the Contra War in Nicaragua against the Sandinista revolution. That insurrection (coming to power in 1979) was the first to enlist in its ranks masses of Christians specifically motivated by reflection on their religious faith. Once again, this caused panic in centers of power.

In reaction, U.S. funding subsidized evangelicals such as Jerry Falwell, Pat Robertson, and Jimmy Swaggart, whose programs were beamed into poor barrios, *favelas*, and *poblaciones* across Latin America. Meanwhile in the United States, the Christian right became openly political as never before. Under the leadership of Ralph Reed, Evangelicals increasingly identified with the politics of the Republican Party. As a result, for the last 25 years and more God and theology have been playing increasingly central roles in American politics.

In other words, the Third Great Awakening and the ascendancy of conservative fundamentalist Christianity were intimately connected with the threat to the capitalist order on the one hand, and with the rise of liberation theology on the other. The Awakening was an antidote to interpretations of the gospel which insisted that the struggle for social justice is part and parcel of being Christian.

Socialist vs. Capitalist Christianity

Put differently, Weaver is correct when she identifies the great intra-Christian "battle of the 20th century" as that between what she terms fundamentalism and liberalism (173). However by keeping focus on the religious dimensions of that "battle," she stops short of penetrating to the connections between those "isms" and the more basic 20th century battle, viz. that between free market capitalism and socialism. It turns out that each of those systems has its version of the Christian faith. Fundamentalists embrace the free market version of Christianity. Radicals embrace the socialist version.

Free Market Christians

More specifically, free market advocates worship a Christian God who favors the winners in economic competition. Typically, the winners are perceived as the hard workers, the moral people whose wealth will "trickle down" in the form of the jobs they provide and the charity they are moved to give on a free will basis. Apart from charity, these worshippers often advocate "tough love" towards the poor who need the stimulus of hunger and poverty to get them into the workforce. Meanwhile the more virtuous wealthy need tax breaks to stimulate their job-creative investments.

The "social issues" which concern this God are most prominently abortion, pre-marital sex, homosexuality, sobriety, and freedom from big government with its wasteful programs of welfare, affirmative action, and over-regulation of the environment. At the same time, these worshippers favor increased government spending on police forces and on the military to protect against those who threaten the prosperity of "the free world" [e.g. during the '80s, Salvadoran rebels and their sympathizers (such as Oscar Romero), and today the indigenous rebels in Chiapas and leaders of "rogue nations" like Cuba, Libya, Iraq, etc.].

Favorite biblical texts of free market advocates include "The poor you will always have with you" (Mk. 14:7). "Render to Caesar the things that are Caesar's and to God the things that are God's" (Mk. 12:17). "Let every person be subject to governing authorities" (Rms. 13:1).

Socialist Christians

Christian advocates of socialism worship a God who favors those at the bottom of the economic ladder. Typically, these believers are (or side with) those the mainstream culture tends to despise or devalue: the working poor, unemployed, welfare mothers, homosexuals, undocumented aliens, prisoners, the homeless, AIDS patients, the addicted, Third World peoples. . . .

Socialist Christians argue that such people are in fact God's "chosen." God has shown throughout the Bible, and especially in the person of Jesus, that God favors those the mainstream despises. In the person of Jesus, God chose specifically to reveal Godself in such a despised person. The "social issues" which concern Christians on the left are most prominently the free market's tendency to concentrate wealth and to exclude the ones God favors. Accordingly, radical Christians favor a comprehensive "pro-life" agenda which provides a welcoming context for all children (thus making abortion less likely) and protects the environment; they advocate full employment at a "living wage;" they oppose capital punishment, harsh laws against immigrants, homosexuals, the homeless. . . .

These worshippers favor increased social spending on

'HE STIRRETH UP THE PEOPLE'

JESUS CHRIST
THE WORKINGMAN OF NAZARETH
WILL SPEAK
AT BROTHERHOOD HALL
— SUBJECT —
— THE RIGHTS OF LABOR —
Art Young, The Masses, December 1913

A radically historical, contextualized depiction of the Biblical God fully is revealed in the prophet from Nazareth. This image comes from the Social Gospel Movement of the early 20th century.

provision of jobs, on assistance for the working poor and unemployed. They favor environmental regulation, affirmative action, elimination of capital punishment, and equal rights for women, homosexuals, resident aliens . . . They favor decreased government spending on prisons, the military and programs to assist large corporations. Their tendency is to oppose military interventions abroad which are typically perceived as attempts to protect the basically immoral maldistribution of wealth in the world. These Christians often interpret as just, revolutions against the prevailing capitalist order (e.g. in El Salvador during the 1980s and in Chiapas in the 1990s) and identify persons such as Oscar Romero as saints, and Fidel Castro and subcomandante Marcos as heroes.

Favorite biblical texts include "Blessed are you poor, for yours is the kingdom of God" (Lk. 6:20-23); "But woe to you that are rich, for you have received your consolation" (Lk. 6:24-26); "You lack one thing; go sell what you have, and give to the poor, and you will have treasure in heaven; and come follow me" (Mark 10:21); "It is easier for a camel to go through the eye of a needle than for a rich man to enter the kingdom of God" (Mt. 19:24).

Conclusion

An old saying has it that when anyone says, "It's not the money; it's the principle," it's the money. The argument of this chapter has been something like that. It says that what separates Third Great Awakening fundamentalists from radical Christians who advocate liberation theology are not primarily issues like scriptural inerrancy or refusal to accommodate "old time religion" to the modern world. Rather, what divides two sides in Weaver's "Battle of the Century" is commitment or opposition to the modern world's prevailing economic system. It's the money. That is, the battle between capitalism and socialism is the real fight of the century – or of the last century and a half.

Liberation Theology's discovery of the fact that modern biblical scholarship reveals a Jesus and early church highly concerned with social justice for the poor is what has sparked an Awakening of its antithesis, viz. the conservative fundamentalism of the last quarter century.

And so conservative fundamentalists have embraced the capitalist system and accommodated their faith to American Empire. The issues fundamentalists champion are all dear to the hearts of white middle class people. Weaver's list makes this clear. Conservative fundamentalists are anti-communist, anti-welfare, pro-capital punishment and pro-conservative fiscal policy.

Meanwhile, as we shall see in subsequent chapters, Christian radicals find capitalism's exaltation of the individual and competition, its tolerance of unemployment and low wages, its need for conquest and empire, all antithetical to the biblical tradition. So radicals reject such antitheses and struggle to replace prevailing economic arrangements. In doing so, they recognize that Jesus did something like that. His example in identifying with the poor and outcast of his day is the "old time religion" they seek to embrace. Their aspiration follows the lead of those who over the centuries have recognized what they consider the patent historical fact that Christian faith and biblical religion have been exploited by the rich to keep the poor in line. They charge that the Third Great Awakening and the latest version of politically conservative Christian fundamentalism have embraced that unfortunate tradition.

Misunderstanding Five:

Fundamentalists Interpret the Bible Literally (Sometimes)

> An extreme fundamentalist believes that there are no mistakes in the Bible and that every word means exactly what it says: the Bible is to be read as fully and literally true. (Weaver 176)

Fundamentalists like I was almost universally claim to interpret the Bible literally. German theologian, Ulrich Duchrow, has a nice response whenever he hears fundamentalists make that claim. He says, "Congratulations; I'm glad you've had the faith and courage to sell everything you have, and to give it to the poor in order to follow Jesus."

Of course, few fundamentalists (or liberals or radicals for that matter) have actually done that. Instead, they've found ways to "interpret" Jesus' words so that they can claim to be Christian without actually giving away all their possessions. Despite such interpretational jujitsu (and it is not limited to Jesus' words about wealth and possessions), fundamentalists persist in claiming to be biblical literalists. This amounts to a radical denial of history and the power of cultural conditioning. Radicalism of this sort seems odd, since on the one hand fundamentalists keep reminding us of the centrality of culture in shaping thought, values and personal identities. So they untiringly denounce the pervasive influence of American modernity with its relativity, uncommitted sexuality, permissiveness, and its claim to rights without responsibility.

On the other hand, however, fundamentalists don't accord that same power of influence to the cultural contexts of the Bible. To do so would threaten their understanding of revelation and biblical inspiration, and their belief that "sacred texts" came down to us in the King James form just as found in the leather-bound copies loving parents gave them for Baptism. To avoid such threat, fundamentalists reject biblical scholarship which highlights the fact that "sacred text" authors were also culturally conditioned.

Additionally, fundamentalists reject the premise that it is difficult to distinguish the cultural assumptions of biblical authors from what those same sources were actually teaching. This is most clear in the biblical stories of creation. These texts seem to assume a flat earth, covered by a blue bowl decorated by sun, moon and stars, and under-girded by an abode of the dead, *Sheol*. The stories also say that the universe was created in a relatively short time. But do such assertions constitute the teaching of the biblical stories, and do they thus necessitate rejection of modern astronomy, physics and of evolutionary theory? Or do the assertions merely reflect the *cultural assumptions* of the author? Could other assumptions have been used as vehicles for whatever the text intends to teach? And just what is that teaching?

Such questions are not so easy to answer. For instance, is it taught in the Bible that women should remain silent in church (I Tim. 2:11)? Or is that part of Paul's cultural baggage? Is it biblical teaching that lending money to the poor for profit is a deadly sin (Ex. 22:25-27)? Or is that too a cultural assumption? What about homosexuality (See Chapter 18)? And is rebellion against established authority (after the manner of the U.S. Founding Fathers) equivalent to rebelling against God (Romans 13:1-2)? Once again, recognizing the cultural conditionality of scriptural texts strikes at the very foundations of fundamentalist certainties. It would put them in league with mainstream biblical scholars who often appeal to St. Paul's evidently repressed sexuality in explaining his teaching, for example, on women and homosexuality. Appeals like these end up treating some of Paul's teachings as rants rather than revelations.

Sacred Texts and Revelation

The approach taken here is that "sacred" texts contain both revelation and rants. The revelation is progressive or "evolutionary." It begins from an idea of God that was originally patriarchal, tribal, violent, and incredibly blood thirsty. This understanding recognized the existence of other Gods; they, however, were considered inferior and subordinate, because, while patriarchal, they were less effectively violent and blood thirsty. From there biblical revelation proceeded sporadically to a more universal understanding of God. This issued from prophets like Second Isaiah, and reached full flowering in the person of Jesus. He spoke of a Father God and of himself acting like a mother concerned for all her children (Lk. 13:34-35). The Jesus of this approach defended women, and included them in his inner circle (Mk. 14:6-9). At the same time, he rejected violence as a means of responding to hostility (Mt. 2651-54). With all this in mind, determining the meaning of "sacred" texts entails development of historical perspective, along with identifying and analyzing historical and cultural contexts.

Such analysis exposes something else about the revelatory component of the "sacred" texts. They are themselves "contested terrain." Contest is evident not only in contemporary "battles" over fundamentalist vs. liberal interpretations, but in the ancient texts themselves. There Israel's royalty fights the poor and the prophets over ownership of the stories and their promises. The poor find the narratives promising them liberation and a land of their own to farm. Meanwhile, the rich read the basic tradition as promising the royal family a perpetual dynasty. Given such contest, the *lasting "revelation" communicated by biblical literature seems to be that warring groups will inevitably manipulate inspired literature to suit their own group projects and to discredit interpretations which do not favor those schemes.* Evidence of manipulation surfaces at every step of textual transmission. The message of the Bible, then, is "beware;" the God the Bible portrays may in reality be an idol – perhaps, as we shall see, even Satan himself.

More specifically, a kind of "battle of Gods" has dominated not only biblical literature, but all of western history. It emerges immediately with the creation stories themselves. There, in the myth of the first woman and the first man, the ancient Mother God joins combat with the Patriarchal God of Solomon's court. As will be indicated (Chapter 8), she wins the fight's initial round, and (in the Book of Revelation) is promised ultimate victory (Chapter 11). In the interim, however, the macho God of the royal court holds sway. Under David and Solomon, he becomes the violent God of the Rich who subdues the God of the Poor, championed not only by Moses, but by prophets like Amos, and ultimately by Jesus as well. Ignorance of primordial battles like these has transformed the Bible's "revelation" into a tool fashioned to maintain the male privileges of the well-to-do dominant class, and to discredit interpretations which challenge such privileges. They take the God of the Rich (of David, Solomon, and the royal court) to be God himself, while ignoring the prophetic God of the Poor. This is the nature of biblical revelation.

Revelation like this is virtually unknown in fundamentalist circles. Biblical rants, on the other hand, are centralized and embraced with passion. Here the reference is not merely to Paul's questionable theories on sexuality. They include more especially and fatefully biblical approaches to violence, of which the Bible approves whole heartedly (Chapter 18). In fact, as Jack Nelson-Pallmeyer has recently argued, any reasonable person reading the "sacred" texts would draw the conclusion that their main teaching is that God is violent, and that his violence saves. From Genesis (where God repents of having created the human race, and destroys it by flood) to Revelation (where the entire earth is obliterated to punish the Roman Empire), the Bible is full of violence of the very worst kind – directed at innocent children, women, the elderly, and even animals by a raging God (E.g., Ex. 8:18-29).

Augustinian Theology

In subsequent Augustinian theology, divine violence is even directed at God's own son. The story goes that the deity had been so offended by "original sin" that he required the sacrifice of one equal to him. So he sent his son to earth to be sacrificed, and thus to appease the God's otherwise insatiable wrath. Only in this way are human beings saved – from a vengeful God. Those not so fortunate are consigned to hell, where God sentences them to eternal torture beyond the wildest nightmares anyone can conceive. A sadistic God even infects his "saints" with his psychosis. Thomas Aquinas held that one of the greatest delights of the saved would be witnessing the torments of the damned, because their anguish was such an exquisite expression of God's justice.[9]

Literal Interpretation And Original Sin

It should be noted that Augustine's emphasis on original sin is central to this theology. As we shall see, however the term "sin" is nowhere found in the key biblical texts upon which the great Church Father built his theology. It is entirely ironic, then, that those who would be biblical literalists accept Augustine's theology completely. They base their theology on a concept completely absent from the biblical text which they claim to be interpreting literally.

---

[9] In the face of such violence, Walter Wink has argued that violence is not merely condoned in the Bible, but that the God of Violence there portrayed is none other than Marduk, the vengeful Babylonian God centralized in what Wink indicates is the oldest story incorporated into western literature. In the Marduk myth, violence stands behind the act of creation itself. Marduk murders the female principle, Tiamat, the "mother of the all." He dismembers her body from which the earth is formed. But Tiamat will not stay dead. Each year it is necessary to ritually repeat the act of creative violence to make sure that the chaos the female represents will not triumph over Marduk's order. In other words, male patriarchy can only be maintained by continually subduing the female who constantly threatens to destroy patriarchal order. According to this story, violence stands at the heart of creation. Evil precedes good. Woman needs to be controlled by violence. These are, in fact, the foundational beliefs of American culture—and often of biblical fundamentalists. This is true, despite the fact that none of this is found in the biblical creation story. There everything is good from the beginning. Woman is man's equal ("flesh of my flesh, and bone of my bone"). Violence does not enter the picture till the first pair's son kills his brother. From then on, however, the violent Yahweh who saves by murder, pillage and genocide transforms into Marduk. It is no wonder, then, that the Marduk tale is the one embraced by fundamentalists and by American culture in general. The story is endlessly repeated in contemporary stories, films and cartoons known to every American who has ever read a"Popeye" cartoon, or seen "Walking Tall," or "Teenage Mutant Ninja Turtles" (Wink 17-25).

In fact a comparison of typical fundamentalist theology with the actual biblical narrative reveals a transformation on the part of fundamentalists from the Bible's basically historical approach to "salvation history" to a mythological one—i.e. to an account of what the God was doing "up there" in the heavens above history before its beginning and after its end. This theological approach virtually ignores the historical nature of biblical revelation. It denies the consequent need to understand the social, economic, political and cultural contexts of divine disclosure in order to grasp the meaning of the texts involved. The allusion here is especially to fundamentalist centralization of the stories of Genesis and the Book of Revelation. Consider the basic story of salvation as told by fundamentalists.

I remember our parish priest years ago helping our congregation recall the Catholic version of its details. He said, "I'm going to treat you all this morning as if you were back in CCD class.[10] I'll give you some prompts; you fill in the blanks.

He said, "In the beginning, God . . . ."

We in the congregation responded, "Created the heavens and the earth."

The pastor continued, "But Adam and Eve . . ."

We all said "Sinned."

"Yes," said the priest. "They committed original sin. In doing so, they corrupted human nature and creation itself. They passed on their sin to all of us.

"Now let's continue. . . . So God got angry and . . . ."

Here our answer was not so swift. Someone ventured, "Closed the gates of heaven?"

"That's right," our pastor said.

Well, he continued in this vein. And so did we. Eventually, the rest of the story came out. God sent his only begotten son. He died for our sins, reopened the gates of heaven, and founded his church. The church supplies the sacraments, which are for believers "keys" to heaven. All who are baptized are saved. The unbaptized are justly condemned forever to hell.

That's the basic account. Protestant fundamentalists would replace the sacraments as opening the path to heaven with "accepting Jesus as your personal savior." They might also want to add something about the rapture, Armageddon, and the end of the world.

Be that as it may. What's interesting about all of this is how unbiblical it is – how pre-historic and ahistoric. Again, this is especially ironic for those who claim to be basing their faith on the Bible. It mostly happens up there in heaven, just like the Greco-Roman tales of Zeus and Jupiter. And

---

[10] Confraternity of Christian Doctrine—the Catholic version of Sunday school.

A depiction of the Blessed Trinity found throughout Latin America. Here God is depicted not as the God of History, much less as the God of the Poor, but (Zeus-like) above History, in the clouds, surrounded by angels reminiscent of Cupids.

that's part of the point here. As we shall see presently, with Augustine, the Church accommodated its belief to the Roman Empire. It transformed the biblical account with its emphasis on history, into a mythological belief with its emphasis on what divine persons were doing "up there."

The importance of the transformation is revealed by comparing the above summary of Augustine's narrative with the story modern biblical scholarship uncovers for us. In simple summary it goes something like the following:

- God's first revelation came to a group of Hebrew (i.e. rebel) slaves, when "Yahweh" liberated them from captivity in Egypt.
- Yahweh made a covenant with his people promising them a homeland, and to be their God as long as they obeyed his law and protected the widows, orphans, slaves and resident aliens among them.
- Once in the Promised Land, the Hebrews lived in a loose confederation of tribes until security considerations provoked by a threat from the Sea People (the Philistines) led them (after much controversy) to change their loose confederacy to a united monarchy.
- The monarchs changed the understanding of the covenant from one insuring God's protection for the entire people, to a covenant guaranteeing that a particular dynasty (of King David) would last forever.
- When kings neglected the widows, orphans, slaves and resident aliens, social critics called "prophets" threatened punishments of disobedient kings. When the punishments occurred, other prophets arose to give hope to the suffering people.
- About 1000 B.C.E., under David's son Solomon, the early traditions of the Hebrew people were written down for the first time by Solomon's court scribes (called "Yahwists"). Most prominently, the accounts included the story of Hebrew liberation from Egypt, and the establishment of the Davidic dynasty. The scribes also recorded legends of ancient Hebrew ancestors such as Abraham, Isaac and Jacob and the fathers of the 12 original Hebrew tribes. Included as well were prehistoric mythological accounts of the origin of the world, of suffering, of sexual attraction between men and women, of linguistic variety, and natural phenomena such as floods and rainbows.
- Following the death of Solomon, the united monarchy was split in two – Israel in the north of Palestine, and Judah in the south.
- In 722 the northern kingdom was defeated by the Assyrians.
- In 587 the southern kingdom was defeated by Babylon (modern Iraq), and its leading figures were taken into exile in Babylon.
- When the Great Exile ended, the Hebrews returned to their homeland and reinterpreted (largely rewrote) their holy texts to respond to their changed historical situation.
- Still, they were controlled successively by the Persians, Greeks and Romans.
- Jesus was born during the Roman occupation.
- He was identified as a social critic or prophet. His teachings afflicted

the comfortable and brought hope to the afflicted.
- He preached Good News not about himself, but about a utopia he referred to as the Kingdom of God, where the Covenant would be renewed and fulfilled for widows, orphans, slaves, resident aliens, and other social outcasts. His preaching thus raised the hopes of the poor, and the ire of the rich and powerful, including the Roman occupiers.
- A conspiracy between Jewish and Roman authorities executed Jesus as a revolutionary.
- Three days later, his followers claimed that he was alive again, raised from the dead.
- They formed a kingdom community where a kind of primitive communism was practiced, exhibiting special care for widows, orphans, slaves, aliens and other social outcasts.
- Baptism was a sign of membership in and commitment to that community which eventually evolved into a "church."

Conclusion

The argument here is that the second narrative is much truer to biblical content than is the Augustinian version. Augustine's theology is a late development, originating in the 4th century of the Common Era. It is questionably biblical, and very mythological in character.[11] It emphasizes points of doctrine such as original sin and the corruption of human nature and of creation itself. Such elements are not found, strictly speaking, in the first two chapters of Genesis. As indicated earlier, the term "sin" does not even appear in the account of the first woman and the first man. Neither are doctrines such as predestination, human corruption, original sin and its connection with baptism clearly present in the writings of Paul especially as those doctrines later came to be understood.

All of these themes will be elaborated in the chapters which follow.

---

[11] Mythological as used here does not refer to explanations humans once took to be true, but now no longer believe because scientific evidence has disproved them. Rather, myth is a reference to stories (usually about the gods setting patterns for humans and for human history) which people have understood as revealing the order of the universe and the meaning of human life.

Misunderstanding Six:
God Supports Conservative Politics

> Perhaps (Ralph) Reed's most notable achievement has been the tremendous influence of the Christian Coalition on the outcome of the 1994 congressional elections. Reed claimed that one in three voters at the polls that November were conservative Christians who shared the values of the Coalition. During the Republican convention in 1996, it was clear that Christian Coalition members gained control of the party platform. (Weaver 249)

This chapter will show that the political struggle for the ownership of God between empire and its victims is not a recent phenomenon. On the contrary, the contest finds its roots in the biblical texts themselves. It is by no means new.

What is new, however, is the post-colonial politicization of the Judeo-Christian tradition, specifically in terms of a struggle between the elite right and the oppressed left, since it was from the former colonies that liberation theology emerged as a force for social change. It was countered in the 1980s by a politically conservative theology that has progressively assumed an indispensable role in today's globalized order and its maintenance by force. Christianity has been and continues to be used as a key weapon of destruction and of death.

This should come as no surprise. Every established order and its defense are routinely supported by appeal to a transcendent power which sanctions them – whether the power is called "God" or "History" or "Manifest Destiny." The given order, it is implied, reflects a transcendent realm, which finds expression in the statutes belonging to the order's culture. Normally laws rationalized in this way have been made to protect the interests of the rich and powerful who control most societies. Since the laws allegedly reflect the divine will, they are routinely sacrificial, in the sense that human welfare, especially of those eventually classified as "collateral damage," must be subordinated to divinely endorsed law and order. Such need for human sacrifice was a favorite theme of Greek tragedy from *Iphigenia* to *Antigone*. Analyzing theology's content and usages therefore, is essential for anyone wishing to make sense of public discourse.

Invoking a conservative God to support the interests of the rich does not, it is argued here, agree with the main thrust of the Jewish Testament tradition—nor, as we shall see, of its Christian Testament counterpart. As Brazil's Carlos Mesters has argued, virtually alone among the founding documents of Western culture, these traditions preserve and centralize the memory, spirituality, aspirations and social ordering principles of a largely poor and oppressed people seeking liberation from exploitation by the rich and powerful. The biblical conception of law, for instance, can be understood as protecting the poor against their exploiters. "Thou shalt not steal" was directed primarily against the rich who normally appropriated peasants' farms to enlarge their own holdings, and who routinely paid their workers far less than was due.

Yet, throughout the Bible and in the traditions of the post-biblical period, we find a struggle between this majoritarian understanding of Yahweh as a legislator on behalf of the poor, dispensing them from law when it works against their interests, and a rich minority's contradictory conception of God as the enforcer of law favoring the elite. The struggle between these Gods—the one the oppressor of the poor, and the other their liberator, expresses a leitmotif running through most of the Bible's inclusions; it represents the theogony, or Battle of the Gods, within the Judeo-Christian tradition itself. As already indicated, and as will be elaborated below, this theogony continues with a vengeance in our own day.

Jewish Testament Battle of the Gods

The Jewish Testament struggle between Gods and their laws appears in three basic movements—each connected with socio-political orders and their laws. The first surfaces in the Hebrews' earliest traditions and is codified in the Mosaic Law. It is the tradition of the God who protects the enslaved and poor. The second tradition presents a God of the elite and powerful. It emerges at the outset of the final millennium before our era, and is reflected in the Davidic Law. The third Jewish Testament tradition is that of the prophets and apocalyptic writers. Speaking on behalf of the Mosaic Law, Yahweh's spokespersons call the elite and powerful to task for perverting God's intended order.

The Mosaic Covenant

The earliest biblical traditions are not about the creation of the world. Even less are they about reward and punishment in some afterlife. Instead, they concern the liberation of a people enslaved by an oppressive order specifically sanctioned by Egyptian law underwritten by the Sun

God, Ra.[12] A charismatic prophet, Moses, demanded release of the slaves, calling on a subversive God who came to be called "Yahweh." Egypt's pharaoh, however, refused in the name of Ra. At times the struggle between the two divinities took on the character of an actual contest of magical powers (e.g. Exodus 7:8-13). In the end, though, Exodus contends that the slave God proved victorious. Moses led the Hebrews (*apiru* or "rebels") out of slavery, northward to a "promised land" called Canaan.

Once there, the former slaves joined other Hebrews who found themselves in rebellion against the burdensome laws of local kings. This Canaanite rebellion was inspired by the heavy tributes and taxes the kings imposed on local farmers they considered their subjects. Each of the potentates had his God who guaranteed and enforced the reigning system. Clearly, then, seizing Canaan from the oppressive kings would require another theogony between Yahweh and the Gods in question. A victory by the rebel God would enable the allied tribes to proceed with their project— the creation of a "liberated zone" where they might live without foreign kings and their oppressive laws and deities.

As they pursued their project, the two groups of Hebrews founded their unity in name, shared history and, above all, in their allegiance to Yahweh, the God of the Poor. The Hebrews called themselves "Israel," and ancestral name belonging to one of the tribal patriarchs whose descendents were among the hordes who fled Egypt. However, the group's unity stemmed more from a shared history of oppression than from common ethnic or tribal factors. A revolutionary project cemented this alliance of poor people.

Legally, the Israelite community was ordered by a set of statutes which came to be known as the Mosaic Law. It underlined and enshrined

---

[12] Among the first expressions of biblical faith we find:

> A wandering Aramean was my ancestor; he went down into Egypt and lived there as an alien, few in number, and there he became a great nation, mighty and populous. When the Egyptians treated us harshly and afflicted us, by imposing hard labor on us, we cried to the LORD, the God of our ancestors; the LORD heard our voice and saw our affliction, our toil and our oppression. The LORD brought us out of Egypt with a mighty hand and an outstretched arm, with a terrifying display of power, and with signs and wonders; and he brought us into this place and gave us this land, a land flowing with milk and honey. So now I bring the first of the fruit of the ground that you, O Lord, have given me. (Deuteronomy 26:2-11)

This text and others like it (e.g. Joshua 24) refer to Israel's struggle against oppressive legal orders which began among a tribally mixed horde of impoverished peoples held in bondage by Egyptian pharaohs roughly 1200 years before the Common Era. Forced to labor in extensive Egyptian building projects, the slaves rebelled. Their resistance involved atheogony from the outset.

Yahweh's character as the savior of the poor and enslaved. The overriding purpose of the Mosaic Law was to insure that Israelites would not return to the slavery and oppression from which they had escaped at such great cost. In a sense, then, it was an anti-law legislation framed against structures of oppression ratified by foreign Gods. Accordingly, both the practices and beliefs which traditionally prepare the way for slavery's return were forbidden. And since it is the poor who are predominantly threatened by oppressive servitude, protective statutes made them its primary beneficiaries. Widows, orphans, resident aliens, poor farmers and slaves themselves: these enjoyed the special protection of the law.[13] Such groups represent precisely the ones for whom Yahweh revealed particular concern in the primordial and defining act of liberation.

> You shall not wrong or oppress a resident alien, for you were aliens in the land of Egypt. You shall not abuse any widow or orphan. If you abuse them, when they cry out to me, I will surely heed their cry; my wrath will burn, and I will kill you with the sword, and your wives shall become widows and your children orphans. (Exodus 22:21-24)

The Davidic Covenant

According to the Biblical narratives, the Mosaic covenant remained in force through the period of Israel's settlement in "the Promised Land" and during its phase of tribal confederacy (1250-1020 B.C.E.). Afterwards, however, pressure from coastal enemies (the Philistines) possessing superior military organization and technology made it possible for elite elements within Israel politically to reorganize the confederacy into a centralized nation-state and to seize power setting themselves up as a royal class. To meet the Philistine threat, the new director class argued that the Israelites required a centralized government, a professionalized military force and the draft, taxes and public works that went along with such developments. In I Sam 9:1-10:16; 11, the prophet Samuel is presented as advancing such claims in the name of the Lord.

However, the transition to a new social order also required a new theology—one is tempted to say "a new God." Israel's elite had to reinterpret and appropriate the Covenant of Moses in a way that made them its direct beneficiaries rather than the lower classes. In this way, the

---
[13] Clearly, the ancient Hebrews were not successful in resisting slavery's reintroduction. The best they could do was to establish laws mitigating the institution's harshness.

elite set the stage for yet another battle of the Gods over laws and their orders. This time the contestants were not so much Israel's God and foreign counterparts, but the Yahweh of the Elite vs. the Yahweh of the Poor.[14]

The group of royal historians whom scholars have called "the Yahwists" advanced the cause of the royal God, the God of the Elite. They supplied the radically new understanding of covenant which changes the party of the second part in Israel's pact with the Lord. Thus under Yahwist influence, the covenant's provisions fundamentally transform so that its clauses no longer primarily concern land given to ordinary people nor justice to the widow, the orphan, the slave and the stranger. Instead, covenant concern is directed towards the royal family. God promises to raise up a successor to King David. The royal covenant's fundamental pledge changes from "I will be their (i.e. the Israelites) God and they will be my people," to I will be his (i.e. the king's) father and he shall be my son" (II Samuel 7:13-14).

With these words, kingship is divinely guaranteed to a single royal family. Specific divine election is no longer necessary, nor is confirmation by the assembly of the people. Now justice is administered indirectly through the king and the royal bureaucracy.[15]

The Prophetic Tradition

This eclipse of the God of the poor eventually gave rise to the prophetic movement, which fiercely confronted the elite usurpation of a poor people's tradition, while championing the cause of Israel's liberating God as originally

---

[14] Evidence of the contest between Israelite Gods appears among the same Samuel traditions which at first endorse the change considered here. In a precise expression of the biblical battle of the Gods with their divergent ordering principles and statutes, the very prophet who is earlier presented as arguing for changes in Israel's organization, warns of the dire consequences entailed in such novelties. In I Sam 7:3-8:22; 10:17-27, Samuel rejects what he says the Lord considers heretical "developments" in the nation's understanding of the covenant. The existence of such contrary traditions side by side not only indicates a Jewish Testament Battle of the Gods, but the urgency perceived by Israel's elite to legitimate the practical transformations under consideration. Accordingly, they forged their own theological rationalizations.
[15] Of course, in theory the basis of the king's judgment continues to be the Mosaic Law. But the very "succession narratives" the Yahwists used to establish the God-sanctioned validity of David's line through Solomon, amply indicate that royal families were little concerned with the common people (II Sam. 7-20; I Kings 1-2; II Sam. 23:1-7). Instead their interests predictably revolved around the court, the king's machismo, sexual conquests, and self-promotion, his imperialistic wars, the internecine struggles of his sons to inherit his throne, and around royal family, Mafia-style vendettas. Similarly, the court prophets, like Nathan, even when critical of the king, exhibited little attention to events reaching outside the orbit of the elite classes. In other words, the thrust of the Davidic covenant was towards swallowing entirely the spirit of its Mosaic counterpart. The Lord originally revealed in the liberation of slaves from Egypt faced reduction to being a God like the rest—the guarantor of elite privilege secured at the expense of the majority.

expressed in the Mosaic tradition. Prophets arose in force after historical events profoundly called into question the Davidic Pact. Following the death of David's son and successor, Solomon, the nation of Israel was split in two – a kingdom of the South (Judah) and that of the North (Israel). So in terms of a united kingdom, David's "eternal" dynasty lasted but 100 years (roughly 1020-920), though his successors continued to rule in Jerusalem for 350 additional years – till Babylon conquered Judah in 587.

Prophets of Denunciation

Before the advent of those national tragedies, however, prophets like Amos vindicated the God of the Poor by harshly criticizing the laws and order endorsed by Israel's rich and famous who had forgotten the demands of the Mosaic Covenant protecting the community's least well-off. The words of Amos reveal such commitment of the God of the Poor in an unparalleled way,

> "The end has come upon my people Israel; I will never again pass them by. The songs of the temple shall become wailing in that day," says the Lord God. Hear this, you that trample on the needy and bring to ruin the poor of the land . . . and practice deceit with false balances, buying the poor for silver and the needy for a pair of sandals, and selling the sweepings of the wheat. The Lord has sworn by the pride of Jacob: surely I will never forget any of their deeds. (8:2-7)

Prophets of Annunciation

Once in exile and reduced to a state reminiscent of their ancestors in Egypt, Israelites encountered prophets like Isaiah II. Speaking for the divine champion of the poor, these prophets consoled the descendents of Abraham, Isaac and Jacob after the Lord's people themselves had been reduced to poverty by the Assyrians (in 722), and by the Babylonians (in 587). For example, Isaiah II appeals to the God of the poor requesting a new Exodus for his compatriots in exile.

> Was it not you who dried up the sea, the waters of the great deep, who made the depths of the sea a way for the redeemed to cross over? So the ransomed of the LORD shall return and come to Zion with singing, everlasting joy shall be upon their heads; they shall

obtain joy and gladness and sorrow and sighing shall flee away. (51:10-11)

What is important to note with both prophets of denunciation and annunciation is that their fundamental imagery is not that of the court—anointing, dynasty, succession, and enthronement—the imagery of the elite. Rather, prophetic imagery is basically that of liberation: Egypt, slavery, Exodus, sea, desert and Promised Land. In the case of Amos, Israelites are expected to treat the poor justly, because they themselves were once poor and enslaved; yet God had liberated them from that condition. With Isaiah II, the re-enslaved captives in Babylonia are urged to keep vivid their memory of the first Exodus in order to preserve hope that the miracle of liberation will be eventually reenacted.

Apocalypse

In terms of opposition to Empire (as will become clear in Chapter 13), the literary type, apocalypse, is of special importance. This genre continued to champion the Mosaic Tradition, the God of the Poor, and the order God sanctioned against all rivals. Apocalypse was a form of resistance literature – once again, against particular oppressive orders.[16] The Book of Daniel is the most important apocalyptic work stemming from the period of supreme crisis embodied in the regime of Antiochus IV Epiphanes.

Disguised as a book written centuries earlier and using the enigmatic style typical of the literary genre, Daniel promises an end to the persecution of Antiochus IV.[17] The book centralizes the character of "the Son of Man." This mysterious figure is the vindicating judge of Israel's imperialistic enemies in any age. Later, Mark's gospel tradition identifies Jesus of Nazareth with this resistance figure. For his part, Daniel describes the liberating "Human One" as communicating encouragement and promising victory to the victims of imperialism whether Persian or Greek (11:19-21).

---

[16] The most notable apocalyptic writings were provoked by an unprecedentedly fierce persecution which followed in the wake of Persia's defeat at the hands of the Greeks who subsequently controlled the destiny of Palestine from 331-167. Departing from Persian policy of religious tolerance, Antiochus IV Epiphanes (176-163) tried systematically to liquidate Jewish culture and to impose Greek ways on everyone. By 167 the Seleucid king had actually outlawed the Jewish faith entirely. Observing the Mosaic Law's Sabbath rest and its dietary restrictions were forbidden; "crimes" of circumcision and possession of the Torah were punishable by death. As a result, thousands of Jews were martyred.

[17] The end of Greek persecution finally came when "the Maccabees," the priestly family of Matthias of Modin and his sons Yohannan, Simon, Judah, Eleazar and Jonathan waged a successful guerrilla campaign against the Seleucids. It proved victorious in 142 BCE. Led by the high priest, Simon Maccabee, the Jews finally experienced return to self-government under the regime known as the Hasmonean dynasty.

Conclusion

The Jewish Testament tradition reveals a true struggle of the Gods played out on the pages of the sacred texts themselves. On the one hand, the God of the Elite supports orders where the affluent and powerful are the chosen of God. The poor exist to serve those superior to them. Accordingly, the elite God sanctifies oppressive laws, human sacrifice and debt, even when repaying loans means the death or involuntary servitude of the indebted. At times, the God of the Elite is identified as Yahweh. Such identification, however, is revealed as false by the main thrust of the Jewish tradition. For at least 90% of the ancient texts celebrate the God of the poor. This Yahweh is atheistic relative to all other Gods. The God of the Poor stands against oppressive laws, human sacrifice, debt and the conditions which inevitably lead to such practices. This is the God of Moses, of the prophets and of Daniel, who is revealed by Jesus of Nazareth in the New Testament. All other Gods even if they go by the name "Yahweh," are idols—and are even diabolical.

To reiterate, the argument here is that for centuries Christians have primarily been worshipping an idol, calling him "Yahweh." Even more, that idol is actually Satan in disguise. We turn now to that argument.

Part II

MISUNDERSTANDINGS ABOUT THE BIBLE

Misunderstanding Seven:
There is Only One God

> We can find echoes of the Babylonian (creation) story in the Hebrew Bible (God speaking, for example, saying, "Let us create humankind"), and there are obvious word plays (God's spirit hovers over a "deep," which is *tehom* in Hebrew, a word that comes from Tiamat). (Weaver 12)

Despite the efforts of the prophets and apocalyptic writers, the elite God of empire ultimately prevailed in his theogony with the God of the poor and oppressed. To understand this argument, one must realize that in the biblical tradition, the term "God" is not univocal. Neither is the designation "devil." As Costa Rica's Franz Hinkelammert has argued, both are "hollow concepts" (*El Asalto* 128). They are generic terms whose specific attributes are then filled in after proper names are assigned. For instance, in the Bible, "God" can be identified as Elohim (a curiously plural form appearing in the Book of Genesis), Yahweh (the proper name of the God of Abraham), or with the more generic term – the equivalent of the English word, "God," (which can refer to a variety of Canaanite deities identified as "Baal"). Meanwhile, the hollow concept, "devil," can be "filled in" with names such as Satan or Lucifer. This point must be made here, before specific and telling examples of the pluriform terms can be investigated in Chapters 8 and 9.

Let's begin by considering the divine name. Believers often make the mistake of assuming that whenever the term "God" appears in the Bible, it refers to Yahweh, the God of Israel.[18] This often results in great confusion. It causes Christian readers, for instance, to conclude that the same God revealed in Jesus ordered holy wars involving horrendous slaughters of children, women, the aged and any other innocents who stood in the way of "his people's" military conquests. Inability to see that such a God stands at odds with Jesus' revelation leads to contemporary support for "shock and awe" military operations in which (literally) untold thousands of innocent civilians

---

[18] There are, in fact, several names used for God within the biblical tradition. Yahweh, Elohim (a plural form) and the more generic equivalent of "Lord," Adonai, are among them. The point here is that even when the proper name of God as revealed to Moses—Yahweh—appears, it does not necessarily coincide with its referent as used and displayed by Jesus whom Christians believe represents the fullness of Yahweh's revelations.

are slaughtered when they find themselves in harm's way at the hands, for example, of the United States military. The confusion is compounded when political, military and even religious leaders identify armed aggression with God's purposes, and the enemy's resistance with those of the devil.

Support for such slaughter is most frequently based on the clearly apparent meanings of the sacred texts themselves. That is, it need not be argued that one can easily find texts that in fact support dreadfully gory understandings of God's will. This is because the images of God within Sacred Scripture are themselves contradictory. Sometimes the God is understood as supporting the law; at other times he is the law's harshest critic. On the one hand, he gives minute instructions for his proper worship; then, on the other, he excoriates those who observe such laws. Sometimes the Bible's God demands child sacrifice; then soon afterwards, he opposes it. Sometimes the God revealed in the sacred texts seems bloodthirsty, arbitrary, petulant, and despotic. At other times, he is full of mercy, forgiveness and compassion.

More liberal commentators often explain away such contradictions by referring to "primitive" understandings that later matured to become clarified, nuanced, refined, and revised till finally, in Jesus, they receive their ultimate correction. For these interpreters, Jesus' revelation cancels all previous partial, and for that reason, inadequate, distorted and erroneous understandings of God.

Meanwhile, more conservative analysts accept the apparent contradictions at face value. They observe that God indeed can seem arbitrary and cruel to limited human perceptions. This, however, is due to the failings of human understanding. God's apparent cruelty is actually a manifestation of mercy and love. Strangely, such commentators and believers influenced by them seem to prioritize the apparently cruel understandings of God over those advanced by Jesus himself – almost as if Jesus' own teaching on forgiveness, violence, war and peace were somehow too soft, too liberal, and too feminine. It is nearly as if Jesus' words, rather than the God who apparently contradicts them, represent the teachings that have to be "explained away." However, as will be seen below, the need to explain away the clear teachings of Jesus stems from the conflict between his words and the principles of empire, which Christianity has supported at least since the 4th century. Once again, they are the satanic principles which necessitate the demonization of Jesus' own Spirit' – which tradition refers to as the Holy Spirit.

A better way to explain the Bible's contradictory understandings of God is to join fundamentalists in accepting them at face value. However, in accord with the thesis presented here, it seems best to understand such contradictions, not (as fundamentalists do) in terms of applying them to the Bible's Yahweh. Rather, they should be comprehended in terms of the already-referenced "Battle of the Gods," which Pablo Richard, for instance, finds contained within the Judeo-Christian tradition itself.

As elaborated by Richard and Hinkelammert, then, the Bible's revelation largely centers on the story of how Israel's God, Yahweh, revealed himself to oppressed slaves. He was their champion; they were his chosen people. As seen in Chapter 6, however, the rich and powerful tried to appropriate that God for themselves and their projects. This resulted in a conflict which stretches across the books of the Bible. It is a contest between conflicting Gods—for instance (as will be seen) the God of Eve vs. the God of Cain; the God of Abraham and Moses vs. God-as-Baal; and the God of Jesus vs. the God of Rome (and eventually Constantine and St. Augustine).

On this understanding, Jesus becomes the prophet whose revelation decided ultimately which is the true God of Israel. Jesus decided in favor of the God of Abraham and Moses, i.e. in favor of the God of the poor and oppressed. Eventually, though, the Constantinian decision to incorporate Christianity into the Roman Empire necessitated the reversal of Jesus' judgment. Not only Jesus' God, but Jesus himself had to be demonized, and Satan put in Yahweh's place. Thus the God of Cain, the Canaanites, Rome – and Satan—was returned to power.

Understanding all of this requires clarification of Satan's identity, and distinguishing him from Lucifer and "the devil."

Satan, Lucifer and the Devil

The shock of identifying Christian faith with a satanic cult, no doubt seems harsh. However, its impact is somewhat lessened by realizing that in the biblical tradition, Satan is not the same as the devil. Neither is the devil the same as Lucifer. In fact, both Satan and Lucifer were highly respected figures in biblical literature and in ancient traditions based on those sources. The same cannot be said for the devil, who in all accounts remains an evil spirit. As a "hollow concept" however, his identity nonetheless becomes confounded with both Satan and Lucifer throughout the Judeo-Christian tradition.

Satan

To begin with, in scripture-based mythology, Satan was one of the chief members of the heavenly court. In fact, Satan was originally the representative of the Persian Empire in those celestial precincts. It was evidently impossible for the ancient biblical authors to believe that an entity as powerful as Persia could not be represented in the ultimate seat of power. As imperial advisor of Yahweh, then, Satan was the defender of law and order – a kind of heavenly Attorney-General, or better yet, a personage modeled on the feared Persian Secret Police (Wink 100). As seen in the Book of Job, Satan kept close watch over human affairs on earth, reporting them scrupulously to Yahweh himself, and insisting that justice be accomplished, come what may (Job 1:6).

It is Satan's imperial penchant for making the law absolute that results in his downfall. In a familiar myth found in the Book of Revelation, he thus incites a rebellion against himself on the part of the Archangel Michael, who is Yahweh's defender against idolatry (see Chapter 11). A cosmic battle ensues. Satan and the angels allied with him are defeated. Significantly, Satan is hurled from heaven and cast down to earth where his legalistic spirit continues as the order of the day (see below).

Satan, then, is the spirit who absolutizes the law of the patriarchal order. He is masculine. His order stands in sharp contrast to that of Yahweh, which is one of love and mercy—feminine.

So the claim that Christians are devotees of a satanic cult is to assert that they have accepted Satan's imperial order, absolutizing law. They have rejected the God of love and mercy, particularly as revealed in the person of Jesus, who subordinates all law to human well-being.

Lucifer

Rejecting the God revealed in Jesus means that Jesus himself had to be demonized. This requirement follows the principle that when evil becomes good, good must be considered evil. The process of demonizing Jesus can be observed in the transformation of one of his principal early titles, Lucifer. From ancient times, this name which means "bearer of light," was consistently associated with the morning star, with the planet Venus, and with the feminine spirit of rebellion against the patriarchy, which, as we saw, eventually became identified with Satan.[19] For more than three centuries in early Christian tradition, Lucifer was associated directly with Jesus who also rebelled against patriarchal law. In fact, the title itself was commonly conferred on Christians at baptism. Up until the 4th century, the cult of St. Lucifer was observed in Italy. Even today the Holy Saturday liturgy of the Catholic Church continues to refer to Jesus himself as Lucifer.

---

[19] The author of the Book of Revelation has Jesus identify himself with Lucifer in this sense in 22:16, "I Jesus have sent my angel to you with this testimony for the churches. I am the root and the offspring of David, the bright morning star." (See Hinkelammert, "El Apocalipsis," p. 4.)

The demonizing of Jesus as Lucifer was demanded by the fact that as Lucifer, he relativized the law so dear to empire, rather than absolutizing it, as empire always demands. He consistently put human welfare above the law. In doing so, he embodied fulfillment of Yahweh's heavenly law by breaking even the most sacred of laws on earth (i.e., the Sabbath law). All of this will be elaborated below. Suffice it here to reiterate that the entire process entailed transforming Lucifer into a diabolic character.

The Devil

The devil, even in serious studies such as Elaine Pagels', is a kind of general personification of the great force of evil not clearly distinguished from Satan and Lucifer. Historically the term "the devil" has been used interchangeably with Satan and Lucifer, ignoring the more accurate distinctions indicated above. Ignored, for instance, is Satan's overriding concern for power – specifically the power of empire, as will be indicated in the temptation of Jesus, and in the Book of Revelation, where the satanic dragon is identified as the source of empire's authority (Rev. 13:4). Ignored too is the fact just mentioned that Lucifer was originally a Jesus figure – rebellious against despotic patriarchal law.

Jesus-Lucifer's rebellion followed the spirit of female revolt which, as will be shown below, initially finds expression in the decision of the First Woman to eat from the Tree of Knowledge of Good and Evil. Since such rebellion conflicted with empire's requirement of unquestioning obedience, that Spirit (of Jesus) had to be quashed. Demonizing it (and with it, the authentic figure of Jesus) was a necessary first step in doing so. As a result, all interpretations of Christian faith sympathetic to the insurgency of those routinely oppressed by empire had to be deemed "heresy." In other words, if one is seeking the most authentic version of Christian faith, heresy is a good place to start looking.

As opposed to Satan's concern with power, the unqualified and generic "devil's" domain has been traditionally associated with personal morality. Often represented as a seductive woman, the devil legendarily tempted holy men to break their vow of chastity. This was the case with Origen, St. Anthony, Augustine, Abelard and St. Thomas Aquinas. Put otherwise, like Lucifer, the devil too came to represent female subversive power. However, that power was not political but personal, and, once again, usually associated with sex.

Conclusion

Distinguishing Satan from Lucifer and the Devil as noted above will help the reader remain clear about the argument unfolding here. That argument is not that fundamentalists (both Catholic and Evangelical) are devil worshippers. Nor (unfortunately) is it that they offer incense at the altar of Lucifer. Rather, the case is that they are unwitting followers of Satan, the author and defender of empire. As such they have set themselves against Jesus-Lucifer, and against the God who the Bible indicates has chosen the poor as his own people. They have also set themselves against the God of Eve, who is responsible for the humanization of "earth creatures."

Misunderstanding Eight:
Eve Sinned First

Some church leaders (mostly male) would say that, indeed, God did create women with natures and attributes that are different from those of men: men are strong, rational, naturally inclined towards philosophical speculation, and meant to rule, whereas women are weak, emotional, naturally inclined toward bodily life (motherhood), and meant to be ruled (Weaver 251).

A number of years ago, I remember being unusually surprised while teaching an introductory class in biblical interpretation. My students and I were reading the Book of Genesis together – specifically with the story of the First Man and the First Woman. I wanted my students to understand that narrative in terms of myth. My point was to get them beyond that word's definition as a story we once thought true, but now realize is fictional. Instead, my intention was to help them to see myth as a rich and insightful complex of stories that transcend questions of fact or fiction. "They're all true," I told them. "Some of them even happened."

My meaning was that myths are stories human beings have remembered and revered because they somehow resonate as true in the sense of uncovering the meaning of human life in relation to God, fellow humans and nature. As such, any mythology worth its salt represents a "rabbit hole" of interminable depth. There is no end to the insights it evokes. As our faculty development group traveling to the Middle East was reminded by a Jewish speaker from the ultra-conservative wing of Judaism, it is odd to imagine that the word of an infinite God can have only one meaning. If it is God's word, it too should have infinite meaning. Every day's reading should find something new and startling.

To make a similar point, I had the brilliant (I thought) idea of demonstrating for students the incredible richness of biblical mythology as discovered by smart and informed people of faith. So I showed them the first episode of Bill Moyers' series on Genesis. The installment kicked off the popular PBS program which gathered together theologians, historians, scripture scholars, pastors, poets, and philosophers – men and women "of the Book," from the Christian, Jewish and Islamic traditions. Their round table unraveled particular episodes in the one book of the Jewish Testament that comprises, no doubt, that volume's most familiar stories. The conversation in Episode One, I thought, was exceptionally rich, full of insight and marked by a consistent creativity of interpretation.

My surprise came when students responded lukewarmly at best to our shared viewing. "They didn't seem to know what they were talking about," students commented. "I mean these people are ministers and rabbis, right? Hardly any of them seemed to know what the Adam and Eve story really means. They all seemed confused. Hardly any of them even talked about original sin, and how Jesus came to take it away."

I was surprised and a bit disappointed by that response. No doubt that reflected naivety on my part, even after decades of teaching basically fundamentalist students in college religion classes. Student reaction in effect denied the heuristic value of the mythology we had been discussing. It showed how strongly a single interpretation of a highly multivalent story has taken hold to the exclusion of myriad interpretations that arguably make more sense. According to the received interpretation, the "Adam and Eve" story is about an original sin that has been passed down from generation to generation, profoundly corrupted human nature, and the cosmos itself. The "sin of our first parents" necessitated the sacrificial death of Jesus without which all of us would deservedly end up in hell – cast into its depths by a justly wrathful God.

In all of this, Eve was the main culprit. She sinned first, and then inveigled her hapless, unsuspecting spouse to follow her sinful example. Eve's punishment, inherited by every woman since, is to be subordinate to her husband in a God-sanctioned patriarchy which demands that female irrationality, emotion and passion be moderated by the male reason and control.

But is that really what the story of the First Man and the First Woman is about? And where did the story about original sin, human corruption, and woman's part in "the Fall" come from? The argument here is that it's all connected with empire's co-option of Christianity. Consider the history.

Original Sin and Imperial Interests

As will become clear in Chapter 10, the crucial historical juncture which necessitated the received interpretation of the Genesis myth came during the reign of the Emperor Constantine. The emperor's politically astute decision to embrace Christianity involved reinterpreting the entire Christian tradition. To that end, the "Adam and Eve" story was crucial.

Constantine's decision to embrace Christianity occurred near the year 313 C.E., with its promulgation of the Edict of Milan. The Edict made the religion of Jesus legal for the first time. Years later, in 381, the Emperor Theodosius made Christianity the official religion of Rome. By the end of the 4th century, then, Christianity had been radically changed. As we will see, by then it had replaced the worship of the biblical God with adoration of Satan.

The transition from worship of Yahweh to worship of Satan was not simple. The whole Judeo-Christian tradition had to be turned on its head – changed from one that sanctioned disobedience to law (especially imperial law) to one that demanded unquestioning compliance. This involved reversing the significance of key events and persons within the tradition.

To begin with, the biblical center of gravity had to be relocated, from the main event of the Exodus to the comparatively minor mythological story of the First Man and the First Woman. Christians had felt an imperative to do so ever since it became apparent that gentiles were replacing Jews as the majority within the primitive community. Non-Jews, of course, would have had difficulty relating to the Exodus which seemed so highly foreign, belonging as it did to a marginal ethnic group distinguished by odd dietary customs, and by the even stranger and more repulsive practice of circumcision. Exodus was a story of national liberation. What was needed was a narrative center to which even sophisticated Romans might relate. That story turned out to be the myth of the First Woman and First Man.

But even that narrative had to be reinterpreted. Until Augustine, the story, like all good mythology, had been open to many explanations. Ignoring the absence of the term "sin" in the text, most nonetheless understood the myth as an account of the first human transgression. But at most the lasting impact of the act was taken in terms of negative example. It represented the kind of choice believers should not make in their quest for self-rule and autonomy. Gnostic Christians, on the other hand, often interpreted the myth allegorically, as an account of liberation through disobedience, i.e. how the first humans became free by disobeying a command of a tyrannical and jealous God (Pagels, *Adam and Eve* xxiv).

Only with Augustine, however, did his highly idiosyncratic understanding of Genesis and related texts take root (109). He described First Parents with god-like decision-making power to corrupt the entire human race and all of creation, for all time (128). The story's moral – to obey blindly even the most despotic orders – fit in nicely with imperial needs. Little wonder, then, that following the wedding of Christianity to empire, the Augustinian understanding eliminated its rival alternatives.

It wasn't, however, Genesis alone that called for reinterpretation. The character of Israel's furthest back ancestor, Abraham, had to be changed as well. He was transformed from the one whose heroism consisted in his refusal to obey a capricious command to kill his son, to the man who found identity and reward in his willingness to offer child sacrifice. In this way, the religion of Israel (and of Christianity) was transformed from a faith forbidding the murder of one's children to a belief system that required blind obedience to highly arbitrary orders even those demanding sacrifice of one's offspring (again, an important requirement of empire).

Above all, the person and teachings of Jesus had to be radically altered to make his teachings compatible with empire. He had been the prophetic figure who fulfilled God's law by prioritizing human welfare over even the most sacred of laws. With accession to empire, Jesus became the model of obedience – to a God who, like Abraham's Baal (see below), and the emperor whom Yahweh was transformed to represent, demanded sacrifice of one's offspring. Thus Jesus' death was interpreted as fulfilling God's law.

Similarly, Jesus' life and particularly his death needed reinterpretation. Rather than completely invalidating the law, as Paul had taught, both became events that affirmed its supreme validity. In fact, the imperial interpretation of Jesus changed him precisely into the giver of a New Law. It also misrepresented him as a God who had been murdered by those refusing to accept his legislation, and who were deicides as a result. These God killers were originally understood to be Jews. Over the centuries, they became all who refused the Law of Christ, which had become co-extensive with the law of empire. Jews or not, any of these law-breakers could be pursued, persecuted and killed with impunity.

Finally, the most anti-imperial of the Bible's traditions, the apocalyptic, had to be depoliticized and tamed in order to enlist it in the service of Roman domination. Accordingly, it was reinterpreted to address the end of the world, rather than with the end of empire. In the process, Satan became simply the devil, the Great Tempter – overwhelmingly in the domain of personal sexuality.

The chapters which follow consider each of these transformations one-by-one. Let's begin in this chapter, with examination of the myth of the First Man and the First Woman.

Adam and Eve, The Tradition's New Center of Gravity

Once again, an important step in the inversion of Christianity's meaning was the centralization of the account of the First Woman and the First Man. The story is virtually ignored in the teachings of Jesus. Paul, it's true, uses that account to explain Jesus' significance. But even Paul does not refer to the story in terms of redemption from "original sin" as understood since Augustine. There is not even any mention of "sin" in the Genesis story itself. In fact, as already indicated, the earliest use of the term in Genesis surfaces in the account of Abel's murder at the hands of Cain. In a literal sense, *that* was the original sin. Likewise, in the New Testament, sin remains unconnected with the First Parents until the Letter to Timothy, one of the Christian Testament's latest inclusions. It was not until the 5th century that the doctrine of original sin took shape at all, when St. Augustine centralized it as the cornerstone of his theology.

With Augustine, then, the Judeo-Christian tradition's center of gravity shifted from liberation from (the Egyptian) empire—which in the Exodus accounts provided the foundation for Israel's faith—to one of blind obedience to law. It shifted from disobedience to (Egypt's) imperial law to obedience to despotic and patriarchal legislation characteristic of any empire. Making that shift required an unprecedented focalizing and reinterpretation of the "Adam and Eve" account.

At the risk of irreverence, consider the Genesis narrative in terms of "Cool Hand Luke." Before Augustine distorted it, the "Adam and Eve" story was more like that than of an account of "Original Sin." The Paul Newman character, of course, was a prisoner who asserted his human dignity before the despotic, arbitrary commands of a prison warden who tried repeatedly but unsuccessfully to confine and "break his spirit." In so doing, Luke awakens the kindred spirits of a whole prison population, and presumably of the film's audience as well.

The story of the First Woman and First Man was something like that. A patriarchal and despotic God gives an arbitrary command to the first couple. That sort of God happens to be the very image of Solomon, the king of Israel from whose court the "Paradise" story originates. "Adam" and "Eve" are not to eat of the mythological tree of "knowledge of good and evil" – the attainment of which would humanize them.

The serpent, however, the traditional symbol for the goddess, advises the Woman of the benefits of disobeying the God's command. As serpent, the goddess counsels that eating the forbidden fruit will make Eve like God and will besides give her eternal life; she will not die. Commenting on this interaction, Hinkelammert observes,

> In the final analysis, the opposition between God and the serpent does not embody a simple dualism. The serpent is not the devil, and God is not the God of Abraham. The serpent is a double figure. On the one hand, it says "You will be like God." In this it tells no lie, given that God himself confirms that the humans

> indeed became like God as a direct result of eating of the forbidden tree. But the serpent also lies, when it promises that the humans will not die. Despite that promise, the result of (Eve's) rebellion is that the humans are confronted with the inevitability of death, as they discover that they are mortal. (81)

This analysis insightfully distinguishes the God of Abraham and the God of the Genesis account. This hints at a solution to the puzzle of the plural references to that God in the story (Gen. 3:22). However, Hinkelammert questionably identifies the serpent as lying to the woman when it promises that humans will not die. This judgment might have been different had Hinkelammert consistently recognized the serpent as a goddess figure associated with the theology that frequently characterized ancient goddess worship. That theology, like the promise of "eternal life" attributed to Jesus by early Christian tradition, identified as the specifically human vocation the attainment of unending life (in what Paul refers to as the "spiritual body"). In the goddess tradition, undifferentiated eternal life transcended the death of the physical body (80).[20] Put otherwise, far from representing a lie, the words of the serpent express what later Christian theology was to characterize as a "proto-evangelium,"—the announcement of the true human vocation to appropriate as their authentic life the indwelling transcendent divine spirit common to all of creation.[21]

In any case, the Woman listens to the serpent/goddess. By this act, Eve becomes the heroine—the "Cool Hand Luke" in the story. As a result, the account recognizes the woman's newly attained divine condition by awarding her the name "Life," Eva (80). With that title, she becomes identified with the triumphant goddess figure—the female aspect of the

---

[20] This is not to say that goddess traditions (and much less, the Judeo-Christian tradition) fall into what Eckart Tolle criticizes as the "You are not your body" school of spirituality (95). Instead, typical goddess spiritualities acknowledge an underlying life force common to all living beings and shared by all of creation. Tolle calls this an "inner body" which remains unchanged even in the face of the sickness and death of the physical body (96). Hindu spirituality calls the underlying life force prakriti and, at times, kundalini (Easwaran, Like 428). Both differ slightly from one another, but are closely related to Atman, "'The Self ',the innermost soul of every creature, which is divine"(426). Such understandings seem compatible with the "spiritual body" to which Paul refers (Hinkelammert, El asalto 80). Realities like these also appear to be what mystics of all traditions understand as embodied in the lives of all "Spirit Persons," such as Jesus (see below), and as surviving after death.

[21] As Hinkelammert indicates, the positive representation of the serpent is found elsewhere in the Judeo-Christian tradition. In Numbers 21:4-9, Moses erects a bronze serpent to miraculously save the Israelites from sickness and death resulting from an attack of ferocious snakes. Later on, Jesus is presented as comparing himself to that same Mosaic serpent (Jn. 3:14). During the Middle Ages it was common for crucifixes to replace the corpus of Jesus with that of a serpent wound around the cross' horizontal beam (82).

creative force, and the antithesis of the patriarchal, despotic God of arbitrary commands. In this first Battle of Gods, then, the Goddess wins.[22] In other words, the myth of the First Woman and the First Man is the story of Life attaining the human condition. Life personified in the first woman accords to the human race not only the knowledge separating it from the animal kingdom, but also what would later be termed "critical consciousness." That is, the knowledge Eve obtains from following the serpent's advice is not only the crucial distinction between good and evil.

More basically, it is knowledge of the patriarchy, its oppression and fundamental lie—Do what you are told, even if it does not make sense, even if it prevents you from realizing your humanity itself. In uncovering that lie, Eve becomes the proto-typical liberator—the rebel against the patriarchy. Her spirit surfaces continuously among human beings who disobey the arbitrary, senseless and self-serving commands of patriarchal law-givers. It appears in Moses, the prophets, in Jesus and among the early Christians.[23] In Augustine's distortion of the story, the command not to know good and evil is taken at face value, and as the very foundation of the Judeo-Christian tradition. The Genesis story, sans its liberation leitmotif, is foregrounded. Meanwhile, the Exodus account of liberation from empire is ignored as such. The Woman is transformed from heroine to villain for listening to "the devil." Her naive husband is seduced by her, and so is castigated along with his wife and all of creation. Human beings and all of creation are cursed, mortally weakened, and rendered incapable of pleasing God. Forever, "Adam and Eve" become the prototypical sinners. The moral of the story is to obey the patriarch's arbitrary commands or justly suffer the terrible consequences. It is a story perfectly shaped for empire's purposes.

---

[21] It is interesting to note, however, that the goddess' victory is short-lived. In Genesis 3:14-15, the patriarchal God addresses the serpent goddess figure, predicting alienation between the woman, her descendants and the Goddess. He foretells the coming victory of the patriarchal God, whose order replaces the reign of the goddess. The divine patriarch's victory is established in what Hinkelammert calls the "foundational murder" of Abel by this brother, Cain. With that assassination, as we shall see, the vengeful patriarchal order is sealed. "And I will put enmity between you and the woman, and between your offspring and hers; he will crush your head, and you will strike his heel."

[22] None of this is to deny that the First Couple's new condition was experienced negatively as well as positively. Attaining the human condition and the beginnings of critical consciousness proves to be a curse as well as a blessing. However, here it should be noted that a curse is not the same as a punishment (87). Nevertheless, along with the joys of being human come sickness, pain, fruitless work and death of the physical body. The human condition is ambivalent, and one can never return to the bliss of animal ignorance.

Cain's Original Sin
The Triumph of His God

In embracing the patriarchal and imperial order, the church endorses as sanctioned by God the order of Cain and the order of Lemech – i.e., the structures of empire. That is, it accepts as the inevitable consequence of Adam and Eve's "original sin," a world-wide corruption whereby fratricide and overwhelming retaliatory murders are standard operating procedure. So as a consequence of his parents' sin, Cain kills his brother, Abel. The normal misunderstanding has it that in doing so, Cain is inevitably following the footsteps of Eve and Adam. No one can expect more in a fallen world. To do so is unrealistic, utopian and even contrary to God's will, which is that humans be punished for the sin of their First Parents.

In the Augustinian interpretation, then, the punishment continues following Cain's fratricide. History persists in its downward trajectory, and nothing can be done to remediate the downhill slide. Cain founds the first city. There a patriarchal order is institutionalized wherein those who kill a member of Cain's family will lose seven members of their own tribe (Gen. 4:15). Subsequently, that arrangement is intensified to the extreme point celebrated in the macho braggadocio of Cain's offspring, Lemech, who sings before his harem, "If Cain is avenged seven times, then Lemech will be avenged seventy times seven." It is the response of patriarchy and of empire to those who dare raise their fists in resistance.

However, in the biblical tradition, Cain's murder of Abel is not presented as the consequence of his parents' "original sin." Rather it counteracts the liberation achieved by Eve. Cain's act is presented as a Foundational Murder. In itself, it sets the tone – creates an order – for the rest of human history. It sets in motion the gory arithmetic of the fratricide enforced by all patriarchies, from the single digit retaliation of Cain to the fearful retaliation of Lemech, mirrored in the triple digit vengeance of Hitler in Poland and of the United States in Iraq. More specifically, Cain's calculation and Lemech's is the typical reaction of Egyptians to rebellious slaves and of Babylonians, Persians, Greeks and Romans to Jewish insurrection. It is the procedure followed by the United States in reply to Iraqi resistance, in its current war, as indicated by the body counts – approximately 700,000 Iraqi dead compared with about 5000 U.S. dead.

However, in Genesis, though Cain's murder of Abel is foundational, it is not the consequence of any "Original Sin." To reiterate, Eve's action was a liberation from the animal state. Instead, as noted earlier, the term "sin" appears in the written text for the first time in connection with Cain and Abel. There God says to Cain,

> Why are you angry? Why is your face downcast? If you do what is right, will you not be accepted? But if you do not do what is right, sin is crouching at your door; it desires to have you, but you must master it. (Gen. 3:6-7)

These words precede the murder of Abel at Cain's hands and anticipate the action that is "not right." What is noteworthy is that the "original sin" referred to here is not something to be surrendered to as an inevitable punishment for another's failing, or as the best that can be hoped for in a fallen world. Instead the sinful order represented by the first fratricide is an obstacle to be overcome – to be mastered.

Attempts to master Cain's impulse appear in the Bible, where the scope of vengeance is reduced by law from 70x7 to 1x1 – "an eye for an eye and a tooth for a tooth." Finally, Jesus does away with vengeance altogether. He says,

> You have heard that it was said, "Eye for eye, and tooth for tooth." But I tell you, do not resist an evil person. If someone strikes you on the right cheek, turn to him the other also. (Mt. 5:38-40)

Jesus' teaching goes even further and substitutes overwhelming forgiveness for Lemech's overwhelming vengeance. In a direct reference to Lemech, Jesus' mandated response to injury is not injury 70x7, but forgiveness in the same proportion.

> Then Peter came to Jesus and asked, "Lord, how many times shall I forgive my brother when he sins against me? Up to seven times?" Jesus answered, "I tell you, not seven times, but seventy times seven."

Conclusion

Despite Jesus' clear words, Christian fundamentalism in both its Catholic and Protestant forms typically rejects Jesus' prescription. At best it endorses the Law of the Talion. At worst it embraces the arithmetic of Empire— 70x7—or even an ethic of using nuclear weapons against those who dare offend the United States. Such calculations represent not merely surrender to "Original Sin." They represent a rejection of the God of the Bible and of Jesus himself in favor of Satan, the one who gives authority to Empire (Rev. 13:4).

Misunderstanding Nine:
Abraham Would Have Killed His Son for God

> . . . God tested Abraham's faith and obedience by asking him to sacrifice Isaac. Faith and trust in God is not a one-time event, but part of an ongoing relationship that requires heroic obedience. (Weaver 13)

The Christian Church's decision to endorse empire, and to accept the order of Satan, necessitated not merely the defamation of Eve, and the embrace of Cain's fratricide as an inevitable order willed by God. It required as well the taming of Israel's hallowed ancestor, Abraham, and the biblical rationalization of infanticide and human sacrifice as a way of honoring God. Empires of every era are founded on the willingness of parents to surrender the lives of their children for the supposed "Greater Good" represented by imperial wars of conquest. Patriotic Americans today routinely invoke Bible-based faith in surrendering their sons and daughters to the military, even when the reasons for doing so are unclear, arbitrary, or even mendacious. Similarly, people of faith demonstrate little problem with accepting the deaths of huge numbers of innocent children as "collateral damage" during bombing raids, or as the outcome of economic embargoes and sanctions placed on designated enemies such as Cuba and Iraq. The deaths of millions of children associated with the simple outworking of the free market are accepted and therefore endorsed as inevitable consequences of laws of supply and demand instituted by God himself.

The difficulty with such acceptance, however, has always been that the Jewish biblical tradition took a clear stance against child sacrifice, which was routinely practiced among the neighboring tribes of the ancient Israelites. In this connection, the Abraham-Isaac story found in Genesis 22:1-19 is key:

> . . . God tested Abraham. He said to him . . .
> "Take your son, your only son Isaac, whom you love, and go to the land of Moriah, and offer him there as a burnt offering on one of the mountains that I shall show you." So Abraham rose early in the morning, saddled his donkey, and took two of his young men with him, and his son Isaac. . . Abraham took the wood of the burnt offering and laid it on his son Isaac, and he

> himself carried the fire and the knife. . . . Isaac said to his father Abraham . . . "The fire and the wood are here, but where is the lamb for a burnt offering?" Abraham said, "God himself will provide the lamb for a burnt offering, my son" . . . . When they came to the place that God had shown him, Abraham built an altar there and laid the wood in order. He bound his son Isaac, and laid him on the altar, on top of the wood. Then Abraham reached out his hand and took the knife to kill his son. But the angel of the LORD called to him from heaven and said . . . "Do not lay your hand on the boy or do anything to him; **for now I know that you fear God, since you have not withheld your son, your only son, from me**." And Abraham looked up and saw a ram, caught in a thicket by its horns. Abraham went and took the ram and offered it up as a burnt offering instead of his son. (Emphasis added)

Traditionally, this story has been interpreted to say that faith is demonstrated by willingness to sacrifice one's children—especially in wars that are invariably presented as willed by God. However, the narrative's close examination shows that it attributes the elimination, not the acceptance, of child sacrifice to a revelation made to the founding father of the people of Israel. That is, like the Mosaic Law itself, the story is essentially subversive of an oppressive legal order – this one demanding human sacrifice on the conviction that death brings life. According to this legend, Abraham's original perception was that Yahweh, like other Gods, operated according to this logic. Prepared to fulfill a sacrificial law, he receives a special revelation nullifying the reigning legalism of his day. The story reveals the God of Israel as the one for whom life brings life. It roots Israelite faith in a non-sacrificial tradition.

Nonetheless, there are indications within the text of attempts to obscure its subversive character. The passage thus reflects yet another "Battle of the Gods" within the Bible itself. The battle is indicated by the change in the identity of the one who orders Isaac's sacrifice. (The amendment is reflected in The New Oxford Annotated Bible translation above.) It is "God" who tells Abraham to sacrifice his son. But it is "Yahweh" (the LORD), the God of Israel who, at the story's end calls to Abraham from heaven and says, "Do not lay your hand on the boy or do anything to him. . ." The distinction is important, since it contrasts the will of "God" (i.e. the reigning Babylonian deity, Baal) with that of Israel's God. The former led Abraham's contemporaries to routinely sacrifice their firstborn. Nothing heroic was involved in doing so. It was the common practice of the day. By contrast, what distinguished the God of Israel was his rejection of human sacrifice.

We have the priest-redactors of the Davidic dynasty with its own imperial pretensions, to thank for adding the words printed above in bold, "... for now I know that you fear God, since you have not withheld your son, your only son, from me." The words are later additions which have caused the text to be remembered as immortalizing an Israelite patriarch whose virtue was found in his willingness to sacrifice his first born son, rather than as a person embracing a faith which enabled him to refuse child sacrifice. Franz Hinkelammert traces the added words to temple priests who during the Davidic dynasty (c. 1000 BCE), were, like ruling classes everywhere, anxious to establish the necessity of sacrificing children to the existing social order.[24] Their addition converts Abraham into a pedestrian man of his time without heroism or originality.

> ... (W)e know who made the insertions which invert the text's meaning. It was the temple priests who had to affirm the new law of Sinai. Child sacrifice in all human myths represents affirmation of law. In order to link this law with the history of Abraham, they had to reinterpret that tradition so Abraham would end up affirming the law's binding force. ... To fulfill the law he was prepared to kill his own son. The law, any law, says we must be similarly prepared. (Hinkelammert, *Fe de Abraham* 19)

In other words, Christian apologists for empire did not have to start from scratch in reversing Abraham's identity from the one who distin-

---

[24] Hinkelammert bases his position that the words in bold were later additions on four considerations: (A.) The text is apparently ignorant of the reigning custom of child sacrifice in Near Eastern patriarchal times. In such context, all good fathers would be willing to sacrifice their firstborn sons. There would have been nothing especially extraordinary about Abraham's intention. An audience without this knowledge would find a father willing to kill his son an admirable example of an exceptional father (*Fe de Abraham* 17). (B.) The text is incoherent with the overall thrust of the Abraham tradition, which is about a God who primarily dispenses life, not death. (C.) The additions are ambiguous. They do not explicitly say that Abraham's faith was found precisely in his willingness to kill his son. Instead, they pinpoint the patriarch's fidelity in his refusal to deny Isaac to Yahweh. Such negation could just as well indicate a refusal to deliver Isaac to death, in view of Abraham's dedication to the God of life. In the end, Hinkelammert notes, it is the reader's socialization that facilitates the common understanding of Abraham's father (19). (D.) The story is easily seen as an example of a "divine temptation" tradition. It was not unusual for Israelite tradition to present God as commanding a "sinful" act, and then as rewarding the one who disobeys the command (108–113).

guished himself by refusing to offer child sacrifice, to the one who was exceptional because of his willingness to sacrifice his son. Their work had long been anticipated by their Jewish counterparts who, like them, needed a God supportive of a primary requirement of empire – the willingness to surrender sons (and daughters) to the exigencies of conquest.

Conclusion

Following the precedent of the Abraham tale, today's Christians have been led to understand their God as one who is pleased with the sacrifice of sons and daughters to meet the requirements of empire. In effect, then they honor the will of one of the Canaanite Baals, rather than of Yahweh. Ultimately, however, in supporting the imperial interpretation of the Abraham and Isaac story, they honor Satan – the source of empire's authority.

Misunderstanding Ten:
Jesus is God's Only Son

> Politically astute, (Constantine) saw that the Roman Empire needed a unifying ideology that a geographically massive empire with a variety of philosophical schools and cultures needed some common belief to bind people together. Constantine saw Christianity as the perfect unifying force. Universal in scope, it was beginning to take hold of people's religious imaginations. It combined some rituals and beliefs of the mystery religions with belief in a historically concrete savior-God, and it had developed a sophisticated philosophical and political framework that enabled discussion of issues and evaluation of positions. And it was *organized*. (Weaver 68)

In order to accomplish the 4th century transition from worship of the God of liberation to worship of the God of empire, the understanding of Jesus required radical overhaul. It meant a complete makeover of his character, changing his identity from the prophet who obeyed God's law by disobeying God's law—i.e., by prioritizing human welfare above particular (even divine) laws, to the very embodiment of obedience to law, and as the giver of a New Law. That law, universal in scope, ultimately came to coincide with the empire's legal system.

Put otherwise, Jesus was changed from the martyr whose assassination committed in the name of divine law itself, had invalidated all legal orders —even as found in the holiest of traditions.[25] Thus, the practical impact of Jesus' death, as understood by the apostle, Paul, was turned on its head. Paul had drawn the conclusion that Jesus' murder had annulled the law itself, since Jesus' assassins had killed him in the name of religion's precepts. Now, however, with the incorporation of Jesus into the ideology

---

[25] Jesus' own relativization of divine law is implied in his frequent violations of Sabbath regulations as understood by his contemporaries. Paul's relativization of all law is made explicit in his argument, especially Galatians and Romans, that the strict interpretation of God's law has been invalidated, since its literal observance by the priestly establishment was responsible for Jesus' condemnation and death. The early church's relativization of biblical law is embodied in the decision of the Council of Jerusalem as recorded in the Acts of the Apostles, removing obligation resulting from dietary legislation and the law of circumcision. See Elsa Tamez: *Contra Toda Condena*.

of empire, Jesus had become the giver of a New Law that was absolute, universal and divine. That law gradually became identified with the law of the Roman Empire. Little by little, all who rebelled against Imperial Law might now be seen as rebelling against God himself, even to the point of repeating the crucifixion of Jesus. As God killers, they could then be punished with death. To accomplish all of this, Jesus had to be made into a God himself.

Such conversion involved theological acrobatics. As Hinkelammert has concluded, Jesus never understood himself as uniquely divine (Hinkelammert, *El Alsalto. . .*, 206). Instead, Marcus Borg and others explain that Jesus was a Jewish layman, an eloquent teacher who taught unconventional wisdom in stories and parables. He appeared within the Jewish prophetic tradition and proclaimed a message not about himself, but about a utopia he referred to as the Kingdom of God. In that utopia all human relationships would be reversed. Those considered worthless and "sinners" by the "virtuous" would be given priority by God. Prostitutes and publicans would enter the Kingdom, Jesus promised, before priests and teachers. The pure of heart, the poor, bereaved, gentle, merciful, persecuted, peacemakers and those committed to justice would be blessed.

To demonstrate the immanence and even the very presence of the Kingdom, Jesus performed faith healings, mostly among those considered unworthy and unclean within the religious and political mainstreams. As a result, he was considered a great faith healer. Most basically, though, Jesus was what Borg calls a "Spirit-Person." In this he was God's son – one who recognized the indwelling of a divine presence within himself. This indwelling united him with God in the most intimate way. However he also recognized that presence within all other humans, and within all of creation. In other words, Jesus was aware both of his own divine sonship and of an identical relationship enjoyed by all other men and women. He acknowledged that presence in nature as well. In that sense, as God's son, he was *primus inter pares*—the first among equals. Consequently, his death was understood by the first Christians, not as the death of a God, but of a brother (206).

This sort of sonship, however, was not sufficient for Constantine's purposes. As we will soon see, for the emperor, Jesus had to be a God in the sense that the emperors had always understood themselves as Gods—a condition which set them apart from the unwashed multitudes, rather than placing them in solidarity with "the least." Constantine's concern was demonstrated in the year 325, when he convoked and presided over the Council of Nicea. Its task was to define the nature of Jesus. With the emperor's approval, the Council concluded that Jesus was a divine person who was fully God. Moreover, his mother had been impregnated directly by the Holy Spirit. (A later Council, Ephesus in 431, would actually conclude that Mary merited the title Mother of God.) Of course, the "fully

God" part of such definition might easily be understood in the spirit-person sense earlier explained. As mystics of all traditions, and as Christian Gnostics held, it is by surrendering to the divine spark within that human beings realize their identity as God's children (Easwaran 6). However, the virgin birth factor of the Jesus equation is what separated him from other humans in the radical way Constantine required. It guaranteed the absolutely unique identity of Jesus as a "Son of God" belonging to an entirely singular order of reality. He was God in a way Roman emperors had rarely pretended to be.[26] At best, they could be considered Gods of the Roman people. Jesus, however, was now a universal God, the very presence of the creator of heaven and earth.

This identification of Jesus with a universal God accorded Jesus divine authority over the whole of creation. Consequently, his word now represented a New Divine Law.[27] That law mandated that all peoples

---

[26] The Roman philosophy, Stoicism, was a key element in connecting Jesus as Son of God with the Roman emperor as Son of God and the latter's connection with imperial law. Stoicism held that the Divine Law, or Logos, was inscribed within each creature, and profoundly within each human being. That Law, Stoics taught, was knowable to some chosen human beings, who, in turn, could fulfill it perfectly. Some strains of Stoicism even asserted that the Roman emperor, as God's Son, not only knew the Divine order and its governing Law perfectly; his word represented that law, and had to be obeyed accordingly. At the very least, the Roman law itself was a reflection of the divine order. Thus Logos, Son of God and imperial law were linked. John the Evangelist facilitated the addition of Jesus to that progression. In the Prologue to his Gospel, he identified Jesus with the divine Logos. However, his intention in doing so was the essentially political one of contrasting Jesus and his law with the Roman emperor and his. John's point was that the universe is not governed by Roman imperial law, but by the Law of Christ, whose way of fulfilling the Divine Law was by disobeying the written law—i.e. by prioritizing human well-being over the a law's inevitable tendency to become absolute. This liberating understanding of Logos and son of god was obscured to the point of erasure by the process presently under discussion. On this point, see Hinkelammert, *El Grito* . . . .

[27] Jesus is indeed presented in the Christian tradition as a law giver. In particular the Gospel of Matthew portrays the Nazarene as a New Moses promulgating a New Law. That law Matthew summarizes in a Sermon delivered specifically from a "Mount"—a clear parallel with Moses bringing the Law from Mount Sinai. When asked to summarize the most important of God's laws, Jesus followed the example of Rabbi Hillel, saying it was to love the Lord with one's whole heart, mind and spirit, and one's neighbor as one's self. Then in instance after instance within Matthew's gospel, Jesus proceeds to illustrate his understanding of that law's fulfillment. He does so by prioritizing human welfare above what his co-religionists considered the most sacred of God's laws—the law of the Sabbath. Jesus explains his conduct by asserting that such law was made for the sake of human well-being; human beings were not made for the law. Simply put, Jesus, the law giver, subordinates law to human welfare, specifically, the welfare of those Jesus describes as the beneficiaries of the New Order he proposes as God's reign—the poor, pure of heart, lowly, bereaved, persecuted, merciful, peacemakers, and those who hunger and thirst for justice. Jesus' New Law was clearly out-of-step with the requirements of the Roman Empire, and of church leaders like Augustine, intent on making Christianity empire-friendly. So following Constantine's conversion, Jesus' law had to be identified with the Rome's imperial law.

become Christians and in so doing come under the aegis of the Roman Empire, in which, after Theodosius in 381, Christianity was the official religion. Thus the conquered were to capitulate to Rome in a way never before even imagined by any empire—by surrendering their own Gods, their own cultures, their very souls.

Constantine: Agent of Theological Transformation

The Roman emperor, Constantine, was the first to perceive this necessity, and the possibility inherent in Christianity and in his own identification as Jesus' vicar. However, to realize that potential, he first of all needed a radical change of Roman imperial policy. That policy had been severely anti-Christian for more than a decade immediately preceding Constantine's accession to power.

For a century and a half before Constantine, the Roman domain had experienced appalling social and economic conditions everywhere. The empire was disintegrating, beginning with the Eternal City itself.[28] Resistance was especially strong in the East— in western Asia and in Egypt where imposition of a Rome's economic, legal and cultural control was stubbornly resisted. Just before Constantine, the emperor Diocletian had been elected by the military to prevent complete imperial collapse by using a firm hand. Accordingly, Diocletian instituted policies of heavy taxation, forced labor, and military conscription. In Egypt especially, the empire's breadbasket and granary, Diocletian had confiscated land to make sure that the food needs of the imperial center would be met. The result was open rebellion (Kamil 111).

In such highly charged circumstances, and in a hugely pluralistic Christian community, with multiple and often conflicting understandings of Jesus, certain of those interpretations were seen as politically dangerous. For instance, the Jesus of the community that produced the Gospel of Mark

---

[28] More specifically, the empire had been weakened both legally and ideologically. Legally, it had trouble controlling its provinces. There were many reasons for this. One was that Rome had allowed too many of them the semi-autonomy afforded by retention of their own laws (as happened in the case of Israel) or by the *Jus Gentium*, a particular form of law meant to govern those without Roman citizenship. Naturally local tribal laws, but also the *Jus Gentium* differed significantly from Imperial Law governing Rome and Romans themselves. In other words, there was missing a universal and absolute law to control the centrifugal tendencies of an empire embracing so many different nations, cultures, customs and interests. The situation could not be corrected, since there existed no successful ideological rationale for imposing a single, controlling, universal law on so many restive" barbarians." Rome had never been very successful in persuading conquered tribes that the Emperor was God, and that they should therefore render him homage and obedience.

proclaimed a revolutionary God, not the God of empire. Jesus himself was presented as resisting empire specifically.

There are numerous indications of Jesus' revolutionary identity throughout the Gospels. For instance, the term "gospel" itself takes a swipe at the Roman Empire. So does the title "Son of God." "Gospel" (*evangelium*) was the title given to what amounted to the emperor's "state of the union" message each year. It was an annual account of his *res gestae*, of his wonderful accomplishments on behalf of the empire. "Son of God" was a title traditionally claimed by the Caesar himself. However the Gospel of Mark, written by the man who invented that literary form, identifies Jesus as God's Son, and Jesus' proclamation of good news specifically to the poor as the genuine Good News. Both literary devices imply criticism and contradiction of empire. They say Jesus is God's son, not the emperor. The good news is what Jesus proclaimed, not that of the emperor.

There are other elements in Mark that might well be termed "anti-imperial." For instance the title "Son of Man," the one most often attributed to Jesus, was a revolutionary identification. Taken from the Book of Daniel, this figure represented the judge of all Israel's imperial enemies including the Assyrians, Babylonians, Persians and Greeks. In Mark's context, it portrayed Jesus as judge of Rome as well.

Also, the fact that Jesus was by all accounts executed by crucifixion indicates that the Romans perceived him as an insurgent. Crucifixion was the mode of capital punishment reserved for revolutionaries. Then there's the account in Mark of the Gerasene demoniac (5:1-20). It's where Jesus encounters a very powerful demon-possessed man who lives among the dead – in the tombs, the most unclean place that a Jew might imagine. The man perceives Jesus as a threat, and his demons within ask permission, rather than being destroyed, to enter a "herd of pigs," the filthiest of animals according to the Jews. Jesus gives the demons leave. They enter the pigs and race headlong over a cliff and into the waters below where they are "drowned in the sea."

Before releasing the demons, Jesus asks them to identify themselves. "My name is Legion," they reply, "for we are many" (5:9). The identification is significant in terms of understanding Jesus as a anti-imperial. When Mark was writing his gospel (around 70 C.E.), his people, the Jews, were in full blown war with the Romans (66-74 C.E.). In that context, the name "Legion" could have meant only one thing for Mark's readers – the hated Roman Legions who were killing their brothers and sisters in resistance.

Additionally, as Myers indicates, recruits for the Roman Army were called "herds of pigs." Further still, having the "legion" "drowned in the sea" would inevitably hark back in the mind of any Jew to Israel's Exodus experience, where the military hosts of the quintessential imperial enemy, Egypt, were "drowned in the sea" when Moses stretched his rod. In other words, what we have in the story of the Gerasene demoniac is a symbolic annihilation of the Roman Army by Jesus – clearly a story full of anti-imperial, revolutionary symbolism.

However, the best illustration of Jesus' resistance to empire is in the famous story of his temptations in the desert. Jesus has just been baptized by John (Mark 1:9-12). A voice has told him that he is somehow the "Son of God" (1:11). He goes out to the desert to discover what that might mean. He prays and fasts for 40 days. Afterwards he's presented with three temptations.

In Matthew's account of the same story, the culminating temptation is nothing if not imperial (4:1-11). The devil takes Jesus to a high mountain. He shows Jesus all the kingdoms of the earth – an empire much more vast than Rome's at the time. Significantly, as we shall see, at this point the "hollow" figure "devil" turns into "Satan." He says, "All of this can be yours, if only you bow down and worship me." Jesus, of course, refuses. He says, "Be gone, Satan! It is written, the Lord God only shall you adore; him only shall you serve." In other words, Jesus rejects empire in no uncertain terms.

The story's identification of seduction to empire by Satan is important to note because, in the Christian Testament Satan is often identified as the author of empire (e.g. Revelation 13:4). So in the temptation story, Jesus not only refuses empire, he also refuses to worship the "god" of empire, Satan, to whom worship must be given in order for any to attain imperial power.

How Christianity Became Imperial

Christians who understood Jesus in anti-imperial terms like those just described, were identified as "subversives." Christian resistance to Rome was widespread especially in the East. To avoid taxation, many there had fled to the desert to join the monks who had long since established a tradition of Christian asceticism in the wilderness.

Moreover, Christians nearly always refused military conscription. From the beginning, they had been doctrinally committed to pacifism.[29] Such forms of opposition to imperial authority made Christians appear as enemies of Rome. As part of his "strong hand" policy, Diocletian published

---

[29] They had even incurred the wrath and persecution of Jewish confreres during the mid-first century uprising against Rome. At that time, the followers of the Nazarene refused to take up arms to defend Jerusalem and its temple in support of their Jewish brothers and sisters.

a decree in 304 requiring sacrifice to pagan gods, and veneration of imperial statues. Anyone who refused was identified as a member of the subversive Christian sect. Recalcitrants were rounded up for trial and execution. None of this worked. Christian presence in the empire spread inexorably.

So when Constantine was crowned emperor in 312, he saw clearly that a change of policy was due. If the Christians could not be defeated, it was necessary to somehow incorporate them into the imperial project. So like Moses with his burning bush, and Paul with his vision on the road to Damascus, Constantine claimed a vision and miraculous story to justify a radical change of heart.

Recall the well-known legend just before the Battle of the Milvian Bridge. The details vary. According to one version, Constantine is at prayer; the sky opens; the cross appears, and the emperor was made to understand, "*In hoc signo vinces*" (by this sign you will achieve victory). Constantine makes sure the cross is emblazoned on the shields of his infantry. Victory is achieved. The Roman Empire is solidified in the West. With that, Constantine has his justification for legalizing the faith which had just recently been so severely persecuted.

Accordingly, the Edict of Milan was proclaimed in 313, making Christianity legal for the first time. By such publication, Constantine realized that stimulating, rather than discouraging the new religion's dissemination, would free up resources wasted already for centuries in policing Christians. Constantine also probably hoped (in vain) that legalization would make available to the empire's armed forces, hosts of new recruits to fight "barbarians" who were becoming ever more restive in their opposition to Rome.

Moreover, as we shall see presently, the ideological possibilities inherent for Constantine as an imperial "son of god" in co-opting a faith that centralized a figure believed to be God's son, were immense. That is, though Roman emperors had traditionally claimed divine status as sons of the gods, their claims had never really found popular resonance, especially in their colonies. However, it would be a short step from becoming the protector of a religion whose central figure was recognized as God's Son to being recognized as the vicar of that figure. This, in fact, is what happened not long after Constantine issued the Edict of Milan.[30]

---

[30] Of course it is not necessary to conclude, nor is it even likely that Constantine somehow all at once foresaw the implications inherent in his personal acceptance of Christianity, nor in his Edict. It seems much more likely that those possibilities unfolded gradually, perhaps even after a sincere conversion on the emperor's part. In any case, it is not difficult to believe that following his conversion, this political ruler whose predecessors had consistently claimed the title "Son of God," reflected on the relationships between that title and the Nazarene, who followers referred to him by that same title.

Christianity and Religious Ideology

Apart from the political, there were particularly religious reasons for Constantine's concern with Christianity. Like all oppressors, he realized that religion represented an incomparable tool for controlling people. If he (or any emperor) could convince people that in obeying him they were obeying God, he had won the day. In fact it is the job of any state religion to make people believe that God's interests and the state's interests are the same.

What Constantine saw in the 4th century was that Rome's state religion was losing power. Meanwhile, Christianity seemed to be spreading like wildfire, even though only about 5% of empire's inhabitants had accepted the new religion. Still Christianity was perceived as politically dangerous. Understandably, the message of Jesus was particularly attractive to the lower classes. It affirmed their dignity in the clearest of terms. Often the message incited slaves and others to rebel rather than obey. For centuries, Rome's knee-jerk response had been repression and persecution. But, as already indicated, by Constantine's day, Rome's repression had proved ineffective. Despite Rome's throwing Christians to the lions for decade after decade, the faith of Jesus was more popular than ever.

Once again, Constantine decided that if he couldn't beat the Christians, he had to join them. He would do so by robbing Christianity of its revolutionary potential. This he would accomplish by favoring a segment of the Christian community whose faith was highly influenced by Roman "mystery cults."

Mystery cults had been extremely popular in Rome. Basically they were "salvation religions" that worshipped gods with names like Isis, Osiris, the Great Mother and Mithra. Mithra was particularly popular in the Roman army. He was the Sun God, whose feast day and birth was celebrated, by the way, on December 25th.

Typically the "story" celebrated in mystery cults was of a god who descended from heaven, lived on earth for a while, died, rose from the dead, ascended back to heaven. From above the deity offered worshippers "eternal life," if they joined in the cults where the god's body was eaten under the form of bread, and the god's blood was drunk under the form of wine.

To convert Christianity into a mystery cult, Constantine (who wasn't even a Christian at the time) convoked a church council – the Council of Nicaea in 325. There the question of the day became who was Jesus of Nazareth? Was he just a human being? Some believed that militantly. Was he just a God and not a human being at all? Some were convinced that Jesus was a God disguised as a human. Was he some combination of God and man? Did he have to eat? Did he have to defecate or urinate? Those were the questions.

For Constantine's purposes, the more divine and otherworldly Jesus was the better. That would make him less a threat to the emperor's very this-worldly dominion.

The result of all the deliberations was codified in what became known as the Nicene Creed. Many of us know it by heart. Roman Catholics recite it nearly every Sunday. Consider what it says . . . .

> We believe in one God the Father Almighty, Maker of heaven and earth, and of all things visible and invisible. And in one Lord Jesus Christ, the only-begotten Son of God, begotten of the Father before all worlds, God of God, Light of Light, Very God of Very God, begotten, not made, being of one substance with the Father by whom all things were made; who for us men, and for our salvation, came down from heaven, and was incarnate by the Holy Spirit of the Virgin Mary, and was made man, and was crucified also for us under Pontius Pilate. He suffered and was buried, and the third day he rose again according to the Scriptures, and ascended into heaven, and sitteth on the right hand of the Father. And he shall come again with glory to judge both the quick and the dead, whose kingdom shall have no end. And we believe in the Holy Spirit, the Lord and Giver of Life, who proceedeth from the Father and the Son, who with the Father and the Son together is worshipped and glorified, who spoke by the prophets. And we believe one holy catholic and apostolic Church. We acknowledge one baptism for the remission of sins. And we look for the resurrection of the dead, and the life of the world to come. Amen.

The statement is amazing. It jumps from the conception and birth of Jesus to his death and resurrection. It leaves out entirely any reference to what Jesus said and did. For all practical purposes it ignores the historical Jesus and pays attention only to a God who comes down from heaven, dies, rises, ascends back to heaven and offers eternal life to those who believe. It's a nearly perfect reflection of "mystery cult" belief. The revolutionary potential of Jesus' words and actions relative to justice, wealth, poverty and revolution are lost. Not only that, but subsequent to Nicaea, anyone connecting Jesus to a struggle for justice, sharing and communal life is rendered suspect and is very often classified as heretical. That is, mystery cult becomes "orthodoxy." The example and teaching of Jesus (and of the early church) becomes heresy.

Recovering Jesus' Lost Identity

How are we to recover the revolutionary Jesus? Is there some strategy to overcome the amnesia that has afflicted Christians to such an extent that they have ended up worshipping not Yahweh, but Jupiter, not Jesus, but Mithra – and even Satan? Can we escape from an imperial religion that deifies the United States, its president and army?

There is only one way. That is to recover the "lost middle" of the Nicene Creed – to fill in the blank and make sure that any discussions of faith take into account the Jesus rediscovered in the liberation theology movement and by the Jesus Seminar. Ironically that "lost Jesus" turns out to be the very kind of person conservative Americans tend to reject and actually despise.

Who is this Jesus? He's the son of an unwed teenage mother . . . . A homeless person at the beginning of his life . . . . An immigrant in Egypt for a while . . . . Someone thought irreligious by the "church" authorities of his time, who considered him as demon-possessed (the equivalent of being called a "communist" or "terrorist" in our own day). . . . He was under investigation by the Jewish authorities from the very beginning of his life . . . . Then he was arrested . . . . A victim of torture . . . . And of capital punishment. . . . Once again, the nearly perfect portrait of a person hated by the Christian right.

Moreover, Jesus was concerned with remedying poverty and its effects. He healed sick people, fed the hungry, and cast out evil spirits. He announced and embodied a new reality for the poor. In the "reign of God" justice would replace exploitation; the positions of rich and poor would be reversed, and a sharing ethic would take the place of competition and oppression.

This sharing ethic was lived communally (one might say "communistically") by Jesus' earliest followers. Consider the description of their life together:

> Now the whole group of those who believed were of one heart and soul, and no one claimed private ownership of any possessions, but everything they owned was held in common. . . . There was not a needy person among them, for as many as owned lands or houses sold them and brought the proceeds of what was sold. They laid it at the apostles' feet, and it was distributed to each as any had need. (Acts 4:32-36).

As Mexican scripture scholar, Jose Miranda indicates, this is a perfect description of communism. That aspiration, he reminds us, doesn't originate with Louis Blanc or with Karl Marx. It comes from the Bible.

Yet most Christians are silent about this passage. They live and speak as though life in the primitive church were instead described as follows:

> Now the whole group of those who believed lived in fierce competition with each other, and made sure that rights to private property were respected. They expelled from their midst any who practiced communalism. As a consequence God's "invisible hand" brought prosperity to some. Many however found themselves in need. The Christians responded with "tough love" demanding that the lazy either work or starve. The unfit, especially the children, the elderly and those who cared for them starved. Others raised themselves by their own bootstraps, and were stronger as a result. In this way, the industrious increased their land holdings, and banked their profits. The rich got richer and the poor, poorer. Of course, all of this was seen as God's will and a positive response to the teaching of Jesus.

Conclusion

As Elaine Pagels has recently argued, multiple interpretations of Jesus' identity circulated among the early Christians. As reflected in the Gospel of Thomas, Gnostics in particular viewed Jesus as a brother who demonstrated the possibilities inherent within all human beings. All could be daughters and sons of God in the sense manifested in the person of Jesus. The purpose of life, then, was to be a seeker, one who sought to discover and "realize" (in the sense of make real) the universal God presence within her, within him. The tendency (though quite ambiguous) in the synoptic gospels is to present Jesus in this universal sense. It is only with the Gospel of John that a clear, contrary, and exclusivist understanding of Jesus' identity emerges. In John, Jesus is understood as God's son in a unique sense that no one else can imitate. In the 2nd century, Irenaeus, the Christian leader from provincial Gaul, embraced this inimitable understanding of Jesus' nature. In doing so, he branded as heretical the belief that the image of God is embedded in each and every human being, thus linking God to every member of the human race.

By the 4th century (367C.E.) Athanasius, an admirer of Irenaeus, and bishop of Alexandria, ordered all versions of the gospel destroyed, except those he identified as "acceptable" and "canonical" (Pagels, *Beyond* 97). The latter embraced virtually all of the entries in the "New Testament" recognized by Western Christians today. Like Constantine before him, Athanasius was interested in uniformity of belief among Christians. Both thought unified creeds would rein in the centrifugal tendencies of rival religious and political groups during the tumultuous 4th century.

Uniformity, they thought, would lead to order in both venues. However, the order imposed by Constantine and Athanasius also led to the eclipsing and denigration of the faith-enriching understandings of Jesus that flourished during the first three centuries of the Common Era. Such exclusion of perspective has given birth to many of the misunderstandings of Christianity summarized here.

Misunderstanding Eleven:
Apocalypse Is about the End of the World

> What Then should be the believer's attitude to the destruction of the world by fire? First of all, he should welcome it and pray for its nearness. (Robert Gromacki, 1970)

The central place of the Book of Revelation in many prominent branches of Christian fundamentalism is both fascinating and puzzling. This final entry of the Christian Testament is perhaps the most obscure book in the entire scriptural corpus. It wasn't even part of the canon when the first list of Christian inspired books was compiled after the end of the fourth century. Revelation is filled with fantastic imagery and fiery poetic language. For that very reason, the book would seem open to multiple interpretations. Its obscurity alone would explain why many exegetes have steered clear of the book altogether. Some Catholic Bibles have prefaced Revelation with disclaimers notifying prospective readers that, though the book contained wonderful images and poetry, it was not to be taken literally. Most especially, the warning went, the book was not to be used to calculate the precise time of the end of the world. According to Jesus' own word, readers were reminded, not even the angels of God know when the Christ will return.

Until recently, those who have dared to comment have treated the book as a description of the "end of the world" (Weaver 33). Contemporary scholarship, however, has interpreted Revelation as describing the end of empire—specifically the Roman Empire whose rule defined the context of the book's composition. While acknowledging this context, Walter Wink, for example, generalizes the book's prediction to the termination of "the domination system."

None of this, however, has prevented fundamentalist preachers from finding in Revelation exquisite detail describing today's world. For example, T.V. Pentecostal evangelist, John Hagee, explains how the book offers precise descriptions of present day reality in the Middle East. To begin with, he says, the reestablishment of Israel is a clear part of God's plan described in Revelation. So Christians must support Jewish Israelis unconditionally. Secondly, in the "Holy Land" itself, according to this vision, a final battle between Good and Evil will be fought on the plain of Armageddon. Two billion people will die as a result—including 2/3 of the Jewish people. The remaining 1/3 of the Jews will be converted to Jesus, because his final revelation will be so convincing. Thirdly, the Rapture will occur at this point, taking all followers of Christ into heaven, while leaving others behind for a period of "tribulation."[31]

Influenced by such theology, Hagee convoked an assembly of 3500 evangelicals in August of 2006; it was a meeting of Christians Unified for Israel. In attendance were three members of Congress, including the head of the Republican National Committee. In his remarks, Hagee referred to Israel's attack on Lebanon as "a miracle of God." He characterized calls for a ceasefire as a violation of "God's foreign policy statement." In response, President Bush sent a note of congratulations thanking Hagee for "spreading the hope of God's love and the universal gift of freedom." From the perspective delineated here, all of this expresses contemporary fundamentalism's surrender to and manipulation by empire—a capitulation that began in the 4th century. Preachers like Hagee take a book whose central message is the end of empire, and convert it into an imperial celebration. Such misuse illustrates the usurpation of the Judeo-Christian tradition by fundamentalists who, it has been argued, have replaced the biblical Yahweh with Satan, and who have demonized the Jesus figure, Lucifer, equating him with the devil.

As seen earlier, the first usurpation surfaced with the Genesis narrative about the First Woman and the First Man. Fundamentalists take the theme of Genesis as a literal account of the beginnings of the world. In Revelation, they find a prediction of the end of the world. In Genesis the world is created. Revelation foretells that world will soon be destroyed.

---

[31] This is the "pre-millennial" understanding. "Millennial" refers to a period of 1000 years. Pre-millennialists believe that Jesus will return soon, and that Christians alive at that time will be assumed into heaven in an event called the "rapture." The raptured will escape the "tribulations" which will follow, and will culminate in a final confrontation between Good and Evil in a battle of Armageddon. Following that battle, 1000 years of divine rule and peace will ensue. Most Christian Evangelicals are pre-millenialists. A minority, however, are postmillenialists. These subscribe to "dominion theology," and believe that Christians must achieve political control (dominion) of the world before Christ can return. They must exercise Christian control of secular politics for 1000 years before the Second Coming of Christ. Both pre-millennialists and post-millennialists represent a peculiarly American interpretation of both the Bible and the Book of Revelation. "Rapture" is also a relatively new concept; it is found nowhere in the Jewish Testament nor in the Christian Testament. It originated in the 19th century with preachers like John Darby (1880-1882) who based his understanding on I Thessalonians 4:16-17:

> For the Lord himself, with a cry of command, with the archangel's call and with the sound of God's trumpet, will descend from heaven, and the dead in Christ will rise first. Then we who are alive, who are left, will be caught up in the clouds together with them to meet the Lord in the air; and so we will be with the Lord forever.

Both books describe a rebellion against God's own order and a need to reestablish that order and the law that supports it. Morally speaking, in the contemporary world, the law in question is the Ten Commandments as interpreted and enforced by empire now given form by the United States.

The imminent end of the world rendered by a fundamentalist reading of Revelation has practical political implications that go beyond U.S. support for Israel. For example, Christian conservatives typically find no need to protect the environment from the depredations of the globalized industrial system. In fact, "the worse the better," since environmental deterioration signals the proximity of an avenging Jesus' imminent return. Additionally, the U.S. arsenal of nuclear weapons will likely be the instruments for the final destruction of the world. As such they are godly; their use is welcomed as hastening the return of Jesus. In other words, there is no need to oppose the new generations of weapons of mass destruction being developed by a now openly imperial United States. Put succinctly, the Book of Revelation confirms the message fundamentalists find in Genesis. The world and human nature are corrupt, since they are rebellious against God's law. As such both humans and their world are objects of God's righteous anger. Both will rightfully be destroyed in short order. The U.S. Empire, like Rome before it, is the agent of God—this time bringing about final punishment for the sin of Adam and Eve, for the murder of Jesus and the general corruption of the world.

Contextualist Reading of Revelation

This fundamentalist reading of Revelation stands in sharp contrast to the competing, more contextualized understandings advanced by analysts such as Pablo Richard and Franz Hinkelammert. These read the book as a defense of sisters and brothers in the believing community oppressed by patriarchal forces analogous to those undergirding Solomon's rule in 10th century Israel. Hinkelammert in particular sees it as a promise of the return of Eve's order displaced by the original sin of Cain ("Apocalipsis" 7).

To begin with, contextualists point out that Revelation was written at the end of the 1st century C.E., during a severe persecution by Rome, and long before Constantine's cooptation of Christianity in the 4th century. In that context, Revelation is a specifically anti-Roman tract. It is not about the end of the world, but the end of the Roman Empire. As such, it is an example of "apocalypse," a kind of resistance literature that became popular among the persecuted Jewish community beginning in the 3rd century before the onset of the Common Era. This literature was written in code understandable to those the literary form addressed, but incomprehensible to their persecutors. Invariably, apocalypse promised an end to persecution and to empire, whether that of Antiochus IV Epiphanes (in the case of the apocalyptic Book of Daniel), or of the Roman Empire (in the case of the Book of Revelation).

The author of Revelation, John of Patmos, was a Christian thinker of highly developed political sensitivity. In this he stood within Israel's prophetic tradition of extremely politicized analysts reflecting on their contemporary situations in the light of their community's faith traditions.

These "seers" were able to project the nascent trends of their times towards likely or inevitable outcomes that remained opaque to most of their contemporaries (8). During the persecution at the end of the first century, the Roman Empire appeared mighty, indomitable and permanent to most Christians. In contrast, John saw Rome as fragile and in decline. He recognized that it would eventually fall to the Christians, that they would take severe vengeance on their former persecutors, ruling them with "a rod of iron" (2:27, 12:5, and 19:15). They would establish a long patriarchal Christian reign characterized by harsh repression of all resembling those who had previously persecuted them.

John, however, was skeptical about the longevity of such a patriarchal order. He recognized that the endorsement of violence would be self-defeating.

So he announced what he saw as God's plan ("the mystery of God") for the direction of history. That was the purpose of his book. According to God's mysterious plan, the violence of patriarchy is to be replaced by the return of Eve's order, the order of the Great Goddess, the feminine face of Yahweh, which was responsible for the humanization of the "earth creatures" in the creation myth. It would be the order of a God without authority in the patriarchal sense—a return to Paradise with abundant trees of life, without prohibitions, and devoid of curses. As is indicated by the descent of the New Jerusalem from heaven to earth, the final stage is located here on earth, not in an above-the-world after-life.

Textual Analysis

More particularly, following a three-chapter introduction saluting the seven Asian churches, John of Patmos reviews all of history. He sees it as a succession of catastrophes and salvations. The mostly unrelieved tragedy of it all, culminating in persecution under the Romans (Babylon), leads God's suffering people to cry out, "When will it all end?" (4:1-11:9). That question is answered in a series of visions revealing "the mystery of God," and centralizing "The Woman," and her son, "The Lamb." The visions assert that Rome will indeed fall, and that its domination will be replaced by its mirror image, viz., by Christians repressing Romans and other similar enemies (12-21). Finally, beginning in chapter 21, a new order takes shape. There human beings live without need of patriarchal authority or of a Christ ruling with an iron rod. To reiterate, Christ's new order reflects the feminine face of God first glimpsed in Eve, the Mother of all the living (Hinkelammert, "El Apocalipsis" 4).

The Woman Appears

The heart of John's understanding of history is found in a key passage beginning with Chapter 12. It centralizes "the Woman," and very ancient matricentric traditions (4). The passage has three movements. In the first the Mother-Goddess appears. She gives birth to a child who is menaced by a great red dragon. The woman escapes the dragon's threats to devour her child.

> And a great portent appeared in heaven, a woman clothed with the sun, with the moon under her feet, and on her head a crown of twelve stars; she was with child and she cried out in her pangs of birth, in anguish for delivery. And another portent appeared in heaven; behold, a great red dragon, with seven heads and ten horns, and seven diadems upon his heads. His tail swept down a third of the stars of heaven, and cast them to the earth. And the dragon stood before the woman who was about to bear a child, that he might devour her child when she brought it forth; she brought forth a male child, one who is to rule all the nations with a rod of iron, but her child was caught up to God and to his throne, and the woman fled into the wilderness, where she has a place prepared by God, in which to be nourished for one thousand two hundred and sixty days, (Rev. 12:1-6)

A woman clothed in the sun and stars, and standing on the moon is a clear reference to the Great Mother God of matricentric mythology, which, as already indicated, is not at all foreign to the biblical tradition. It had appeared in the account of the First Woman, who was also a figure of the Great Goddess. Recall that Genesis had identified the First Woman as the mother of all the living not merely of all human beings (Gen. 3:20); she was the mother of plants and animals as well—a clear goddess figure (5). The point is that in our bookend appearances of "a woman" in both Genesis and Revelation, references to the goddess and the feminine order she represents are implicit.

In Goddess theology, the natural cycles were typically explained by the Mother Deity who gave birth to a child of destiny. The child flourished for a year, and then died, only to be resurrected, and born again to repeat the natural cycle (5). In the text at hand, the familiar cycle is referenced; however the woman's child is only threatened, not killed, and the cycle is not repeated.

Here readers are being introduced to the mystery inherent in goddess mythology that all of history embodies the sequence of birth, death and rebirth culminating with the production of an entirely new world. That world, like the idealized world of Genesis, is somehow linked to the feminine and represents the mysterious goal of all history.

Rebellion in Heaven

The second movement in the Goddess story follows immediately in chapter 12, verses 7-12. It is a story that illustrates for both fundamentalists and contextualists how the earthly rebellion depicted in the first book of the Bible was reflected in the heavenly rebellion portrayed in the final book. (Recall that for fundamentalists the Genesis rebellion was against God pure and simple – the Original Sin. For contextualists, as we have seen, rebellion was against a patriarchal despot modeled on the kingship of Solomon—an act of liberation led by a woman.) In any case, in Revelation, the heavenly rebellion is precipitated by the Dragon's persecution of the woman and her child. It helps to cite the passage in its entirety.

> And there was a war in heaven. Michael and his angels fought against the dragon, and the dragon and his angels fought back. But he was not strong enough, and they lost their place in heaven. The great dragon was hurled down—that ancient serpent called the devil or Satan, who leads the whole world astray. He was hurled to the earth, and his angels with him.
> Then I heard a loud voice in heaven say: "Now have come the salvation and the power and the kingdom of our God, and the authority of his Christ. For the accuser of our brothers, who accuses them before our God day and night, has been hurled down. They overcame him by the blood of the Lamb and by the word of their testimony; they did not love their lives so much as to shrink from death. Therefore rejoice, you heavens and you who dwell in them! But woe to the earth and the sea, because the devil has gone down to

You! He is filled with fury, because he knows that his time is short."

The Fundamentalist Understanding of Satan's Rebellion

Traditionally, this passage has been read as the description of a heavenly rebellion against God and his order. The mutiny is led by angelic forces under the leadership of Satan himself, who, like Adam and Eve, aspired to be "like God." Such arrogant ambition is indicated in the name of the rebellion's opponent, the archangel, Michael, who defends God's uniquely divine identity and rule. Michael's name, which means "Who is like God?" itself addresses a rhetorical question to the rebellious Satan. It connects Satan's insurrection with that of humanity's first parents. They were promised by the Tempter that they would be "like God" if they ate of the fruit of the Tree of Knowledge of Good and Evil. The answer to Michael's question is implied in the story's development. "No one is like God," it says. To illustrate the point, Satan is expelled from heaven just as Adam and Eve were thrust out of Paradise. He and his minions are hurled down to hell from which they emerge constantly as devils (often depicted as women) tempting human beings – chiefly to commit sins of a sexual nature (Hinkelammert, *El Asalto* 128-31).

With this interpretation, the proclamation of the "loud voice" which is heard following Satan's defeat becomes a reassertion of God's identity and his law and order. The law becomes the expression of Jesus' "authority" as the upholder of the New Law interpreted as synonymous, in medieval interpretations, with Roman law.

> Then I heard a loud voice in heaven say: Now have come the salvation and the power of the kingdom of our God, and the authority of his Christ. (Rev. 12:10)

The problems with this reading are manifold. To begin with, it does not recognize that the contestants in the heavenly battle described in Revelation 12:7-12 are not Satan and God, but Satan and Michael.

Secondly, the reading ignores the crime of Satan, viz., that he has been accusing members of the Christian community ("our brothers") continually before God. He is not rebelling against law, but enforcing it. In this he is fulfilling his traditional role as the representative of empire in Yahweh's heavenly court. In the Christian community's context at the end of the first century, Satan is portrayed here as reproducing in heaven, the accusations against Christians on earth. Once again, he appears to be supporting the Roman imperial order. Thirdly, Satan, now become "the devil," is not thrust down into hell, but onto the earth, where according to

Rev. 13:4, he gives the authority (presumably that he exercised in heaven) to "the Beast," the actual ruling power identified in the book of Revelation, the Roman Empire. Fourthly, the authority of Christ is established by the very expulsion of Satan from heaven to earth, i.e., in ending Satan's support for an order inimical to "the brothers." All of these misreadings and exegetical silences are overcome in a more contextualized reading.

The Contextualist Understanding Of Michael's Rebellion

To reiterate: in the context of Roman persecution of Christians at the end of the first century C.E., the story of heavenly rebellion represents encouragement for Christians who found themselves accused "day and night" for not obeying the Roman law requiring formal worship of the Roman emperor. The convicted were punished—often tortured and even thrown to the lions. The situation seemed hopeless, especially in the face of Christian faith that the early martyrs had overcome Satan, their Great Accuser, "by the blood of the Lamb and by the word of their testimony." Once again, the apocalyptic book of Revelation was written to encourage the faithful in such trying circumstances. "This too will pass" is the message of that book. History is in God's hands. The victory over evil has already been won by the enthronement of the Christ in heaven.

In this context, verses 7-12 of Chapter 12 are understood to describe a heavenly rebellion led by the Archangel Michael and his hosts against the forces of Satan and his angels. The rebellion is precipitated by the arrival of the woman's son, the Christ, before the throne of God (12:5, 10-11).[32] As just indicated, the rebellion thus fomented is not against God—except in so far as Satan represents the authoritarian side of God previously depicted in the Genesis story of the Forbidden Tree.[33] Neither is Satan the rebel. Instead, Michael is the rebellious one. Satan is the one rebelled against— precisely as the representative of an authoritarian God and his patriarchal order understood as supporting empire. Satan has been "the accuser of our brothers, who accuses them before our God day and night." On behalf of the persecuted "brothers" (and sisters), Michael rebels against Satan and the Roman law requiring emperor worship. The great dragon is expelled from heaven to earth (not to hell). From there he and his minions vent their

---

[32] The assurance here is that the victory over Rome and empire has been achieved by the death of Jesus and his enthronement in heaven.

[33] In other words, the Dragon, or Satan (heaven's imperial spokesperson), the devil, or the authoritarian God is a multivalent character in John's vision (Hinkelammert "El Apocalipsis"6).

fury in efforts to lead "the whole world astray"—precisely by continuing to divinize the law of empire. Thus Satan is understood as the Great Source of the Roman Empire's power against which the entire Book of Revelation was written (Hinkelammert, *El Sujeto* 451).[34]

The Millennial Rule of Christ And the Dethronement of Patriarchy

The third movement in the story leading up to the restoration of Eve's order begins with Revelation's description of the thousand year millennial rule of Christ. Here empire's order is reversed. The destroyers of the earth are themselves destroyed as promised earlier (11: 17-18). Those who persecuted God's people are exterminated with twice the force allowed by the measure of eye for eye and tooth for tooth (18:6). More particularly, the dragon, cast down to earth, pursues the woman in an attempt to destroy her. She, however, is saved by the earth. Angered, the dragon turns his fierce attention to Christians (12:17). He gives authority to the Beast (Rome) to make war on and defeat the Christians (13:7). Without warning, though, Babylon suddenly falls of its own accord, i.e. without divine intervention (14:8). A great blood bath ensues (14:20). Rome's female side (the opposite of the Lamb's mother)—the city of Rome, the Great Whore of Babylon—is stripped naked, devoured and cremated (17:15-18). The Lamb's wrathful, thousand year reign is then inaugurated (19:11-21). After one thousand years, the dragon returns for a final battle. He and his followers are utterly destroyed (20:7-15).

Finally, a new order is inaugurated when the earlier announced (19:7-9) marriage of the Lamb is celebrated (21:1-2). The order is unmistakably feminine.

> Then I saw a new heaven and a new earth; for the first heaven and the first earth had passed away, and the sea was no more. And I saw the holy city, New Jerusalem coming down out of heaven from God, prepared as a bride adorned for her husband; and I heard a great voice from the throne saying, "Behold, the dwelling of God is

---

[34] "Men worshiped the dragon because he had given authority to the beast, and they also worshiped the beast and asked, 'Who is like the beast?'" (Rev. 13;4). Here the "beast" is the Roman Empire. The question, "Who is like the beast?" connects Rome's project with that of Satan in heaven (absolutizing the law responsible for the accusations against "the brothers"). The connection is that Satan's project and that of Rome are countered by the opponent of idolatry, Michael, whose name is translated "Who is like God?"

with men. He will dwell with them, and they shall be his people, and God himself will be with them; he will wipe away every tear from their eyes, and death shall be no more, neither shall there be mourning nor crying nor pain any more, for the former things have passed away. (21:2-4)

Hinkelammert identifies the Lamb's spouse with the Woman introduced in chapter 12. In the long matriarchal tradition, the son weds his mother in order to introduce the New Year following the long winter. Here, however, the wedding of son and mother introduces an entirely new world ("Apocalipsis" 10). The text bears Hinkelammert's reading, though the spouse of chapter 21 is another of Revelation's multivalent characters. True, the "bride adorned for her husband" is The Woman; but she is also Jerusalem, Eve, the Mother of the Lamb, Earth, Life itself and the Great Goddess. Regardless of such identifications, however, the new order, the new city is incontrovertibly female. With God's new order, Eve's order has returned. It represents the horizon, the utopia towards which Christians are called to journey.

Conclusion

The Book of Revelation thus presents readers with what Hinkelammert terms a vision of Western history from the viewpoint of first century Christians. That vision recognized Jesus as put to death by the Roman Empire. Christian faith, however, relocated him to heaven, with the accompanying belief that his enthronement assured the victory of Christians over empires of all kinds. Nonetheless, Jesus' victory was a long time finding historical expression. Rome persecuted Christians unmercifully. Eventually, though, the Empire fell; its rule was replaced by its Christian mirror image, with all the violence and bloodshed that entailed. Yet the earthly utopia promised believers was not to be that characterized by the super-vengeance of the patriarchal order. Instead, the promised order was to be that of the Great Goddess, Eve – the order of life, and of a transformed God without authority or arbitrary prohibition.

In other words, with Revelation's installment of the Goddess order, the circle is complete. Eve and the feminine side of God have been restored to power. God has changed (11). Satan has been banished – except in the Christian fundamentalists' counter-offensive, and its rescue of Satan from the Lake of Fire.

Part III

MISUNDERSTANDINGS ABOUT THE CHURCH

Misunderstanding Twelve:
Christianity Is Compatible with Empire

> And if a sparrow cannot fall without his knowledge, do you think an empire can arise without his permission? (U.S. Vice President Dick Cheney. Quoted in David Ray Griffin, *9/11 and Christian Faith*).

As we have seen, the general thrust of church history from the end of the first century down to our own time depicts the reassertion of imperial law over human life in a way that runs exactly contrary to the holy anarchism of the Old and New Testament traditions about Eve, Abraham, the prophets, Jesus and John of Patmos. Rather than the religion of the great dissenters and disobedient to all but Yahweh, Christianity increasingly becomes an affirmation of law demanding subordination of human life and welfare to empire and imperial wars. Human subordination and sacrifice are exacted not only by empire itself, but by unpayable debts, and an economic system whose natural laws of supply and demand should in principle never be interfered with, even though their outworkings may cost millions of lives.

The pro-imperial distortions of Christianity, which, as already shown, were given decisive impetus under Constantine continued through the medieval period. For instance, in 410 St. Augustine's *City of God* distinguished between God's city and the city of human beings in a way that affirmed the necessity of honoring legal orders imposed by emperors, kings and princes. Augustine wrote,

> The earthly city, which does not live by faith, seeks an earthly peace and the end that it proposes, in the well-ordered concord of civic obedience and rule, is the combination of men's wills to attain the things which are helpful to this life. The heavenly city, or rather the part of it which sojourns on earth and lives by faith, makes use of this peace only because it must, until this mortal condition which necessitates it shall pass away.
>
> Consequently, so long as it lives like a captive and a stranger in the earthly city, though it has already received the promise of redemption, and the gift of the Spirit as the earnest of it, it makes no scruple to obey the laws of the earthly city, whereby the things necessary for the

> maintenance of this mortal life are administered, and thus, as this life is common to both cities, so there is a harmony between them in regard to what belongs to it. (XIX, 17)

With these words, Augustine, on the one hand affirms the function of law as insuring that all human beings have what is necessary to sustain their lives. But on the other, he asserts a harmony between the laws of this world and those of the "heavenly city" which he identifies with a transcendent realm to which access is gained after death. Christians therefore are to make "no scruple to obey the laws of the earthly city." This Augustinian endorsement of imperial law remains even though in his *Commentary on the Psalms*, the great church doctor acknowledges, "even the sons of the pestilence sit sometimes in the seat of Moses. . ." (LI 6). With sentiments like these, then, a pro-imperial, anti-utopian and completely docile interpretation of Christianity is affirmed. It endorses the order of this world and its law, while furthering the transformation of God's Kingdom from an historical reality which comes, to a transcendent realm to which believers go after death.

At the end of the middle ages, this understanding of Christian hope as supporting empire and as focused on the after-life becomes indelibly engraved on the Western mind through Dante's *Divine Comedy*. Whether they know it or not, it is from this source that most in our culture derive their strongest images of heaven, hell, purgatory and Satan. Significantly, in terms of Christianity's wedding to the Roman Empire, Dante places Brutus and Cassius (along with Judas) in hell's worst location for their crime of assassinating Julius Caesar. In other words, by the early 14th century, the meaning of Christianity had become so inverted that rebellion against established law and order – the rebellion against empire – was understood as the most unspeakable offense against God himself. It was equivalent to the betrayal of Jesus by Judas.

Reformation Inversions

The Protestant Reformation continued the medieval trend domesticating the thrust of the Judeo-Christian tradition expressing the hope of the poor in an anarchic God opposing any and all legalized orders of oppression. True, Luther began by centralizing an interpretation of law which annulled its power when legal observance proved harmful to the community. Thus he invoked the Gospel to allow the royal classes to disobey papal directives. But in its dominant form, Reformation reinterpretation stopped well short of extending the privilege of disobedience to the dispossessed centralized in the Mosaic Covenant, in the preaching of Jesus, and in the letters of Paul. In fact, it made the binding force of the law stronger by demanding that believers obey it with enthusiasm. In his *Commentary on Romans*, Luther writes,

> To fulfill the law, we must meet its requirements gladly and lovingly, live virtuous and upright lives without the constraint of the law, and as if neither the law nor its penalties existed. But this joy, this unconstrained love, is put into our hearts by the Holy Spirit, as St. Paul says in Chapter 5. But the Holy Spirit is given only in, with and through faith in Jesus Christ . . .

Theology like this not only robbed those without public power of their right to disobey laws in conflict with human welfare, it turned freedom to disobey the law into "freedom" to obey it. The elite implications of this understanding were illustrated during the peasant rebellions of 1524 and '25, when, in the name of law and order, Luther opposed the German peasantry's rejection of the feudal and manorial burdens placed upon them by the noble classes. In effect, then, Luther helped transfer the seat of absolute authority in Europe from the Vatican in Rome to royal palaces scattered throughout Europe.

Even more to the point, by the time John Calvin systematized Reformation thought in 1536, he specifically denied the right of disobedience in those oppressed by their overlords. In fact, he rendered property owners' authority inviolable. In Book IV, Chapter XX of his *Institutes of the Christian Religion*, Calvin wrote,

> We owe this attitude of piety towards all our rulers in the highest degree, whatever they may be like. I therefore the more often repeat this that we should learn not to examine the men themselves, but take it as enough that they bear by the Lord's will, a character upon which he has imprinted and engraved inviolable majesty ...

More specifically, Calvin states, that authority retains its absolute character even when it is exercised oppressively,

> Therefore, if we are cruelly tormented by a savage prince, if we are greatly despoiled by one who is avaricious or wanton, if we are neglected by a slothful

one, if finally we are vexed for piety's sake by one who is impious and sacrilegious, let us first be mindful of our own misdeeds, which without doubt are chastised by such whips of the Lord (cf. Dan. 9:7). By this, humility will restrain our impatience. Let us then also call this thought to mind, that it is not for us to remedy such evils; that only this remains, to implore the Lord's help, in whose hand are the hearts of kings, and the changing of kingdoms. (Proverbs 21:1)

Later Calvin becomes even more specific in proscribing rebellion against royal authority,

But we must, in the meantime, be very careful not to despise or violate that authority of magistrates, full of venerable majesty, which God has established by the weightiest decrees, even though it may reside with the most unworthy men, who defile it as much as they can with their own wickedness. For, if the correction of unbridled despotism is the Lord's to avenge, let us not at once think that it is entrusted to us to whom no command has been given except to obey and suffer. (Bk. IV, Ch. 22, No. 29)[35]

---

[35] For Calvin, any sort of resistance to governing royalty must come from within the ruling establishment itself. That is, only properly constituted authority—magistrates, he said, can defend the Christian freedom of common people from oppression of their rulers.
 . . . if there are now any magistrates of the people, appointed to restrain the willfulness of kings. . . I am so far from forbidding them to withstand, in accordance with their duty, the fierce licentiousness of kings, that, if they wink at kings who violently fall upon and assault the lowly common folk, I declare that their dissimulation involves nefarious perfidy, because they dishonestly betray the freedom of the people, of which they know that they have been appointed protectors by God's ordinance. (Institutes. . . , No. 31)
Still however, there is a single exception to Calvin's proscription against rebellion of common people against properly constituted authority. In fact, he says, Christians are bound to disobey authority when its legislations run contrary to the law of God. But here, at least according to the supporting evidence he advances, Calvin seems to be referring to laws which destroy the soul by inhibiting the practice of formal religion. This also seems to be the case, since the reformer had already disqualified resistance to acts of oppression affecting "merely" the body.
 In that obedience which we have shown to be due the authority of rulers, we are always to make this exception, indeed to observe it as primary, that such obedience is never to lead us away from obedience to him to whose will the desires of all kings ought to be subject, to whose decrees all their commands ought to yield, to whose majesty their scepters ought to be submitted. . . . if they command anything agains him, let it go unesteemed. . . . on this consideration, Daniel denies that he has committed any offense against the king when he has not obeyed his impious edict

Enlightenment Inversions

With the demise of Christendom, and the accession of the bourgeoisie to political power beginning in the 16th century, a whole new understanding of the law and of Christianity's relation to the law had to be developed—without relinquishing the claim to divine authority. In other words, Christianity long-since alienated from genuine worship of Yahweh, found itself required to reformulate its justification for covertly (and usually unwittingly) offering incense at the altar of Satan. After all, the old justification had empowered the *ancien regime* directed by kings and queens whose "divine right" theory gave theological authority to the medieval law and order. This was unacceptable to the bourgeoisie who seized power all over the world, most notably in the New World in 1776, in France in 1789, and across the European continent in 1848. A new ideology was required to justify the concomitant changing of the guard.

That ideology had presented itself in embryonic form in the 17th century with the dawning of the scientific revolution. The Revolution's implications gradually became clear to the new ruling elite. Newton, of course, had "explained the world," by removing the contradictions inherent in previous attempts to explain motion on a moving planet. Laws of inertia, gravity and those governing colliding bodies seemed to clarify everything.

In formulating such laws, Newton gave impetus to the Enlightenment and to new rational explanations of all aspects of natural and human life. After Newton, theorists in every field claimed to be "scientists;" they viewed their endeavors in political philosophy, economy, biology and psychology as equivalent to those of astronomers and physicists. Consequently, they desperately sought "Newtonian" laws that explained developments in their fields (Rivage-Seul 64).

Most significant to the study at hand were the "discoveries" of Adam Smith, published in the last quarter of the eighteenth century. In his *Wealth of Nations*, Smith found for the science of economics the equivalents of Newton's forces. He found them in the laws of supply and demand and in the iron law of wages deriving from those laws. In fact, Smith saw the whole economic process governed automatically by an "invisible hand," a phrase that itself contained implicit theological overtones. That is, the economic order, which was central to the property owners' universe, was established

---

(Dan. 6:22-2 Vg.). For the king had exceeded his limits, and had not only been a wrongdoer against men, but in lifting up his horns against God, had himself abrogated his power. (Institutes. . . , No. 33)

by a force as close to the divine as Enlightenment thinking would allow. Consequently, any interference in that order to change its quasi-divinely ordained outcomes was anathema and blasphemous.

Conclusions like these made intolerable all the movements for emancipation, from the 18th century on. This was especially true of communism with its doctrinaire atheism. On the one hand, communism's godlessness underlined its unacceptability for Christians. By default (as well as in virtue of arguments like Smith's) capitalism assumed the status of God's own order.

The consequence of all this was that any interference in market law to favor those with whom Jesus identified historically came to be deemed sinful by Christians who became capitalism's staunchest defenders. Those who advocated economic planning and market interference were considered rebels against God himself, on a par with Adam and Eve, with the rebellious Satan, and with the Jews who were considered God-killers by most God-fearing Christians. Meanwhile those who honored the manifest will of the market, refusing (unlike the Godless communists) to interfere with its outworking, became the defenders of God's order, even though such defense might cost tens of thousands of deaths each day.

In light of the arguments presented here, all of this is entirely ironic, since the God atheistic communism rebelled against was really Satan. So Christians rejected communists for not worshipping Satan.

Meanwhile, as defenders of those exploited by respect for reigning market law, the atheists more closely approximated the position of Jesus. In other words, in the name of Jesus, Christians embraced Satanism, while in the name of atheism, communists can be seen as embracing the Spirit of Jesus.

Conclusion

The Judeo-Christian tradition represents a faith that subordinates observance of law to human well-being – to human life. This characteristic perception is embodied in the Genesis account of the first woman and first man, in the narrative about Abraham's refusal to sacrifice his son, and in the person of Jesus who distinguished himself as a prophet who fulfilled God's law by his readiness to disobey legal prescriptions for the sake of human well-being.

This understanding, however, has been challenged throughout the course of the tradition's life. The challenge appears in the stories of Cain and Lemech, as well as in the person of the God, Baal, who appears at both the beginnings of the Eve story, and that of Abraham and Isaac. The God who forbids eating from the Tree of Knowledge of Good and Evil, as well as the God who demands child sacrifice, is a patriarchal God fashioned after the image of a 10th century B.C.E. despot, Solomon of Jerusalem.

The God of Cain and Lemech is that same divinized patriarch who by means of fratricides establishes human culture as an order indelibly marked by vengeance and bloodshed.

That order was continued in the Roman Empire, which after the 4th century co-opted the Judeo-Christian tradition, transforming it from a liberating Gospel of hope for victims of empire into a message requiring the surrender of human subjectivity to the demands of patriarchal, despotic and arbitrary laws serving the elite few at the expense of the non-elite majority. Following the demise of the Roman Empire, such understandings were continued in a medieval system where the nobility "lorded" their power over serfs and commoners – all in the name of a God who was only a masked Satan.

Satan's masquerade continued after the scientific revolution and the subsequent establishment of property-owners' democracies. Now the requirement of subordination to law was secularized. The Deists' "watchmaker" God became responsible for the ordering of the universe by means of natural laws – chief among them, those of supply and demand governing the economic sphere so central to bourgeois concern. To interfere with such laws would identify one with the system of Godless communists. Christians reasoned that since the system opposing the bourgeois order was godless, the property-owners' order itself must be godly. So many of the would-be faithful gave that order their undying allegiance. They remained unaware that in doing so they were worshipping Satan, the one who divinizes law, whatever the cost.

Misunderstanding Thirteen:

Churches Committed to the Rich or to the Poor Worship the Same God

> . . . (S)ome Christian preachers saw riches as a sign of God's favor and the kingdom of God as a kingdom of wealth, as a place where the morally fit should be allowed to make money. Rich Christians acknowledged their great wealth as a sign of approval by divine providence. In contemporary terms, a version of the Gospel of Wealth is supported by some conservative Christians who think Jesus would have supported the American dream had he known about it. According to them, the economic system of America is bound up with God's plan: preachers assure their members that God wants them to be rich, that a believing Christian will never go under financially. In some ways they hope to demonstrate that it "pays to believe in Jesus." The sign of salvation for these preachers—who can be seen regularly on television—is prosperity. (Weaver 217)

> The Social Gospel . . . argued that capitalism and individualism had numbed the Christian conscience. Poverty was not a divine curse (as some had suggested) but the result of human exploitation. (216)

Each semester while I was teaching in the Latin American Studies Program (LASP) of the Council of Christian Colleges and Universities, our group of six staff and 50 students would travel to Nicaragua, the second poorest country in the western hemisphere (after Haiti). We spent two weeks there. Students would live in the countryside or *campo* with Nicaraguan families. The experience was life-changing for many who had never witnessed, must less experienced such poverty.

Before sending our charges into the *campo*, all of us spent three days in Managua. The first point was to give students an orientation towards the city. We visited landmarks including the monument to Nicaragua's poet laureate, Ruben Dario; the memorial with its "eternal flame" dedicated to Carlos Fonseca, the founder of the Sandinista National Liberation Front, and the Plaza de la Revolución, where I had been present in 1990, when nearly a million people gathered at the pre-election rally of the Sandinista Party. Church landmarks included the ruins of the cathedral destroyed in the 1972 earthquake, the new cathedral erected with funds provided by Tom Monahan, the owner of Domino's Pizza, and the liberation theology church, Santa Maria de Los Angeles.

The second point was to orient students towards Nicaragua's extremely bloody history. Our orientation concentrated on the more than 50 years Nicaraguans suffered under the dictatorships of three members of the brutal Somoza family. Our LASP staff wanted students to understand the Sandinista Revolution (which came to power in 1979) in terms of rebellion against that oppression which the U.S. had supported to the hilt. Franklin Roosevelt himself had recognized the tyrannical nature of the regime he and other U.S. presidents had and would underwrite. Describing Anastasio Somoza, Roosevelt admitted, "He's an S.O.B., but he's our S.O.B." F.D.R. meant that Somoza had served U.S. interests quite well (vs. those of the Nicaraguan people, whom Somoza himself referred to as "cattle").

Fifty thousand Nicaraguans lost their lives in the Sandinista uprising against the Somozas. An additional 30,000 were killed during the 1980s, when the United States (successfully) supplied and funded the overthrow of the Sandinistas. That was the period of the so-called Contra War.[36] Those casualty totals were astounding—eighty thousand dead in a country of just over four million people. If the equivalent carnage had been suffered in the United States, the numbers of those slaughtered would reach well into the millions. In Nicaragua, we were indeed in the killing fields. And the head butchers were our own presidents—Hoover, Roosevelt, Truman, Eisenhower, Kennedy, Nixon, Ford, Carter, and Reagan.

---

[36] The term "Contra" was short for the Spanish equivalent of "counter-revolutionary." It referred to a U.S.-constituted and supported army whose core was the National Guard of the Somoza dictatorship. After the triumph of the Sandinista Revolution in 1979, those Guardsmen fled to Honduras, where they were reorganized and trained by the CIA. Later they were joined by others who had issues with the Sandinista government and revolution, and by unemployed Nicaraguans lured into the Contra ranks by promises of money provided by U.S. taxpayers. Other funds were secured by drug trafficking, well-publicized by the U.S. government's own Drug Enforcement Agency. The Contra mercenaries generally avoided direct conflict with the Sandinista Army. Instead, they concentrated on attacking facilities which represented the achievements of the Revolution—schools, hospitals, farming co-ops (See immediately below). When pursued by the Sandinistas, the Contras took refuge across the Honduran border where they found safe haven. They were confident that the Sandinistas would be unable to follow them in "hot pursuit," even as allowed by international law. Had the Sandinistas done so, they would have been accused by the U.S. of invading Honduras, and would have rendered Nicaragua vulnerable to retaliation by way of direct U.S. invasion.

The problem was that both the U.S. support of the Somozas, and especially of the Contras who fought to overthrow the Sandinistas, were inspired by Christians. Cardinal Obando y Bravo, the archbishop of Managua was staunchly in the Contra camp. At the same time, Pat Robertson, Jerry Fallwell, James Dobson and other Evangelical Protestants urged their listeners and viewers to support the Reagan policy of war against the Sandinistas who were identified as Godless Communists. "Marxist-Leninist, totalitarian communists" was the preferred characterization. In other words, the Contra War took on the nature of a crusade against the enemies of God – including, as we shall see, priests, nuns and bishops. As Chomsky indicates, the Contra War was a religious war against the Catholic Church.

That is, many Nicaraguan Christians had taken up arms to overthrow the Somozas on the one hand, and against the Contras on the other, to defend the gains of the Sandinista Revolution. Those achievements had been impressive. Land reform had been implemented to provide fields and work to previously unemployed or underpaid farmers in Nicaragua's basically agrarian economy. A literacy program had raised the number of literate Nicaraguans well above 90%. Health care had been made available to all; the World Health Organization had even cited Nicaragua as offering a splendid example in that field for the rest of the Third World to imitate. Food subsidies made a basket of basic necessities (including rice, beans, oil, sugar, salt . . .) available to all Nicaraguan citizens for the first time. Despite a punitive U.S. embargo, the Sandinistas had attempted to insure that every citizen had a job. In 1986, the country had held its first elections (judged "free and fair" by international observers, with the lone exception of the United States). The Sandinistas had won those elections in a landslide, garnering over 75% of the vote. This meant that continuation of the Contra War represented yet another instance of the United States commitment to reversing democratic choice by the Third World poor.

When many Nicaraguan Christians compared the achievements of the Sandinista Revolution with the extreme oppression of the Somoza decades, it is no wonder they found themselves in support of the revolution, precisely as Christians. This was also true of the Catholic priests who exercised leadership in the new government. Among them was the Jesuit poet, Ernesto Cardenal, who accepted the post of Sandinista Minister of Culture. Maryknoll father, Miguel D'Escoto, was the Minister of the Exterior – what we would call the Secretary of State. In the Sandinistas these priests and many other Christians, found a government attending not to the needs of the rich elite, as the Somozas had done so well, but to the needs of the poor, as Jesus himself had done. Basing their reasoning on traditional Just War theory, Christians supporting the Sandinistas had recognized the rights of poor people to defend themselves against the depredations of the rich, even to the point of taking up arms.

Recalling this history for my LASP students enabled me to introduce a theme quite relevant both to them and to the study at hand—misunderstandings of Christian Faith. That theme is the "Battle of the Gods" which we have already seen foreshadowed in Biblical texts. That is, in Nicaragua, I saw, in effect, that for more than half a century (not to mention the European West's 500 year history of colonialism), a war had been taking place between two Gods, each claiming to be Christian, and each arraigned on an opposite side of a barricade. On one side stood the God of the Rich, on the other, the God of the Poor. The God of the Rich stood with empire and against social changes such as those introduced by the Sandinistas. He was recognized by Obando y Bravo, Robertson, Fallwell and Dobson.

Through such spokespersons, the rich God was urging followers to kill "Godless Communists." At worst, they claimed, the Godless were real Communists manipulating religion to suit their own ideological purposes. At the very least, Sandinista supporters had been duped into supporting a class war that favored the so-called "poor and oppressed." Since the God of the Poor was a biased entity, their God was for that very reason false, and (following the long tradition since Constantine) his devotees could be killed with impunity. After all, it was argued, the God of the Bible is classblind, loving everyone equally both rich and poor.

For their part, the defenders of the Sandinista revolution were also fighting in the name of God—the very one denied by those opposing them. Their claim was that, yes, the God of the Bible is indeed a biased God. Consider the Exodus, they said, the first revelation of God in history. God preferred a group of slaves to their Egyptian slave holders. Besides that, the Mosaic Law went out of its way to protect widows, orphans, foreigners and slaves from those among the People of God who would abuse them— presumably rich and powerful Israelites. Prophets like Amos continually defended the poor and harshly criticized the rich in the name of the Exodus God. And in Jesus himself God made it understood that Godliness could be revealed most fully in the person of a poor working class human being, as opposed to the rich and powerful.

Were these really two Gods at war with each other? My students often objected that they were not really two Gods but two opposed understandings of the one and only God. The students may have been right. Still, however, it must be recognized that the divinity or divinities involved were somehow urging the elimination of the devotees of their opposite number, presumably because those others were idol-worshippers.

In the 1980s, the war of the conservative rich against the revolutionary poor, each with their own version of God, was very like the current war of Christians against Muslims. The Christian version of God tends to be the one supported by the developed world. The Muslim counterpart tends to be recognized by the poor of the Arab world. In fact, in the current conflict, it is not unusual to hear U.S. spokespersons like the U.S. Army's Colonel Boykin speaking directly as if two different Gods are separate contestants in the War on Terror. In speeches given in full military dress, Boykin has claimed centrally that "our God is mightier than their God." The claim is made, even though strictly speaking, the God of Christianity and of Islam is the same.

In any case, given the argument already presented here—that God is a "hollow concept" even in the Bible—it helps (me, at least) to conceptualize the "understandings of Christianity" in terms of a "Battle of the Gods." Such conceptualization forces a choice, at the risk of idolatry, on dialog participants. Which is the God they truly believe in? Is it the God who sides with the rich, or the one who sides with the poor? And if it is neither, what are the class options of the God they worship? If the answer is that God is neutral, how then does one avoid identifying that God with the interests of the rich? After all, the prevailing order is the one favoring the wealthy classes. If God makes no choice in such circumstances, doesn't that mean that God necessarily favors the status quo? And doesn't that make God then, the God of the rich who primarily benefits from the given order? As they say, "not to decide is to decide," even for God.

Hitler's God

While such questions and suggested conclusions might at first seem extreme, the idea of conflicting parties fighting each other in the name of God should not, even apart from current battles between Christians and Muslims. During World War II, for instance, combatants on both sides claimed to be Christian.[37] Hitler's Nazis had the support of Germany's mainline churches. Pius XII called Hitler himself "an indispensable bulwark against the Russians" (Johnson 490).

---

[37] Point #25 of the Nazi Party Program of 1920 read, "We demand freedom of religion for all religious denominations within the state so long as they do not endanger its existence or oppose the moral senses of the German race. The Party as such advocates the standpoint of a positive Christianity without binding itself confessionally to any one denomination" (Qtd. in Kendrick 192).

The leadership of the Catholic Church proudly salutes their Fuhrer.

And der Fuhrer himself was careful to be photographed at prayer and coming in and out of church. (Photos on this and following page taken from collection compiled by Jim Walker, http://nobeliefs.com/nazis.htm)

German soldiers were proud to say they had God on their side

A German Army belt buckle proclaims "God with us."

Were Hitler and his troops really worshipping the same God as the allies who opposed them? Was God neutral in World War II? If not, whose side was God on? And into whose presence did the prayers of Hitler and the Nazis arrive?

Following World War II, and especially after the Second Vatican Council (1962-'65), the Battle of the Gods was intensified. It became especially fierce beginning in the 1960s, with the emergence of Liberation Theology. In 1968, at their Conference in Medellín, Colombia, the Catholic Bishops of the region had recognized that the God of the Bible is not neutral about hunger, poverty, and exploitation. Rather, Yahweh, they said, stands with the poor against their exploiters. As we have already seen, this acknowledgement, and the resulting activism on behalf of the poor by Catholic clergy and lay persons, caused great consternation not only in Washington, but throughout the bastions of the elite in Latin America. In 1987, the confidential documents of the 17th Conference of American Armies held in Mar del Plata, Argentina, devoted fully 15 pages to theological analysis (Duchrow125-140). Two years later, during a major battle in El Salvador's revolutionary war, the U.S.- supported Salvadoran Army brutally assassinated a team of specifically liberation theologians, along with two household attendants.[38] Can you imagine the reaction of the U.S. government if those murdered had been Evangelical ministers in Cuba or in Nicaragua for that matter? It would surely have been taken as a sign of religious persecution by Godless Communists. Instead, the killing of the theologians in El Salvador was written off as strictly political rather than as a sign of church persecution at the hands of a government the U.S. was supporting with more than $1 million per day.

Returning to neighboring Nicaragua during the 1980s, it helps to recall that while President Reagan appealed to Christians to fight "Godless Communism" there, the Sandinista government of that country also claimed allegiance to the Christian God. They minted their coins so that Augusto Caesar Sandino, the "patron saint" of their cause, stood in relief on one side, while on the other were inscribed the words "In God we trust."

1980 Nicaraguan One Cordoba coin. At left, an image of Augusto Caesar Sandino with words, "Republic of Nicaragua." At right, the words, "In God We Trust" (at top), and "Free country or death" (at bottom).

---

[38] Pablo Richard relates the incident to the theological dimensions of the ongoing war of the rich against the poor, each claiming support from the Biblical God "Many people, horrified, condemned these crimes, but very few have reflected upon the meaning of these deaths. In fact, they condemned the crime while simultaneously giving political support to the president of El Salvador. The six priests formed a team that reflected, taught, wrote from within the process of liberation of the Salvadoran people. They were friends; they prayed together; they thought together about the future of the people; they created pastoral strategies and policies of liberation. In the strict sense of the word, they were a team which practiced the Theology of Liberation on a day to day basis. The death of the Jesuits was a terrorist act against the Theology of Liberation. They were killed precisely because they did liberating theology in a concrete process of popular liberation. Witnesses told us that, after murdering these priests, the killers took out their brains—the "de-brained" them, to be very sure that their intelligence was really dead. Within this team, too much holiness and intelligence had been accumulated and that had become unbearable to the powerful. With the death of the Jesuits and of the Theology of Liberation, an effort is made to take from the poor their voice, their hope, their awareness, their faith their spiritual power" (*La Lucha* 202).

Meanwhile, in 1990, the Bush administration aligned itself with the "Godless Communists" themselves in its effort to defeat the Sandinistas, who never enjoyed the support of their country's Communist Party. In one of their election posters immediately below, the Communists explain why they stood within the (U.S. supported) UNO Party (United Nicaraguan Opposition).

Nicaraguan Communist Party (PC de N) poster: "We Communists stand within the UNO (United Nicaraguan Opposition). The UNO government will eliminate predatory merchants. It will distribute all products at controlled prices. Teaching in all our schools will be lay and scientific, without deception. As Marxists-Leninists we stand with the UNO. [Communist Party of Nicaragua (PC de N)]"

The poster suggests strongly that the real enemy of the United States in Nicaragua was not communism; neither were the Sandinistas Communists. Otherwise how could the U.S. align itself with Nicaragua's Communists against the Sandinistas? Does this mean that for the United States, the real enemy was the empowerment of poor people that the Sandinista revolution represented?

As can be seen from these examples and from recent presidential campaigns in the United States, it is easy to argue that the Battle of the Gods is real. The God of Christian fundamentalism, in both Catholic and Protestant forms, currently arrays himself against the One who stands on the side of the poor and their liberation. To better understand this argument, which is important to both this and the following chapter, it helps to look at the stark contradictions between the Gods in opposition—the God of the Rich over against the God of the Poor:

GOD OF THE RICH	GOD OF THE POOR
• God experienced in nature	• Experienced in history
• Mythological, revealed primarily in Genesis	• Historical, revealed primarily in Exodus
• Concerned with orthodoxy & worship	• Concerned with justice as true worship
• Class-blind, politically neutral	• Class-biased, committed to the poor
• Endorses work ethic	• Endorses ethic of love and self-sacrifice
• Protects freedom to compete	• Protects freedom from exploitation
• Riches = sign of God's favor	• Riches presume exploitation
• Poverty = sign of laziness	• Poverty evokes divine anger vs. the rich
• Permits violence to defend capitalist order	• Permits violence to defend poor vs. exploiters
• Jesus = teacher of timeless moral Truth	• Jesus = ultimate revelation that God stands with the poor
• Anti-communist, anti-terrorist	• Anti-imperialist
• Favorite texts: "The poor you will always have with you." "Render to Caesar. . ." "My kingdom is not of this world."	• Favorite texts: Exodus, Prophets, Gospels.

The term "nature God" in the left column is a reference to the belief that the "Supreme Being" is primarily experienced in the act of creation and in the laws established by that act. God made the world as described in the book of Genesis. The laws established there govern every facet of life. Here the "Ten Commandments" are the core of biblical teaching and the basis of morality. They mandate middle class values of sexual purity, individualism, hard work, discipline, respect for parents, church on Sundays, "eye for eye" retribution, the right to bear arms, and rejection of homosexuality, abortion, gambling, cursing and alcohol. Jesus is understood as teaching such values by means of illustrative parables which convey timeless moral lessons and focus the hopes of believers on an afterlife rather than on this world. In the economic and political sphere, God's laws favor something like the "American Way of Life," and seem to single out U.S. Americans as especially holy in God's eyes. More particularly, the divinely established order enshrines the market laws of "supply and demand." To violate freedom of enterprise is a heinous offense against God, for whom capitalism is most coherent with his plan of salvation. As such, God permits the use of any act of violence including nuclear destruction to "save" the divinely favored system.

The term "God of history" in the right hand column, refers to the belief that the biblical God is primarily experienced in this-worldly events. Questions of the afterlife are left in God's hands and are not a main focus of Christian faith. God's first historical intervention coincided with the beginning of the people of Israel, about 1200 B.C.E. The group was distinguished by shared oppression rather than by ethnicity. The experience of liberation convinced them that their God favored the oppressed in their midst. That conviction was written into their politics and economics as expressed in the biblical books of Exodus, Numbers, Leviticus and Deuteronomy. To repeat: in all cases, special provision was made for the poor, the enslaved, widows, orphans and resident aliens. The law also enshrined continuous land reform protecting the property rights of the poor against natural tendencies of buying and selling to concentrate land holdings in the hands of a few. Protection of the poor was supported by the prophets who continually confronted the rich for their neglect of the least well off. Jesus assumed the mantle of the prophetic tradition. Class mattered for Jesus who delivered his message specifically to "the poor," while harshly criticizing "the rich." In defense of the poor, he modified the law's harsh provisions. He set it aside entirely if it caused hardship for the hungry. As the very incarnation of God, he reiterated divine identification with the poor by living as a poor man himself. A member of an imperialized people, Jesus is recorded as opposing capital punishment, and himself was its victim. His execution came at the hands of an alliance of his time's religious conservatives and imperial powers.

As will become even clearer in the chapter which follows this one, such reflections face believers and their churches with a stark choice. It uncovers another layer of the "understandings of Christianity" addressed in this book. Understandings and misunderstandings not only involve heresies such as Gnosticism, Arianism, and the rest. They not only entail differences between Western Christianity and Eastern Orthodoxy. Understandings even go beyond variations in belief belonging to Catholics, Anglicans, Episcopalians, Presbyterians, Congregationalists, Baptists, Holiness churches, Methodists, Evangelicals, Mennonites, Quakers, and Churches of God, Christ and of the Brethren.

Conclusion

The point here is that perhaps the most important difference in belief entails commitment to either the God of the Rich or the God of the Poor. The fact is that most of the churches mentioned in the long list just cited have predominantly worshipped the God of the rich. Most are basically patriotic churches that support capitalism and the American empire. In fact, support of empire has been the predominant order of the day since the fateful 4th century, when the church definitively joined forces with imperial Rome.

Since then there have always been dissenters. They've included monks in the Egyptian desert, followers of Francis of Assisi, Anabaptists, proponents of the Social Gospel, and advocates of liberation theology. In each case, those who have insisted that the God of the rich is idolatrous have not only met staunch opposition, they have been routinely persecuted and murdered. During the 1980s in Catholic El Salvador where priests, nuns, catechists and bishops sided with the poor, the going slogan issuing from the Catholic military was "Be a patriot; kill a priest." All of that indicates a strong incompatibility between understandings of God among Christians themselves. The argument here is that at some point incompatibility crosses the line separating different *understandings* of God from different kinds of God. Incompatibility crosses into the realm of idolatry.

Misunderstanding Fourteen:

(Left) Politics Has No Place in Church

> The theology of liberation . . . is based on a reading of the Bible in which God is perceived as a liberator of captives (in the Exodus) and Jesus is identified with the poor. According to this view, God's primary interest lies with the poor: they are the objects of divine concern in the Old Testament (see the Prophets especially) and the ones to whom Jesus brings the message of salvation. It is argued that all Christians who want to imitate Jesus should work for the elimination of oppression, a task that may mean working to overthrow corrupt and exploitive political structures. (Weaver 213)

The offensives of Pope John Paul II and his lieutenant, Joseph Ratzinger (now Pope Benedict XVI), along with fellow fundamentalists from the Protestant community, including Ronald Reagan and the Presidents Bush, tried mightily to kill the God of the Poor, and (unsuspectingly) to replace him with the very Satan Jesus had rejected at the outset of his public life. They have all but succeeded. To get an idea of the object of their wrath, it helps to visit the Third World, especially Latin America, since it was principally in that site that the God of the poor was rediscovered and brought to prominence after long centuries of obscurity, vilification, and satanic transformations on the part of mainstream church officials and theologians. The iconography of four such sites makes clear both the character of the God of the Poor and the battle lines that have been drawn in relation to the God of the Rich. Together the sites illustrate how far from the God of the Bible is the one worshipped today in the churches supporting the current Empire and its governing law.

Catholic Worship of the God of the Poor

Once again, the brightest lines of battle examined here are found in Nicaragua – in the church of Santa Maria de los Angeles, in Managua's Barrio Rigueiro. During the 1980s, while Father Uriel Molina was pastor, Santa Maria was a church specifically dedicated to the worship of the God of the Poor. Then Father Molina was a researcher at the progressive Centro

Antonio Valdivieso a Nicaraguan institute of theological research and publication. In the meantime, however, under the reactionary backlash described above, he was removed and eventually even expelled from his Franciscan Order.

During the 1980s, when Molina was still in charge, he celebrated the *"Misa Campesina"* (Peasant's Mass) each Sunday afternoon. The songs of the Mass connected the revolutionary struggles of the Nicaraguan poor with biblical texts. Sometimes they were performed by prominent, pro-revolutionary artists like Carlos Mejía Godoy. For example, the text of the Creed reads in part,

> I believe in you, Christ the Worker,
> the only begotten of God,
> I believe in you, compañero, the human Christ,
> conqueror of death . . . .
> You are rising from the dead
> in every hand that is raised
> to defend the people
> from domination and exploitation.

Soldiers returned from their mountain struggles against the US.–supported counter-revolutionaries frequently gave reports and testimony about the exploits of *"los cachorros"* (the "Cub Bears," the nickname for Sandinista soldiers). Often returnees with amputated legs and arms occupied places of honor before the altar. Always, Molina's homilies were pointed and unabashedly pro-Sandinista, vilifying the Contras, their leaders and especially the United States. At one *Misa Campesina*, Father Molina reportedly illustrated the U.S. role in his country's suffering by spreading the American flag on the altar where, according to Catholic belief, the "Sacrifice of the Cross" is reenacted during Mass. Invariably a large contingent of foreigners would be present.

The reason for visiting Santa Maria de Los Angeles is the mural iconography which still decorates the church walls and illustrates the Battle of the Gods theme. Centralizing the revolutionary struggle against Somoza, the murals depict what their creators saw as the principal manifestations of the God of the Poor in the lives of Latin Americans in general, and of the Nicaraguan people in particular. Manifestations of that God in indigenous forms are represented in statuary over the church's main entrance.

Depictions of Indigenous Divine Consorts and Corn God over main entrance of Santa Maria de los Ángeles

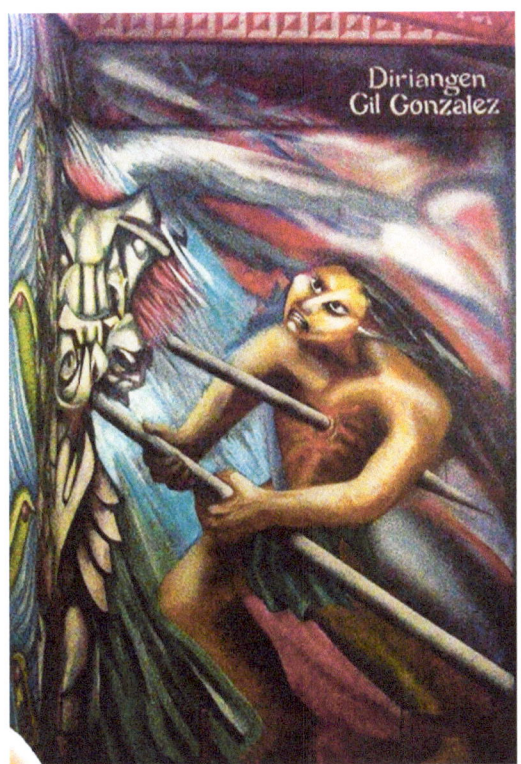

Resistance to the Spanish conquistadors on the part of the heroic indigenous leader, Diriangen comes next. Here he is pictured in direct confrontation with Gil Gonzalez, who subdued "the Indians" on behalf of the Spanish crown.

Then the Spanish missionary, Bartolomé de las Casas, is depicted. He intervened on behalf of Latin America's indigenous when they were mistreated by the Spaniards and Portuguese.

Diriangen and Gil Gonzalez

Latin American priests who championed the cause of the poor exploited by their Spanish overlords, and who in some cases joined armies of the poor as chaplains find prominence as well. Below Camilo Torres of Colombia and Gaspar Garcia Laviana of Spain, both of whom lost their lives while accompanying guerrilla movements, are portrayed above the mutilated bodies of the victims of the U.S.-supported dictators their people were rebelling against.

Bartolomé de Las Casas standing between the Spanish Conquistadors (right) and Native Americans (background)

Camilo Torres and Gaspar Garcia Laviana

Archbishop Oscar Arnulfo Romero

El Salvador's Oscar Romero, advocate of Latin America's poor, who was martyred by a member of a U.S.-supported Salvadoran death squad finds prominent place as Central America's most celebrated martyr. Here he is shown in his priestly vestments (He was murdered while celebrating Mass), blood pouring from his throat, and extending his hands towards another anonymous martyred figure.

Understandably, the Nicaraguan Revolution against U.S.-supported dictator, Anastasio Somoza receives most of the attention from the muralists of Santa Maria de los Angeles.

Carlos Fonseca (left) and Augusto Caesar Sandino (right)

In the mural immediately above, the historical founder of the Sandinistas, Carlos Fonseca, and the spiritual inspiration for the movement, Augusto Caesar Sandino are featured. Sandino is at the right, holding the Nicaraguan flag. Fonseca is on the left holding the red and black Sandinista colors. Three children race off into a bright future. A masked figure (in U.S. sweater and jeans) tries to prevent Fonseca from fulfilling his liberating vocation. Fonseca pays no attention. The words at the mural's top right are "the story of the ants." They refer to Sandino's words that if he were to die before Nicaragua's liberation (which he considered certain), the ants would come to his grave to tell him it had happened.

The panel on the next page celebrates the fourteen year old martyr, Luis Alfonso Velazquez, who was a member of the Santa Maria de los Angeles parish. In the background, under the Sandinista flag emblazoned with the slogan, "Free Country or Death," a group of young musicians from the parish are singing as they used to on Sunday mornings during the insurrection against Somoza – to spread news of resistance acts that had occurred the previous week. One Sunday, Luis Alfonso tried to warn them of the approaching National Guard depicted here as hideous monsters. The Guard killed Luis Alfonso brutally before he could get to his *campañeros*. The sling shot in the boy's right pocket compares him to the biblical David confronting Goliath.

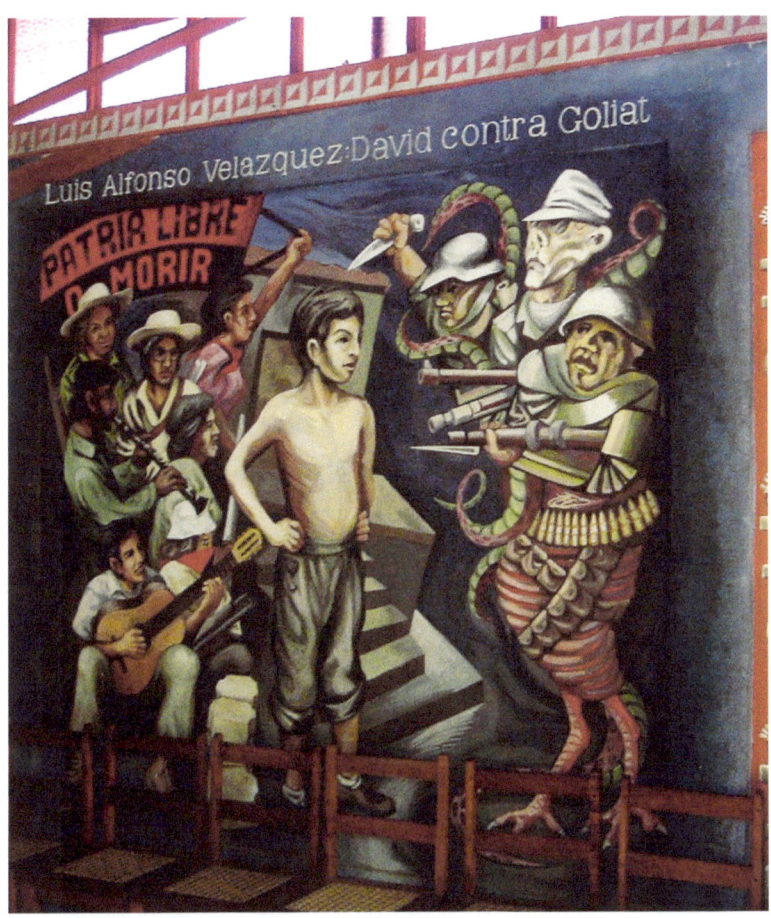

Luis Alfonso Velazquez confronts Nicaragua's monstrous National Guard

The (Indigenous) Risen Lord

The Indian behind the Screen

The culminating mural in Santa Maria de Los Angeles is located behind the church's main altar. It depicts the Risen Christ and the coming of the Reign of God in the theological perspective of the God of the Poor. Jesus is indigenous.

The Reign of God is a Reign of Plenty

And the Reign of God is one of material plenty where there is no hunger.

There will be no more death, or tears from poor mothers carrying pictures of their daughters, sons, and husbands "disappeared" by the death squads of those worshipping the God of the Rich.

Mothers of the Disappeared

Cover-up

The problem is that all this theology of the poor has been literally covered over in the most eloquent expression of the Battle of the Gods.

Following the defeat of the Sandinistas in 1990 by the U.S.-supported United Nicaraguan Opposition (which, as we saw, embraced the Communist Party), a contingent of parishioners at Santa Maria de Los Angeles found the church's murals "too political." Some voted to have them painted over completely, the way other murals throughout Managua were erased immediately after the 1990 elections. Other parishioners defended the murals and their God of the Poor theology. A compromise was struck.

The murals would remain. However, the ones behind the main altar would be covered with a white screen, and a traditional (i.e. white, European) crucified Jesus would become the focus of attention. The whole debate and compromise is emblematic of what has gradually happened to the Catholic version of the "God of the Poor" since the accession of John Paul II to the papacy in 1979.

Sr. Beatriz explains the politics and theology of iconographic cover-up.

The Protestant God of the Poor

Liberation theology even as radical as expressed by Padre Molina, developed out of a conservative movement called "Catholic Action" which took shape following World War II. Its thrust was intensified by missionary movements in the Catholic Church during the 1960s. For example, the Society of St. James, founded by Boston's cardinal archbishop, Richard Cushing, played a key role in sending diocesan priests to "save Latin America from communism" — and, one might add, from Protestantism.

As the result of such efforts, the 1950 total of 1600 U.S. missionaries in the region was raised by 1960 to 2400. By 1968 a total of 3391 missionaries were serving in Latin America, joined by about 2000 Canadians by 1971.

The problems was that given traditional Catholic Church structures, about 40,000 missionaries would have been required to meet the needs of the estimated 80 million Catholics living in Latin America. Priests who plunged into the work soon found themselves massively overwhelmed and spending nearly all of their time "sacramentalizing" – conferring baptism, marrying and burying members of their flocks. Remaining time spent in charitable outreach soon convinced many that their assignment was not only exhausting, but counterproductive. Sacramentalization prevented any meaningful formation of Christian community and faith development.

Though social outreach within the system was creating "rice Christians," it was, in effect, treating hemorrhaging wounds with band aids.

Understanding the systemic nature of problems both within and outside the church, many priests and nuns were radicalized and embraced the approaches of liberation theology. Socially, they concluded that the unbridled system of free marketism was at the root of their problems and that it had to be resisted and changed to favor the increasingly excluded poor they served. Theologically, pastoral workers grasped the reality of the "Battle of the Gods" — the choice facing Christians between idolatry of the God of the Rich or the authentic faith in the God of the Poor. They decided that the quality of Christian community experience was more important than maintaining long parish registry lists. So they concentrated efforts on small communities of faithful committed to action for social change. Worship time was spent in "biblical circles," studying the Bible, praying as led by the Holy Spirit and applying conclusions from Biblical reflections to work within local communities. Many pastoral workers moved out of church buildings, rectories, convents and seminaries, and took up residence in *favelas, colonias* and *barrios* to discover and serve the God of the poor.

Today, Protestant missionaries in Latin America appear to be going through the "Catholic Action" phase Catholics faced in the '50s and '60s. Though large numbers of former Catholics are joining communities of *evangélicos*, and though "rice Christians" are being helped through hard times, many pastors are recognizing that playing the numbers game and fighting socialist tendencies are leading to unwitting cooperation with the deadly system of Free Marketism. So following the example of Catholic pastoral workers, a significant number are studying and even teaching the theology of the God of the Poor. Their work is often less politicized than what Catholics did during the '70s and '80s. Nonetheless, these converted missionaries are working politically as well as pastorally on behalf of the people they serve. Many have moved into slums where they live with the communities they serve.

Thus even among Protestant missionaries, the God of the Poor is increasingly worshipped, not in formal churches and cathedrals, but in homes and humble churches—in groups referred to as Base Christian Communities. There the leader is typically not an ordained minister, but a layperson. The community members resemble the kinds of people to whom Jesus directed his message—poor and simple people without formal education, money or friends in high places, as depicted in this poster from Brazil (c. 1985).

The words say, "The Bible: Hope of a Struggling People."

God of Indigenous Catholicism

In the cathedral of Chichicastenango, Guatemala, a third face of the God of the poor appears. It is different from the ones seen in Santa Maria de los Angeles or among Protestants working with Base Communities. Neither does this version bear exactly the same characteristics summarized under "God of the Poor" in the outline cited earlier. Though definitely on the side of the poor, this deity is an amalgam of colonial Catholic belief and the faith of Guatemala's Mayan people. It demonstrates the resistance of this proud impoverished nation to the destruction of their culture represented precisely by the traditional Catholic God in a land where the indigenous make up about three quarters of the population.

On any Sunday, the Chichicastenango church will suggest a theogony to the attentive observer. The church dominates the market square. The steep stairs leading up to its entrance almost give the appearance of a low stone ziggurat or "high place" devoted to sacrificial worship. Over them hangs a white, sweet smelling smoke coming from the tin cans swung as thuribles by Mayan medicine men, called *curanderos*.

Emergence from the smoke and entrance through the massive front doors will find the main aisle alight with candles. This center walkway is where the *curanderos* do their priestly work. Meanwhile, in the rear of the church, in front of the baptistery, a Ladino Catholic priest (i.e. one who identifies with the white culture), will typically be found giving baptismal

Mayan *curandero* incenses church entrance

instruction to a group of fifteen or so couples presenting their children for initiation into the church. The relative location of the priest and the *curanderos* is significant; it mirrors the proportionality between Catholicism and Mayan belief in Mayan-Catholic syncretism. Indigenous religion is foreground; Catholicism, more marginal.

At least half a dozen circles of candles will line the church's main aisle, tended by the *curanderos*. Some of the circles are made of white candles, others of yellow, blue, red or black. Within each circle flowers and other offerings are found, including money and alcoholic drink. The circles defined by the candles represent prayers offered for various groups within the community: for married couples, children, the sick, women, alcoholics, the recently deceased. Each group has its canonized patron. So prayers at each circle are offered to a particular saint charged with caring for the group concerned. After the prayers are offered in the church, many of the devout follow their *curanderos* to a nearby hill where the traditional Mayan chicken sacrifice is offered for the same groups commemorated on top of the Christian ziggurat. Mayan faithful see no contradiction here.

The pertinent point in this description is not merely that traditional Mayan religious practices have been preserved, but that the saints invoked within the church itself are really Christian reincarnations of Mayan Gods and Goddesses. Those deities were "christened" in response to missionaries' attempts to eliminate polytheism among the indigenous. In effect, the Mayans said, "If we can no longer worship our pantheon under its members' own names, we will call them St. John, St. Sebastian, St. Ann and St. Elizabeth, if you like."

At least one of the saints' disguises is transparent indeed, the lustful St. Simón, incorrigible drinker, smoker and fornicator. St. Simón is really an antisaint. He not only resembles an earthy Mayan God; he also represents an obvious example of resistance to the religious imperialism of Christian missionaries—a *reduction ad absurdum* of their practices which locals saw as literally ridiculous. St. Simón is always pictured sitting on a chair and wearing a hat. Invariably he has a cigar in his mouth and a bottle of liquor in his hand. In some depictions, he is without legs. They've been cut off by

St. Simón

villagers who have tired of his inveterate habit of chasing young women.

The best known case of "christening," among another indigenous group, is Our Lady of Guadalupe in Mexico. The appearance of the Blessed Virgin allegedly came to Juan Diego precisely at the time when the Spaniards were depriving the indigenous there of their Great Mother Goddess. The dark skinned Blessed Virgin with Indian features became that Goddess in disguise, and her cult continued.

For this reason, in the early 19th century, during Mexico's war against Spain, the "Battle of the Gods" actually became the "Battle of the Virgins." Statues of the white skinned virgin led the Spanish troops into battle against the Mexican army headed by the dark skinned Lady of Guadalupe.

Virgin of Guadalupe appearing to Juan Diego, 1531 (Tercera aparicion de la Virgen de Guadalupe, by Jose Mota, 1720)

In 1994, when Mexico's indigenous arose again – this time against the North American Free Trade Agree-ment (NAFTA), they adopted the Virgin of Guadalupe as their icon. All over the area surrounding the Lacandona rainforest, graffiti images of the Virgin were posted on walls – usually depicting her wearing the Zapatista signature hand-kerchief mask covering her nose and mouth. In the image below, The unspoken message is that in the current battle between the God of the Rich and the God of the Poor, the Virgin is on the side of the Zapatistas."

A Zapatista version of Our Lady of Guadalupe

God of the *Iglesia Profunda*

In his book, *Mexico Profundo*, Guillermo Bonfil Batalla contrasts what he calls "Imaginary Mexico," with "Mexico Profundo." Imaginary Mexico is the one most people think of when Mexico crosses their minds. It is the Mexico of mainstream scholars and publicists. It is the Mexico we learn about in school, and which great numbers of Mexicans themselves think they inhabit. Imaginary Mexico is the one shaped by the *conquistadores*. It is a Republic, divided up into a United States of Mexico. The head of state usually comes from the white Creole or Ladino class. People in Imaginary Mexico speak Spanish and English. Their values are increasingly "American," in the sense of U.S. values—individualism, over-work, industrialism, technological innovation, and unlimited consumption . . .

Mexico Profundo, on the other hand, is indigenous. It is a Mexico with which few are acquainted. *Mexico Profundo* is shaped by traditions that stretch thousands of years into the past, and has resisted *Mexico Imaginario* at every step. The leaders of *Mexico Profundo* are tribal caciques, wise women and men, and tribal councils. Its political landscape has nothing to do with a "United States of Mexico," but instead is marked by innumerable boundaries defining areas that together belong ultimately to the Great Creator Spirit. Provisionally, the lands are cared for by tribes, families, and clans, speaking (again) more than twenty-five languages, of which imaginary Mexicans know very little. Values in *Mexico Profundo* are traditional. Work is determined by cargoes—or community service responsibilities. These have little to do with either individualism, the rat race, technology or unlimited consumption. *Mexico Profundo* finds its most recognizable contemporary expression in the Zapatista movement.

In the spirit of Bonfil, we might also speak of a fourth church of the poor as the *Iglesia Profunda*. This "deep church" has little to do with hierarchies, organizations, or church buildings. It is "*profunda*" in the sense that it is much older than any of the Christian traditions reviewed so far. In fact, it preceded the founding of Christianity, which eventually linked up with it, and found expression in Christian mysticism – in the person of Jesus himself, in Paul, in Gnostic Christians, the Desert Fathers, and great mystics such as Francis of Assisi, John of the Cross, Theresa of Avila, Meister Eckhart, John Woolman, Teresa of Lisieux, and uncounted others. Many of these would find themselves perfectly at home with their counterparts living in contexts that are Buddhist, Hindu, Muslim, Jewish, Taoist, Jainist, and, yes, even agnostic and atheist.

Thus, the God of the *iglesia profunda* is broadly ecumenical. The deity is called, God, Allah, Elohim, Yahweh, Adonai, Brahma, Great Spirit, or even "Nature with a capital 'N'." There is no quibbling here over names or orthodoxy.

Similarly, the beliefs of the *iglesia profunda* have nothing to do with dogmas, creeds, of litmus tests of any kind, which are founded on "intellectual assent." Instead, its underlying convictions are based on experience, and appeal to experience alone for verification. That is, adherents to this "church" perform a kind of experiment to verify its tenets. They enter into the "laboratories" of their own lives, and attempt to live by the church's basic convictions. If their lives, if their actions are changed for the better in the process, no further proof is required.

The underlying convictions of the *Iglesia Profunda* are few: (1) a spark of the divine resides within every single human being; (2) that spark can be realized – i.e. made real in one's life; (3) in fact it is the purpose of human life to do so; (4) there are traditional disciplines recognized in all religious traditions for realizing and cultivating the divine spark, and (5) those who do so inevitably recognize the presence of the spark within every other human being, and in all of reality.

The spiritual disciplines which help one realize life's purpose include (1) daily meditation, (2) "praying always" using mantrams or spiritual "aspirations," (3) reading regularly from the great mystics or classic religious texts, such as the Bible, the Holy Koran, and the Bhagavad Gita, (4) training the senses, (5) practicing one-pointed attention, (6) slowing down the pace of life, (7) fostering spiritual companionship with others who are on the same path, and (8) putting the needs of others first.

The *Iglesia Profunda* deserves to be classified here as "Christian," because this tradition recognizes Jesus as one who embodied, practiced and taught the convictions and practices just listed. He, along with the Buddha, Mohammed, Krishna and others, is understood as incarnating the model to be followed. Those raised within the Christian tradition have more reason (or less!) to recognize Jesus in that role, rather than the others just mentioned.

Conclusion

What has been presented so far should reinforce the idea that Christianity is not monolithic. Instead polytheism characterizes it, as well as what are often considered more "primitive" faiths. Many brands of Christianity contradict those who would have the world believe that there is only one kind of Christian. Each variety has its version of the biblical God. At least two such Gods are clear. One stands with the world's dominant business classes, supports its Free Marketism, work ethic and "American Way," while blaming the world's evils on the impoverished majority. The other Christian God opposes the business classes and the culture they represent. This God takes a place alongside the poor in their struggle for survival within economic and political structures that would either exclude them entirely or exploit them unmercifully. Neither the God of the Rich nor the God of the Poor is neutral. Neither can be harmonized with the other into a kind of bland monotheism. In fact, recent history has shown them to be war Gods freely decreeing the deaths of their opponent's followers in the most blood thirsty ways.

It is even possible to discern more Gods than two. In fact, among the indigenous there are unabashedly many, though they appear under the cover of saints' names. Feminists often argue that Our Lady of Guadalupe and the Catholic cult of Mary in general represent the return of the repressed Great Mother Goddess whose recognition and religious following simply will not go away. This cult stretches back some 25,000 years and stubbornly resurfaces in covert forms, despite the opposition of the patriarchy over the last five millennia.

Part IV

Misunderstandings about Contemporary Issues

Misunderstanding Fifteen:

Fundamentalists Reject Darwin

> The work of Charles Darwin on the evolution of the species and the popular slogan about the survival of the fittest led many people to look upon the poor as morally unfit, a position known as Social Darwinism.
> Sociologists linked poverty with crime as surely as some church members associated it with sinfulness. Some Christians saw poverty as a divine curse or punishment for sin, and if poverty was a divine curse, then it was the will of God, and working to eliminate poverty was tantamount to opposing God's will. These Christians took the words of Jesus, "The poor you will always have with you" (Matt. 26:11) as a mandate to leave the structures of poverty in place, while at the same time exhorting the poor to move up out of them. (Weaver 216-17)

There is no single specifically "Christian" alternative to the biological theory of evolution. This is true despite the fact that some would make rejection of the theory a litmus test for separating genuine Christians from inauthentic pretenders. Nevertheless, even summary reflection makes it evident that Christians actually hold a variety of opinions about Darwin, the origin of life in all its forms, and about most other issues one would care to name.

Clearly some Christians are convinced that they reject evolution root and branch. They do not. Their erroneous conviction rests on their unswerving certainty that the words of the Bible must be taken literally, at face value, without interpretation, attenuation, or modification. Understood in this way, would-be literalists hold that evolutionary theory conflicts with the account of creation in the Bible's Book of Genesis, Chapters 1 and 2. Therefore, they are convinced that they recognize nothing positive about Charles Darwin and the theory of evolution.

On the other hand, a great number of believers have little problem with the biological dimensions of evolutionary theory. They point out that the Genesis account is not scientific, but a "myth." The biblically informed among them use that term not in the secular sense of an untrue story, but in the deeply religious sense of a symbolic narrative meant to uncover the truth of an otherwise unspeakable mystery – the origin of the universe, and the nature of human beings' relationships to God, one another and to the non-human world. Myth in this sense is concerned with expressing religious truth – with answering the otherwise unanswerable question "why?" In that sense, the truth of myth is much more valuable than scientific truth, which merely addresses empirical questions such as "what?" and "how?" In other words, many Christians have no trouble recognizing that biological evolution simply appears to represent the divine plan and method of creation.[39]

Virtually All Christians Are Darwinians

That said, it is important in the light of this book's argument to observe that biblical literalists too usually unwittingly endorse an important version of Darwinism – one that arguably should be totally unacceptable to followers of Jesus. In fact such highly questionable endorsement is given at least implicitly by any who accept our era's commercial globalization with its attendant absolutizing of the market, with its unbridled competition, and acceptance of "survival of the fittest" ethic. The reference here, of course, is to "Social Darwinism" – that is to the ideological application of Darwin's biological theory to human beings. In the contemporary world, social Darwinism places market law above human welfare. In so doing, it absolutizes the law, and rejects the teaching and practice of Jesus, who fulfilled the law by disobeying it whenever it conflicted with human well-being.

The distinction between the biological theory of evolution and its ideological application is important to note. The biological theory finds its most famous expression in Darwin's *Origin of Species*, published in 1859. Its ideological application referenced here received its first, fullest development by Herbert Spencer in his *Study of Sociology* in 1873. To put it simply, the biological theory holds that from the very beginning, life on the planet has proliferated in unbelievably abundant forms, varieties and sheer quantities. With such plentiful production, "random variations" occur within individual species — a tooth, a claw, a feather, a fin, where there was none before. These variations equip their beneficiaries with competitive advantage in the struggle for limited supplies of food and other

---

[39] Neither should it be forgotten that indigenous Christians, like the Mayans referred to earlier, easily accept both the biblical creation accounts and their own traditions' myths contained in the Pop Wuj. They place both sets of myths side by side, along with the discoveries of Western science, and learn from all three—usually emphasizing enriching points of agreement, rather than rejecting one or the other.

sources of sustenance. In the ensuing "struggle for survival," those possessing the random variations ("sports" as Darwin termed them) survive and reproduce their kind. The less well-equipped die off. By this process, species change and advance.

Fundamentalist Darwinism

As earlier indicated, most Christians have no trouble reconciling this account with the pre-scientific stories, for instance, of the first woman and the first man as referenced earlier in this book. A great number of believers do not think it necessary to reject what has become a pivotal and highly useful insight of modern science, when it can so easily be reconciled with the clearly mythological character of the Genesis accounts.[40]

What appears to be less easily reconciled with the teachings of Jesus about law and the treatment of human life and of creation itself, is the entirely questionable ideological application by Herbert Spencer and his legions of followers to today's globalized world. Spencer's own words pose the problem.

> Pervading all Nature we may see at work a stern discipline which is a little cruel that it may be very kind ... Meanwhile, the well-being of existing humanity and the unfolding of it into this ultimate perfection, are both secured by the same beneficial though severe discipline to which the animate creation at large is subject. It seems hard that an unskillfulness, which with all his efforts he cannot overcome, should entail hunger upon the artisan. It seems hard that a laborer, incapacitated by sickness from competing with his stronger fellows, should have to bear the resulting privations. It seems hard that widows and orphans should be left to struggle for life or death. Nevertheless, when regarded not separately but in connection with the interests of universal humanity, these harsh fatalities are seen to be full of beneficence–the same which brings to early graves the children of

---

[40] The "markers" of that mythological character appear throughout the accounts. For instance a "Tree of Knowledge of Good and Evil" seems clearly symbolic—as does the God strolling through the Garden with the first woman and first man. The story also centralizes a talking animal (the serpent), which in other circumstances would be indication enough for most adults that the account was not to be understood historically. None of this, of course, threatens the truth of the story. It is completely possible for the sincere believer to affirm that all of the stories in the Bible are true, without exception—and that some of them even happened.

diseased parents, and singles out the intemperate and debilitated as victims of an epidemic (Qtd. in Spielvogel 714-15)

Despite echoes here of concepts such as "tough love," dear to many Christians, this vision does not seem compatible with the teachings or practice of Jesus. In the world of Spencer and tough love advocates, the artisan suffers hunger as part of a divine plan, perhaps to make him work harder or more efficiently. The laborer works long hours, and experiences privations as a result of competition with stronger fellow workers; but that too is part of a beneficent order. Widows and orphans (the phrase is absolutely biblical!) are justly left alone in their struggle for survival. Parents are ill; infant mortality is high; the physically weak and improvident are victims of disease and premature death; but all of that is good too. Spencer (and by extension proponents of free market capitalism's immunity from government intervention) pronounces all of this good and full of benefit for "universal humanity."

Just how universal are the benefits from Spencer's order is illustrated by the following U.N. graph depicting wealth distribution world-wide. The graph was published in 1992, but since then the gaps between the cohorts depicted have widened rather than narrowed.

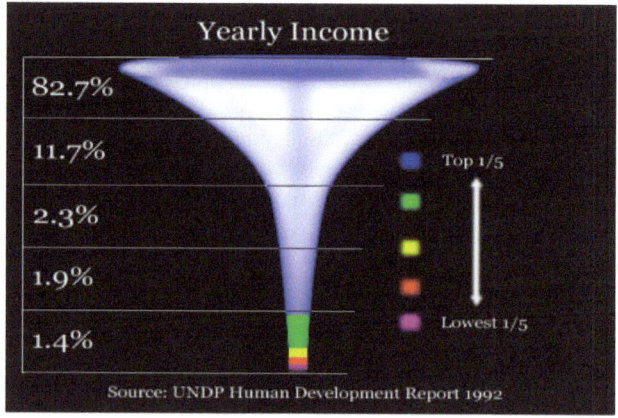

According to this graph 20% of the world's population receives well more than 80% of global yearly income. (What is not depicted is the fact that just 1% receives about 40 %.) The next 20% receives more than 11 % of world income. That leaves something like 6% for the bottom 60% of people. The people at the bottom of the graph are simply dying. Up to forty million of them perish from hunger related causes annually— most of them children. All of this contradicts the impression given by Spencer that benefit is the norm, and exclusion is the exception.

Transcending Polarization over Evolution

Three steps are necessary to overcome the polarization of Christians over the issue of evolution. In the first place, a bit of historical perspective will help all concerned realize that the evolution/creationism conflict has long since been solved. Secondly, the anti-biblical and Darwinian character of Western ideology must be clearly articulated. Finally, all segments of the Christian community must join forces to protect the natural order that all Christians agree is a gift of God. These same steps will blunt the manipulation of the question by politicians. The steps will expose the absurdity of implying that pro-life Christians can accept 40 million annual and utterly preventable deaths as no more than "collateral damage" resulting from a "universally beneficent" order.

17th Century Resolution of the Problem

The problem of the conflict between modern scientific discoveries and the pre-scientific worldview presented in the Bible should have been regarded as solved for Western Christians in the 17th century long before Darwin. It was then that the Roman Catholic Church condemned Galileo Galilei for exactly the same "crime" of which fundamentalists today accuse Charles Darwin and those who accept his theory, viz. contradicting the clear and evident meaning of Sacred Scripture. Galileo's offending assertions were found in his book, *The Starry Messenger*. There he offered evidence to support the heliocentric theory of the cosmos, first advanced by Nicolaus Copernicus in 1543. Copernicus had reasoned that the sun, rather than the earth stands at the center of the universe, but he offered no empirical evidence for his theory. Galileo offered the proof. The earth, he concluded, was moving around the sun, which remained stationary. In 1616, the Office of the Holy Inquisition termed Galileo's theory "absurd in philosophy and formally heretical, because expressly contrary to Scripture" – charges very similar to those made by fundamentalist opponents of evolutionary theory today.

The contradictions between Galileo's findings and the "Sacred Texts" were clear. For instance, in the Book of Joshua, the great Israelite general, famously stops the motion of the sun to gain time to defeat Israel's enemies.

> On the day when the LORD gave the Amorites over to the Israelites, Joshua spoke to the LORD; and he

> said in the sight of Israel, "Sun, stand still at Gibeon, and Moon, in the valley of Aijalon." And the sun stood still, and the moon stopped, until the nation took vengeance on their enemies.
>
> Is this not written in the Book of Jashar? The sun stopped in mid-heaven, and did not hurry to set for about a whole day. There has been no day like it before or since, when the LORD heeded a human voice; for the LORD fought for Israel (Joshua 10: 12-14).

Clearly, the Joshua text describes the sun as moving; it travels across the sky and sets in the evening. It is not stationary as Galileo claimed. The proof advanced by the literalist Catholic Inquisition was incontrovertible. The same was true for another text used against Galileo. The Nineteenth Psalm describes a cosmos seriously at odds with Galileo's conception

> . . . In the heavens he has set a tent for the sun, which comes out like a bridegroom from the wedding canopy, and runs like a strong man runs its course with joy. Its rising is from the end of the heavens, and its circuit to the end of them and nothing is hidden from its heat (Psalm 19:4-6).

This wording is even more specific in claiming that the sun moves. It "rises" and "runs" in a "circuit" from one end of the heavens to the other. (Curiously, an absolutely literal interpretation of the text would seem to demand belief that there is actually a "tent" in the heavens in which the sun rests, it seems, during the night.)

A third scriptural passage used against Galileo is found in the book of Ecclesiastes. It simply says "The sun rises and the sun goes down, and hurries to the place where it rises (Ecclesiastes 1:5).

Very few Christians today, fundamentalist, literalist or not, would adopt the literalist position of the Office of the Holy Inquisition. Almost none would dispute Galileo's fundamental insight, or demand that the three texts just cited be interpreted literally, insisting that we live in a geocentric universe. Galileo explained why in his landmark "Letter to the Grand Duchess Christina." There he argued that God is revealed in two ways, in sacred Scripture and in nature. Sacred Scripture was written for simple folk, he said (Drake 199). Its statements are often ambiguous and metaphorical. These cannot be taken literally in every case. Even St. Jerome, Thomas Aquinas, and other master theologians had recognized this centuries earlier; they were not literalists (200-201). Galileo further reasoned that since it is frequently so difficult to ascertain the exact meaning of biblical passages, one must often resort to God's revelation in nature to determine the truth. When God's written word conflicts with natural revelation, the latter is to prevail, because it is clearer and less ambiguous (182-83).

Whether one agrees with all elements of Galileo's argument, Christians of all stripes have, in fact, set aside literal interpretations of Joshua 10:12-14, Psalms 19:4-6, and Ecclesiastes 1:5. This is because the proof demanding such abandonment is incontrovertible. Fundamentalists might respond that the evidence supporting evolutionary theory is less incontrovertible than for Galileo's case. But such consideration not only conflicts with the general consensus of the scientific community; it is immaterial. Galileo's principle nullifying completely literal interpretation of sacred texts has been established. When the apparent meaning of the Bible conflicts with empirical observation, the text must be reinterpreted in the light of the physical evidence. Once again, virtually all Christians have actually done that in the controversy over heliocentrism vs. geocentrism. So, at the very least, they should not be shocked or scandalized or ready to excommunicate, when they encounter Christians who are persuaded that the scientific evidence calls for yet another reinterpretation of a biblical text.

Still fundamentalists might insist that "Scientific Creationism" be given equal time with evolutionary theory in public schools, for the very reason that not all find the evidence for evolution that convincing. Such insistence is sound. However, the point of the exercise should not simply be to determine which of two apparently conflicting theories is true. That is, the study should not be reduced to a "battle of evidence sets," of claims and counter-claims. Rather, the purpose of the comparative study should be to help students understand the context of the controversy – to help them see (for example, through the Galileo case) that the principle has been established (and implicitly accepted even by them) that the Bible must be interpreted in the light of physical evidence, and not the reverse. The study should also include acquainting students with various literary forms, including "myth" in the sense reiterated throughout this study. Once historical context has been set, and literary forms understood, students can move on to weigh evidence sets to determine whether they find Scientific Creationism or evolutionary theory more helpful, and in what contexts. They might, for instance, find the scientific account better for understanding *what* has happened in the history of the universe, while the biblical account is more useful for understanding the meaning of what occurred.

Confusion of Religion with Science

The controversy about the biological theory of evolution illustrates the bankruptcy of fundamentalist forms of Christian faith, and how thoroughly modern they have become. That is, literalist religion has so comprehensively bought into the secular world vision of the Enlightenment that for its adherents, only facts seem to have meaning. Fundamentalists then would seem to echo the sentiments of schoolmaster Thomas Gradgrind at the very beginning of Dickens *Hard Times*,

> Now, what I want are Facts. Teach these boys and girls nothing but Facts. Facts alone are wanted in life. Plant nothing else, and root out everything else. You can only form the minds of reasoning animals upon Facts: nothing else will ever be of any service to them. This is the principle on which I bring up my own children, and this is the principle on which I bring up these children. Stick to Facts, sir!"

Again, it is ironic that such words well summarize the fundamentalist view. It is basically super-scientific and anti-religious. For religion is the realm of image, metaphor, symbol, myth, legend, poetry, and art. Yet if one were to point out that the creation stories of Genesis 1 and 2 are mythological and highly symbolic, this is understood as a negative comment. No, fundamentalists seem to insist, to have worth, the stories must be factual.

The realms of science and religion have thus been radically confused. On the surface, this seems a rather total sell-out to secularity, and a confusion of science and religion. It is an abdication of the religious sphere where life's meaning is sought—a meaning which can best be expressed through the very media just listed. The confusion results in pro-life fundamentalists lending full support to the economic order that claims 40 million preventable deaths annually. This amounts to accepting as their priests, scientists like economists, Friedrich Hayeck and Milton Friedman. Ironically, these latter and their disciples have become the West's moral guides. They have no trouble issuing statements about human nature, the meaning of life, its possibilities, and the inadvisability of idealistic or utopian thinking. The story they would have us believe is something like the following,

> In the beginning God created the universe (either in 6 days or 15 billion years).

> In doing so, God established "laws of nature."
> These govern every sphere of human life, from the astronomical to the sub-atomic.
> One of the spheres governed by God's natural law is economics.
> Its laws of supply and demand manifest God's will.
> They should not be interfered with, For to do so would disrupt God's order and thus be sinful.

This guiding story, of course, nowhere appears in the Bible, and is nowhere expressed so directly. Nonetheless, it represents the largely unspoken theology which governs our time and which (to repeat) Christians who reject biological Darwinism typically accept, even though the belief is socially Darwinian. In addition, the story absolutizes a set of laws – the laws of economics. Doing so, it has been argued throughout this book, ends up honoring Satan, albeit "anonymously." It also rejects the teaching and practice of Jesus of Nazareth, who placed human welfare above any law whatever.

If Christians are to make a difference in the world described by the U.N. champagne glass graph, they must replace the secular "wisdom" of the above story with the specifically faith-inspired wisdom of an alternative story incorporating both the spiritual insights of Genesis and Jesus with the deeply contemplative and scientific understandings provided by Charles Darwin and those who employ his theory to unlock the secrets of physical creation. The story might sound like this:

> All life forms, including humans are part of a great web of life.
> This web is self-regulating.
> Its processes must be respected, not dominated.
> Humans represent the evolutionary process "coming to itself" in the act of self-consciousness.
> As such they understand the evolutionary process, can admire and celebrate it, and can even use it for their benefit.
> But they must avoid knowingly eliminating life forms, which represent their ancestors, brothers and sisters.
> Much less may humans kill or otherwise harm fellow humans who are united to them by bonds which precede those of nation, culture, language, religion, family, etc.

All humans must care for the planet and for each other.

They must resist the "freedom" of individuals and groups to destroy the common heritage of all creation.

Conclusion

Focusing on the biological theory of evolution as though it represented a problem for Christian faith, while embracing Social Darwinism as though it were somehow compatible with the teachings of Jesus is just another aspect of the anonymous Satanism would-be Christians have unwittingly accepted.

Misunderstanding Sixteen:

Abortion Should Be Outlawed

> Some religious groups use *constitutional* power to promote their views in order to dominate the entire society with them. The campaign on the part of a variety of Christians—Roman Catholic, fundamentalist, and conservative Christian churches—to secure a constitutional amendment against abortion is an example of this strategy. . . . The purpose of the amendment strategy is to make abortion a crime, to put the state in a position to punish those who commit what these Christians perceive as a grave sin. (Weaver 213)

One of the main wedge issues the U.S. politicians of Empire manipulate to gain support from people of conscience is abortion. By virtue of working for the repeal of *Roe v. Wade*, and offering hope for a constitutional amendment outlawing abortion, they claim identity as "pro-life" candidates, because they would eliminate the approximately 1 million abortions that occur in the United States each year. Meanwhile, they champion a world-wide economic system that claims up to 40 million victims annually (mostly children)—from clearly preventable hunger-related causes. As Jeffrey Sachs has recently shown, the vast majority of those victims could be saved if the United States donated a mere 0.5% of its GDP to U.N. programs specifically targeted to provide health care, education, and clean water to the world's 2 billion people living in absolute poverty. Pro-life candidates also tend to support military interventions such as the war in Iraq, and the new Gulag Archipelago of a world-wide U.S. prison camp system, with its systematic torture, abuse and murder of inmates. Additionally, pro-lifers commonly lend support to capital punishment. They typically oppose regulation of fire arms, universal health care, welfare and sex education programs, as well as legislation to protect air, water, soil and the flora and fauna of the natural environment. Despite such contradictions, the self-professed defenders of life carry the day with many Christians, because they promise an "end to abortion."

Their promise, however, is illusory and deceptive. The fact is abortion will never be "ended." It will always be with us, no matter what – with *Roe v. Wade*, without *Roe v. Wade*, with a constitutional amendment or without. Promising an end to abortion is like promising an end to prostitution, the world's oldest profession, or to stop alcoholism, drug addiction, or crime. It just won't happen.

The best pro-life Christians committed to the God of Life can hope for is for a *reduction* in the number of abortions, or for alleviation of the circumstances which make the abortion option acceptable to women with unwanted pregnancies.

Calling attention to such truisms becomes important in election years, when politicians predictably fog this extremely important issue, and manipulate it for their own gain, and when religious leaders give the impression that legal remedies will "end abortion," and that only the legal approach to the abortion question is "Christian."

Instead, the truisms call attention to the fact that what separates so-called "pro-life" Christians from their "pro-choice" brothers and sisters is not necessarily approval or disapproval of the act of abortion itself. Rather, for most, disagreement surfaces over what tactics or strategies are most effective for *reducing* the unacceptably high number of abortions chosen by desperate mothers – usually quite painfully and reluctantly.

In fact, decades and centuries of debate over abortion have identified at least three paths that believers might follow, while remaining loyal to their faith.

To illustrate the choices, imagine yourself standing before three divergent paths (Figure opposite). The problem of unwanted pregnancy is your point of departure. In the distance, you see your goal—not ending abortion, but the protection of unborn children and their mothers. To your right is a legal path, leading to the repeal of *Roe v. Wade*, or to a constitutional amendment outlawing abortion. To your left is a "community-building" path aimed at creating a "welcoming community" for otherwise unwanted children. Down the middle runs a three-lane highway. It combines legal restrictions on abortion with social programs aimed at fostering a welcoming community for children and their mothers; it also has a third specifically Christian "passing lane" of "prophetic witness."

What follows here takes a walk down each of the three paths just described. In the process, we'll examine the pitfalls contained on each one, as well as the advantages each promises. The hope is that these reflections will make it clear that a politician or ordinary citizen who might not favor the repeal of *Roe v. Wade* or the passage of a constitutional amendment to reduce the number of abortions should not thereby be disqualified from claiming specifically Christian motivation in approaching the question of abortion.

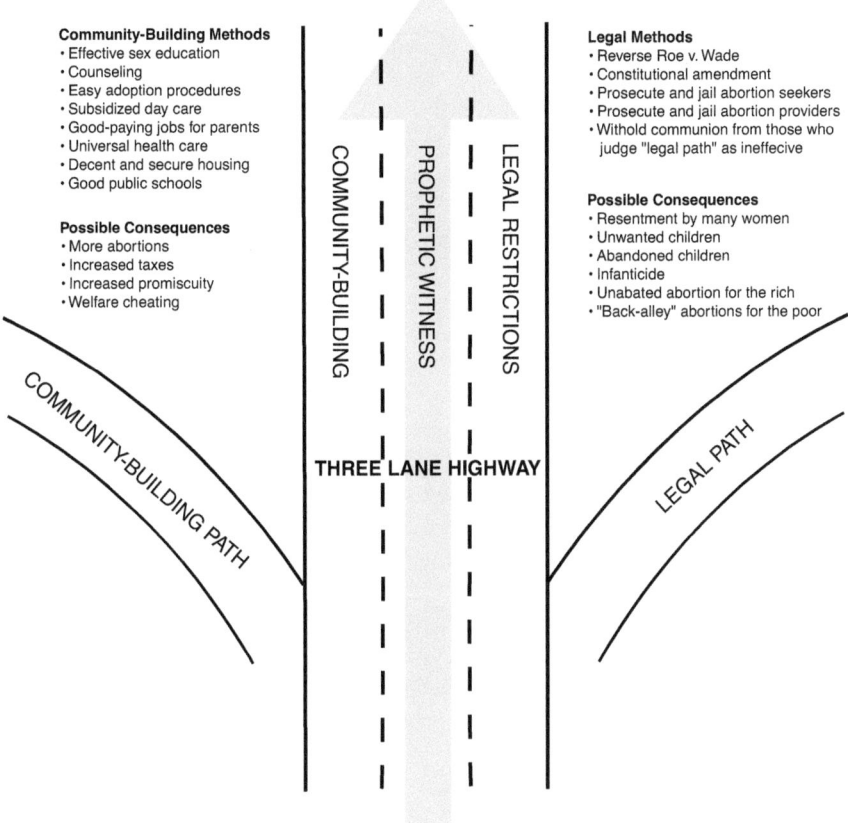

The Legal Path

This is the most familiar path in the current debate. It would criminalize abortions, shutting down clinics, and presumably incarcerating abortion seekers. Certainly, it would imprison abortion providers.

Where does this path lead? First of all, it would possibly lead to a reduction in abortions, and to the birth of many otherwise aborted children who would uniquely grace our planet, and the human community. That would be a most welcome outcome for nearly all concerned. However, honesty also compels admission that such a result is not nearly guaranteed. In fact, according to Mark W. Roche of the University of Notre Dame, the lowest abortion rates in the world are in the Netherlands and Belgium where abortion is legal, but where state programs for mothers, newborns, and children are firmly in place. On the other hand, abortion rates are among the highest in the world, in Latin America, where nearly all abortions are illegal.[41]

In fact, pre-Roe v. Wade experience has illustrated undeniably that, even with abortion outlawed, well-to-do abortion-seekers will merely travel to where the act is legal, and have it performed there. Poor women will either self-administer abortions with coat-hangers, similar instruments or drugs. Alternatively they will find a "back alley" abortionist who stereotypically will operate on a kitchen table. So, once again, the second result will be increased illegal abortions, without benefit of the considerable protections and restrictions that, we will see, have been afforded by Roe v. Wade.

Thirdly, criminalization of abortion will result in yet more prisoners added to a U.S. "corrections system," already distinguished by the highest per capita prison population in the world.

Fourthly, criminalization will alienate huge segments of the U.S. population. This will happen as a result of having a highly debatable opinion of one group forced on those not sharing the opinion. Recall here that very large groups of people espouse respectably defensible positions about the crucial question of when personal (vs. human) life begins, and therefore about when abortion represents the taking of another's life.

The answer to that question is not self-evident, nor has it ever been, even to people of faith. For while it is self-evident that human life begins the moment egg is fertilized by sperm, it is not equally evident that the resulting human life is yet personal.

---

[41] Mark W. Roche. "Voting Our Conscience, Not Our Religion." *The New York Times*. Oct.11, 2004 (http://www.nytimes.com/2004/10/11roche.html. Some statistics in the Roche oped (later cited by Senator Hilary Clinton) drew criticism from Randall K. O'Bannon— "Hilary Clinton Perpetuates Urban Myth of Abortion Increase under Bush" (http://www.nrlc.org/news/2005/NRL02/AbortionIncreaseMyth.html). O'Bannon took issue with assertions by Roche, Clinton, and Professor Glen Harold Stassen of Fuller Theological Seminary that abortions had decreased under Bill Clinton, and increased under George W. Bush. O'Bannon admits that "abortions did decline during Clinton's two terms, but not nearly as much as Roche reported." He also points out that figures showing abortion increases under George W. Bush are based on figures "that state officials were reluctant to endorse as accurate."—Apart from the general argument of the chapter at hand, the point here is that, at the very least, voting for a presidential candidate on the basis of the single abortion issue has not made much difference. Statistics can be marshaled to show that the number of abortions have actually increased under an aggressively "pro life" president. Often those quibbling with such figures end up talking about marginal differences.

That a fertilized egg is a person, represents, of course, the highly respected official position of, for instance, the Roman Catholic Church. But even within the Catholic community, prominent moral theologians beg to differ. Some, for instance, would argue their case by directing attention to the way the medical profession determines death. When the brain stops emitting its waves, "brain death" occurs. Personal life has stopped though bodily life may continue. Plugs may then be legally pulled, even if a patient continues to breathe with artificial assistance. If that is so, these moralists reason, no personal life exists before a fetus' brain begins sending off detectable brain waves. That occurs only several weeks into a pregnancy. Other people of faith have traditionally identified the beginning of personal life with the moment of quickening, with viability outside the womb, with actual emergence from the womb, or (as with some Native Americans) with the "painting" of the emergent child to distinguish it from the animals.

The point here is not to decide who is correct, but simply to point out that all of these positions are traditional; many are inspired by faith; quite a few are well reasoned and both intellectually and scientifically defensible. To impose one of them as correct in a pluralistic society is politically problematic and divisive in the extreme.

Fifthly, such imposition will inevitably alienate a very large number of women, who rightly or wrongly would interpret criminalization of abortion as yet another instance of the patriarchy carrying on its longstanding practice of controlling women's sexuality. The sentiment of this group is captured by the ironic observation that if men could get pregnant, abortion would likely be given the status of an eighth sacrament.

Finally, there is the question of the legal path and its coherence with the Way of Jesus and Paul. Unfortunately, we have no pronouncements from Jesus about abortion. Consequently, we are reduced to surmising what his approach might be, were he confronted with the question. What we know for certain is the point central to the argument of this book: Jesus was the opposite of a legalist. In fact, Jesus was the one who distinguished himself from his co-religionists by claiming to fulfill the law precisely by breaking it—even its most sacred components connected with the Sabbath observance. For his part, Paul was so liberal in his interpretation of Jewish Testament Law that he set it aside entirely—including dietary prescriptions, and even circumcision. It was futile, he said, to seek salvation in law—even in God's law. The argument of this book has been that seeking salvation in law is literally satanic.

The Path of Community Building

As already indicated, the pathway of community building finds its goal in the fostering of a welcoming national context that expresses its pro-life orientation by weaving together a "seamless garment" of respect for all life. Among other elements, this approach would include universally accessible health-care, full employment in well-paying jobs, environmental protection, as well as opposition to war, torture, capital punishment – and to abortion.

Specifically relative to abortion, this community building strategy would begin by providing effective sex education for everyone, so that the problem of unwanted pregnancies might surface less frequently. It would provide pre-abortion counseling so that young women might be fully aware of alternatives. Intense pre- and post-natal medical attention, as well as liberalized adoption procedures would be part of this approach too. It would involve subsidized child care for mothers choosing to work. For those who would rather stay home with their children, subsidies would also be provided, until the child reached the age when maternal presence would no longer be required.

In other words, this strategy would express as much concern for the unwanted children once they emerge from the womb, as it did, while they were unborn. Doing so, "Second Path" travelers say, would remove the adverse economic consequences from unwanted pregnancy, and make women less likely to choose abortion. Thus the goal of protecting the unborn and their mothers would be approximated in a more Christ-like way than by criminalization and punishment – or by the apparently hypocritical approach of grave concern for the child in the womb, followed by societal neglect once the child is born.

But what would be the negative consequences of this policy? Opponents might say it would lead to increased abortions, simply because abortion would be legal. It might also encourage promiscuity, welfare cheating, and having children simply to attain the government subsidies involved. This might lead to backlash against the "welfare mothers" in question, and to an increase in abortions to avoid the stigma. Certainly, taxes would have to be increased to fund this approach – or at least reallocated for that purpose.

Also as was the case with its legal counterpart, it is not entirely clear that this second path would reduce the number of abortions below the level currently experienced, nor below that to be anticipated, should abortion be re-criminalized, as it was before Roe v. Wade.

The Three Lane Highway

Recognizing the advantages and disadvantages of the first two ways towards the goal of reducing (not ending) abortion, and protecting the lives of the unborn and of their mothers, a particularly Christian Way suggests itself – even absent specific teaching about abortion on the parts of Jesus and Paul. This way would join the paths of law and community building, and would add a third "passing lane" of "prophetic witness."

The legal lane would be shaped by *Roe v. Wade*, or by its reform. Here it is essential to recognize that in itself the 1973 decision represents not merely the legalization of abortion. Already *Roe v. Wade* embodies *restrictions* on abortion – perhaps, as already indicated, of the only kind viable in a pluralistic society so defensibly divided on the question of when personal human life begins. That is, *Roe v. Wade*, for better or worse, lays down conditions. During the first trimester, it specifies that the mother may decide about the termination of her pregnancy without consultation. During the second trimester, she must confer with her physician. And during the final three months of pregnancy, the state recognizes its need to protect the unborn; it can accordingly forbid or otherwise condition pregnancy termination.

Some, of course, might charge that such restrictions are not nearly strong enough. However, in lobbying for legal changes, objectors need be aware that *Roe v. Wade* restrictions are barely tolerable to many liberals and to those who belong to communities with diverse convictions about the beginnings of personal human life. So, tightening restrictions might well introduce the negative consequences already discussed, without substantially improving protection of the unborn and their mothers.

This is where the community-building lane comes in. Adding this lane to the legal one is required in order to care for the undeniably human results of pregnancies brought to term because of legal restrictions. But, of course, this path too retains the drawbacks already indicated, especially as far as the politically conservative are concerned. These latter object to "big government" programs, to welfare, welfare cheats, and to increased taxes – all of which, it must be admitted, are part and parcel of traveling the lane given to community building.

It is here that the importance of the specifically Christian third lane of the highway surfaces. It represents the "passing lane," empowering believers to pass or transcend the objections of both liberals and conservatives. The addition of the passing lane represents, on the parts of believers, a practical demonstration (to those on both the left and right) of comprehensive pro-life commitment, regardless of the personal or financial costs. Thus traveling this prophetic corridor would demand that Christians show in their daily living that consistent pro-life choices are indeed possible, including refusal to practice abortion themselves. Accordingly and crucially, it would include a drastic simplification of believers' life styles, as well as opposition to war, capital punishment, torture, and to reduction of public services for the poor. Doing so would thereby empower the Christian community to speak publicly against abortion with a moral authority it currently lacks.

That is, the legal path currently privileged by Christians confers no moral authority. It is easy to traverse for most who (as far as the single issue of abortion is concerned) style themselves "pro-life." Dietrich Bonhoeffer would have called such travel "cheap" rather than "costly." This is because voting for politicians who favor repeal of *Roe v. Wade*, and making grand statements about commitment to every (unborn) child require little or no personal involvement, tax dollars or sacrifice. Most of us can cast our votes for conservatives and offer our impassioned public statements and prayers, while continuing to drive our SUVs; "support the troops;" eat high on the food chain; watch passively as children, many innocent people, and the mentally defective are executed; and while welfare benefits are cut for former fetuses brought to term.

Instead, criminalizing abortion lays a burden on "those others," who end up being mostly poor women. Males pay little direct cost – especially those belonging to the age cohort of our typical legislators. Young men are so often irresponsible when it comes to acknowledging paternity; "deadbeat dads" can escape fatherly obligations quite easily. As already pointed out, well-to-do women and their daughters will get their abortions safely in the Bahamas, Europe or some other venue. It is poor women who virtually alone pay the price.

Similarly, though perhaps a bit more painful, it is relatively easy for liberals to pay higher taxes and vote for politicians who will support social programs for pregnancies brought to term, rather than having been aborted. This too can be done without changing how liberals support preemptive wars, eat, drive, or house their families.

All of this is quite apparent to pro-choice advocates. They observe the cheapness, classism, and one-dimensionality of Christian opposition to abortion. This is why concerted prophetic witness on the part of Christians seems required to bypass and reverse such perceptions. Once again, this would lend a currently absent moral authority to Christian statements about the sacredness of life.

In the context of elections, it might be objected that traveling the three-lane path amounts to an endorsement of one particular party or candidate. In fact, the reverse is true. Instead, present privileging of the legal path ends up offering such endorsement. Recognizing the two other paths as defensibly Christian would, in fact, open the door to more even-handed approaches. Republicans would thus come under closer scrutiny for their unwillingness to pay for social programs that serve the very children they are so anxious to see born. In fact, under the present arrangement of privileging the legal path, those cutting back on social programs for poor children and mothers have been given a free pass by church authorities. This includes Democrats whose "structural adjustment" concessions masquerading as reform of "welfare as we know it" have cooperated with what many believers see as a concerted "war against the poor." Emphasizing the American Catholic Bishops' Conference "seamless garment" of pro-life commitment would pressure both parties to see that congregations understand abortion as inseparable from the creation of a comprehensively pro-life United States more in keeping with the Christian tradition.

Conclusion

The point here has not been to persuade anyone that the two alternatives to the criminalization of abortion are necessarily preferable to the project of making abortion illegal. No doubt, believers will continue to disagree on this point of strategy (not faith). Those who are convinced that the legal strategy is best should, of course, continue their efforts to outlaw a practice that is painful for everyone.

On the contrary, what has been presented here, has been merely a reframing of the question, and in doing so, an attempt to expand awareness of the range of possibilities for combating abortion that are open to people of faith. At the basis of the re-framing is first of all, the recollection that legal approaches to the problem will not result in "the end of abortion." Rather, they will drive it underground, possibly without reducing the number of abortions. Secondly, the point has been to remind Christians that their goal is not passing laws or constitutional amendments in themselves. Instead, the goal is to reduce (not eliminate) the evil of abortion. Thirdly, readers have been reminded that for specifically faith-based reasons, some believers and politicians might well draw the conclusion that the criminalization route is unwise, counter-productive, and even un-Christ-like. Many of these will reject the legal path, and adopt the community building or threefold path, which they might deem more in keeping with the Spirit of Jesus.

Finally, those who adopt these latter approaches should not be denied Holy Communion, any more than should those doubting or denying the effectiveness of fostering community in order to reduce the number of abortions.

Misunderstanding Seventeen:

God Hates Homosexuals

> I'm sick and tired of hearing about all of the radicals, and the perverts, and the liberals, and the leftists, and the communists coming out of the closet! It's time for God's people to come out of the closet, out of the churches, and change America! (James Robinson in "Battle for the Bible." Bill Moyers, 1992).

"The Sabbath was made for humans; human beings were not made for the Sabbath." As we have seen, these words provide a key to understanding Jesus' attitude towards all law and legal arrangements. While Satan absolutized the law and legal institutions, Jesus refused to join his contemporaries in being seduced by what he saw as Satan's infernal logic. Those contemporaries thought, for instance, that the Sabbath law forbade curing on the first day of the week. But Jesus performed his cures anyway, simply because people needed them. Jesus' words about the Sabbath stand as testimony that all laws and legal arrangements must serve human welfare first, or be set aside. Jesus made no exception for marriage. He did not say, "Human beings were made for marriage; marriage was not made for human beings." So, on the face of it, it is not clear that Jesus would oppose homosexual marriage, unless it can be shown that he said something specific to remand his statement about subordinating legal concerns to human well being.

What Jesus Did Not Say

The problem is Jesus said nothing at all about homosexuality, much less about homosexuality and marriage. There is no evidence that the issue played any role whatever in Jesus' concerns, thought or teaching. It is not insignificant, however, that he befriended and created community with people whose social standing was comparable to gays in the contemporary United States. Lepers, prostitutes, drunkards, terrorists, tax collectors, shepherds, the insane, non Jews, and devil-possessed – all these were regarded in Jesus' culture the way our homophobic culture regards homosexuals. Yet Jesus ate with those outcasts, touched them, traveled with them, and considered them his special friends and disciples. He promised that they, rather than good religious people, like the lawyers, scribes and pharisees, would be the first to enter the Reign of God.

As for the rest of Sacred Scripture, it also ignores the question of homosexual marriage. In fact, only five verses in the entire Bible deal with the morality of acts which fundamentalists find so reprehensible. So it seems safe to say not only that the question of homosexuality was not important to Jesus, but that it was less than pressing for biblical authors as well.

What Jesus Did Say

Compare the Bible's relative neglect of homosexuality on the one hand, with issues of economic justice, wealth and poverty on the other. As we will see presently, there is a connection between ways of thinking about the two sets of issues. It turns out that wealth and poverty issues are the ones most frequently addressed by Jesus in the Bible. In fact, one out of ten verses in the Synoptic gospels (Matthew, Mark, and Luke) contains direct teaching on economic issues such as the danger of wealth, and the need to be concerned about the poor. In the entire New Testament, one out of sixteen verses includes direct teachings on economic issues, and there are many more passages of indirect teaching. It is curious, then, that U.S. Christians concentrate so much attention on what Jesus did not say, while being rather good at explaining away what he *did* say.

Perhaps the misdirected concentration is explainable by the fact that Jesus' actual words challenge the entire "American Way of Life." He said "Blessed are you poor" (Lk. 6:20), and "Woe to you rich" (Lk. 6:24), and "It is easier for a camel to pass through the eye of a needle than for a rich person to enter the Kingdom of God" (Mt. 19:24). He told the rich land owner who asked what he must do to inherit eternal life, "Sell all that you have and distribute to the poor, and you will have treasure in heaven; and come follow me" (Lk. 18:22).

By contrast, the words Jesus did not say only challenge "those others who are not like us." The unspoken words challenge *them* to change, leaving the rest of us free merely to criticize, condemn and feel superior. So it makes sense to downplay Jesus' words about wealth and poverty and to act as though Jesus said "Blessed are you heterosexuals." "Woe to you homosexuals." "It is easier for a camel to pass through the eye of a needle than for a homosexual to enter the kingdom of God." Imagine the changes Christians would demand (from others) had Jesus actually uttered such words. Compare that with the changes Christians do not make in response to Jesus' actual words about wealth, poverty and justice.

Texts on Homosexuality

Even the five texts dealing with homosexuality are of questionable relevance to what is meant today by that term. In the Jewish Testament, related terms seem to appear in Leviticus 18:22 and 20:13. In the Christian Testament, references are found in I Corinthians 6-9, in Romans 1:27, and in I Timothy 1:10. All of those passages have problems of applicability to the modern question of sexual orientation and homosexuality. That's because the question of "sexual orientation" is a modern concept—issuing from the post-Enlightenment social sciences. So everyone in the biblical world rightly understood "lying with a man, as if with a woman," as a "perversion"—as heterosexuals engaging in homosexual acts. *That* seems to be what is forbidden.

This is clearly the case in the famous instance of Sodom and Gomorrah, which, in the popular mind, is the text most frequently associated with the question at hand (Genesis 19).[42] However, that text primarily addresses homosexual rape (as well as violation of the sanctity of hospitality). As for the Leviticus texts, they deal with homosexual prostitution in the context of temple worship in pagan sanctuaries, i.e. with idolatry. Idolatry and rape, of course, are always criminal in the eyes of biblical authors—and of Jesus himself.

Rejection of homosexual behavior in Romans is also connected with the worship of idols and with lust—"serving the creature rather than the Creator." The meaning of the word which appears in I Cor. 6:9-10 is unclear; it probably refers to "pederasts." The same appears true of the Timothy passage.

Explaining Away Jesus' Words

Imagine what would happen if Christians emphasized Jesus actual words, and not the more comfortable ones they wish he would have said.

In that case, Christians might have to distance themselves from the culture's consumer society—and maybe even from capitalism, which, after

---

[42] Even if the point of the Genesis text were to condemn homosexual acts in general, the condemnation there is clearly of heterosexuals intending to commit homosexual acts. Otherwise, what would be the sense of Lot offering his two virgin daughters to satisfy the lust of those demanding the surrender of the two men given refuge in Lot's home?

all is based on acquisitiveness, accumulation of property and greed.[43] Those, after all, are the very foundations of our society; and Jesus didn't seem to like any of them. So, taking seriously Jesus' words about poverty and concern for the poor would challenge *all* to give the world a practical example of voluntary simple living. The first Christians, remember, held all things in common, none of them owning anything themselves, but devoting it all to the poor.

> Now the whole group of those who believed were of one heart and soul, and no one claimed private ownership of any possessions, but everything they owned was held in common. With great power the apostles gave their testimony to the resurrection of the Lord Jesus, and great grace was upon them all. There was not a needy person among them, for as many as owned lands or houses sold them and brought the proceeds of what was sold. They laid it at the apostles' feet, and it was distributed to each as any had need. (Acts 4:32-35)

If those words were taken seriously, U.S. Christians might have to distinguish themselves from their non-believing neighbors through their simple living, commitment to the poor, to communal values, and by their abhorrence of all forms of personal possessiveness. They might even have to recognize communism's vision "from each according to his ability to each according to his need," as coming directly from this passage in the Acts of the Apostles. They might even be led to see that ideal as more compatible with Christianity than capitalism's "God takes care of them who take care of themselves."

So, even the most fundamental of fundamentalists among us ends up "explaining away" Jesus' words which so obviously reject the foundational values of our culture. We are quick to point out that Jesus' sayings about wealth and poverty, about living as he did, identifying with the poor and outcast—*becoming* poor and outcast, without two coins to rub together— originate from the first century world, and so have little relevance to contemporary society with its modern approach to economy. The biblical

---

[43] By the way "greed" as well as "drunkenness" and "fornication" all find themselves classified equally by Paul in I Cor. 6:9 as sins excluding people from inheriting the Kingdom. The list includes "fornicators, idolaters, adulterers, thieves, greedy people, and drunkards." One wonders if such people too, along with homosexuals, should be prevented from marrying.

teaching prohibiting the taking of interest on loans comes from an even much more ancient order.

> If you lend money to my people, to the poor among you, you shall not deal with them as a creditor; you shall not exact interest from them. If you take your neighbor's cloak in pawn, you shall restore it before the sun goes down; for it may be your neighbor's only clothing to use as cover; in what else shall that person sleep? And if your neighbor cries out to me, I will listen, for I am compassionate. (Exodus 22:25-27)

Without interest and loans, where would our consumer society or the global economy be? What would we do with our credit cards? By contrast, we assure ourselves, in biblical times, people operated in a peasant economy, where the mysteries of compound interest, supply and demand were unknown. Unknown too was the assurance that the wealth of the extremely rich would "trickle down" to the grateful masses below. The classification of greed as one of the Seven Deadly Sins came before Adam Smith and modern economics helped us realize that greed is actually good, and that an Invisible Hand governs the economic sphere in a miraculous way. Without self-seeking and accumulating wealth, the world as we know it would fall apart. Imagine what Jesus would say to that!

However, once we start setting aside Jesus' actual teaching in favor of a modern social science, like economics, we run the risk of doing the same, for example, with psychology. The door then creaks open to the suggestion that the words we wish Jesus would have said about homosexuality (but actually didn't) also can be "explained away" by *that* modern science. That is, first century Christians and B.C.E. Hebrews knew as much about Freud's psychology as they did about Smith's economics. And if one can explain away Jesus' clear words about wealth, poverty and concern for the poor by appealing to their ignorance of Smith and compound interest, one might just do the same with Jesus' imagined words, in relation to Freud and the superego. In that case, one might be forced to recognize the conclusions of modern psychology that sexual orientation is not a matter of choice, and that homosexual relations are quite natural. Following such thinking, Christians might even reach the conclusion that committed sex within a gay marriage is preferable to promiscuous sexual relationships outside of marriage. But that, of course, would entail accepting the premise that marriage was made for humans, and that human beings were not made for marriage.

Protecting the Children

Still one might object that the question of homosexual marriage is about protecting children and their whole understanding of what marriage and sex are about. Allowing gay marriage is not just a matter of permitting victimless sexual expression between consenting adults. Children are the potential victims here. So is the institution of marriage. Both must be protected from anyone who might call into question the worth of married life as our culture has known it.

Take the institution of marriage first. Set aside for the moment what has already been said about Jesus, law and human well being. Remember that the churches (Catholic and Protestant) have done their own parts to lessen the dignity of that institution. Granted, the Catholic Church had elevated marriage to the dignity of a sacrament. It also forbade divorce under pain of mortal sin. However, from the 13th century on, Rome designated the married state as the refuge of second class members of God's People – for the laity, as opposed to the clergy. Not getting married, practicing celibacy was preferable. From then on, priests have been obliged to refrain from marriage. Martin Luther also did his part to deprive marriage of any undue grace. In the 16th century, he demoted matrimony from the sacramental state to the secular. It became merely a legal arrangement that was blessed by the church. Under the aegis of the Reformation, it became possible for the first time for Christians to divorce and still regard themselves as members in good standing within the Christian community.

Since then, it has been all downhill for the institution of marriage. Around 50% of marriages now end in divorce. Christians (and their pastors) divorce and remarry at about the same rate as non-Christians. And none of the institution's decline is attributable to homosexuals. It is due instead to (presumed) heterosexuals whose behavior has inevitably scandalized the young, impressionable and vulnerable before whom the non-gay parents have disgraced the institution. Children have witnessed the infidelities, quarrels, acts of physical and emotional abuse that lead up to divorce. They have been torn apart and emotionally damaged by tugs of war between parents over their children's affections.

In other words, heterosexuals, not homosexuals, are the ones who have attacked the institution of marriage and corrupted children in the process. So if Christians are worried about the institution of marriage and children's respect for it, perhaps heterosexuals should be the ones prevented from marrying, until we've demonstrated staying power, maturity, and freedom from addictions to the sex, drugs, alcohol, consumerism, and selfishness which are the true enemies of marriage and the children produced from ill-fated unions. With that in mind, it might be best for Christians to drop all the talk about protecting the institution of marriage from homosexuals, and deal with protecting it from heterosexuals.

Conclusion

In the meantime, given the silence of Jesus on homosexuality, the paucity of texts in the entire tradition that deal with the question, and the problematic nature of interpreting the few texts that do seem relevant, it might be more honest for Christians to contemplate their own conversion instead of the conversion of "those others who are not like us." Instead of concentrating on what Jesus did not say, and on the few texts that might have said something about homosexuality, it might be best to concentrate on the issues of poverty, wealth, and justice that Jesus himself seemed most concerned about. Once those matters make it to the radar screens of Christians, there might be time and energy to closely observe the homosexual marriage initiative—to see if homosexuals do better at marriage than heterosexuals have. Given the state of marriage in our culture, there seems little enough to lose.

Misunderstanding Eighteen:

Our Violence is Holy, Not Theirs

> Peace churches . . . argue that experience does not teach us about the efficacy of violence but about its uselessness; violence, they argue, breeds violence. Jesus meant what he said about loving one's enemies and turning the other cheek. They say that nonviolent means have never really been tried and taken seriously. More important, the peace churches argue that Christians must be nonviolent whether nonviolence works or not: their position is not based on a pragmatic judgment about the possible good outcomes of the position but based on Jesus' words and his way of dealing with violence. These people believe that being faithful is more important than determining by violent means what kind of government they will live under. (Weaver 231)

"Crucify him! Crucify him! C'mon, everybody say it. I know you mean it. Crucify him!" Each semester, as my LASP students in Costa Rica completed their study of liberation theology, I placed the picture above before them. I urged them to shout, "Crucify him!" Most were reluctant to do so. I'm convinced it wasn't so much because they had accepted the understanding of Jesus reflected in our semester-long study and here in the peasant art from the Nicaraguan community of Solentiname.[44] Rather, it was because they'd find a similar reluctance before any depiction of Jesus. It just seems so ungodly to stand before any image of the peasant from Nazareth and to shout "Crucify him!"

And yet, I'm also convinced that as believers Christians are somehow forced to decide whether or not they want the Jesus depicted here crucified. In the 1980s many world and ecclesiastical leaders made their own choices clear. They did not hesitate to join the chief priests, scribes and people of Jerusalem in screaming "Crucify him!"

Look at the picture again. That's how Jesus appears in the theology explained in much of this book. There, as in the painting, Jesus is undeniably a human being—clearly a man. His skin is dark. He's stretched out completely vulnerable on an instrument of torture reserved for opponents of empire—in this case, the Roman Empire. He's a victim of capital punishment, expressing solidarity with victims of torture and execution everywhere. At this supreme moment of God's revelation (as understood by Mark, the earliest of the canonical gospels), the places at Jesus' right and left hand are not occupied by James and John as per their request (Mk. 10:35-45). Rather in Mark, the Sons of Zebedee are nowhere to be found (though in the painting John seems to be present). Instead, the places the two fishermen had requested when Jesus "enters into his glory" are filled by insurgents. Jesus' solidarity with their movement, if not with their violent tactics, is indicated by the rebel's beret he's wearing, complete with star. Women are present though. Throughout Mark's Gospel, unlike Peter and the others, women are the ones who most understand Jesus (although he disowned his own mother because she apparently could not— Mk. 3:20-34). Of course, the soldiers are there, this time wearing the uniforms of Somoza's National Guard—stand-ins for the military puppets of the U.S. Empire everywhere. As in Mark, there is no resurrection here, only the word that might be "alleluia" (or is it guerrilla?) over Jesus head, and the bright blue, pink, purple and green flowers everywhere—all suggesting continuity of life despite the painting's unspeakable theme.

Who can accept all that? My students had a hard time doing so, largely because of the misunderstandings of Christianity that have been

---

[44] Solentiname was a "monastic" community of laypeople in Nicaragua living under the direction of Jesuit Priest, Ernesto Cardenal (who later became the Sandinista Minister of Culture). They published their biblical reflections in *The Gospel in Solentiname*, and their art in *The Art of Solentiname* both published by Orbis Books.

part and parcel of their upbringing. But they are in good company. Reagan wanted that Jesus dead. So did John Paul II, and his minion, Joseph Ratzinger, now Benedict XVI. They all wanted liberation theology dead. They wanted the poor robbed of their voice and God, so the elite's own God of the Rich might hold exclusive sway. So the rich and powerful shed no tears when Romero was gunned down at the altar, or when the four American religious and their lay colleague were raped and murdered by the Salvadoran Treasury Police, nor when the six Jesuit liberation theologians and their housekeepers were butchered by the crack Atlacan platoon trained by the United States, and sent to bash in their heads and strew their brains across the convento lawn.

Violence as God

Yes, there's a battle of Gods. Yes, there's a battle of Christs. Yes, there is a battle of the virgins. And the God that has proven victorious in all of this (over Jesus and Yahweh) is Violence itself. Violence has filled the "hollow concept" of God – just as we have seen it being filled at various points in the Bible by the Gods of Eve, Cain, Abraham, David, the prophets and Jesus. From these it is the God of Cain's original sin that has triumphed worldwide. And he has subjected the world to the terrible arithmetic of Lemech, multiplied again by the United States. Not one death for one death, not seven for one, not five hundred for one, but one thousand (and more) for one. Walter Wink said it clearly: Violence itself is America's God. Our creed is that violence saves. "Thou shalt not kill?" As the Bible-reading Staff Sargeant in "Jarhead" instructs his recruits about that commandment, "Well, f – – – that s – – – !"

In the face of such cultural and religious rejection of non-violence, theologians are faced with an overriding necessity to bracket their accustomed theological concerns, and to focus on idology (i.e. the study of idols). They must think specifically about Violence as God.

Under the influence of Third World theologies, many have written about the "spiral of violence" that characterizes the contemporary world. Brazil's Dom Helder Camara, as well as El Salvador's Oscar Romero spoke of that spiral in terms of "three levels" of violence. They did so to place in perspective the spurious accusations that Latin American revolutionary movements were unique in using religion to endorse violence. Both bishops pointed out, for instance, that the acts of revolutionary violence characterizing the world of the '70s and '80s (and, we might add, the terroristic violence expressed in the 9/11 attacks on the World Trade Center and Pentagon) were not unprovoked. Those were "second level" acts of violence – responses to "first level," "structural violence."

The latter refers to social, economic, political, and military systems and arrangements, codified in law and custom that are responsible for tens of thousands of innocent deaths throughout the world each day. Structural violence is that exacted, for instance, by economic "rules of the game" demanding that a world awash with food destroy or warehouse the excess produce rather than share it with the children starving at the bottom of the "champagne glass." As a result, those children die as surely and predictably as if guns had been placed to their heads, and triggers pulled (the U.N. tells us) 21,000 times each day. That is violence, as Camara and Romero explained, every bit as worthy of the term as the revolutionary violence it provokes.

But the spiral doesn't end with rebellion. A third level of violence completes the deadly conjugation. It might be termed "reactionary violence" to distinguish it from "structural violence" (first level), and from "revolutionary violence" (second level). Reactionary violence is the state's reply to acts of rebellion against structural violence. During the 1980s in Central America, it mostly took the form of state terrorism directed at those suspected of being or supporting second level revolutionaries.[45] State terrorism typically expresses itself in death squads, indiscriminate bombings, massacres, mass imprisonments, and torture—the same tactics used by the U.S. military in Vietnam, and today in Iraq.

Violent Trinity

It is easy to take this thought a bit further, and to do so by accepting Wink's premise that Violence is America's real God, and that its creed is that "violence saves." Having accepted that "idological" point, the conclusion surfaces that if violence is God, Camara's and Romero's three levels of violence represent a bloody Trinity that is killing us all.

Violence the Father

Take the trinity's first "person," structural violence—the Father, the patriarch of bloodshed. Largely because of common misunderstandings of Christianity, this dimension of violence, like the biblical tetragrammaton,

---

[45] "Terrorism" is a violent tactic that can be associated either with revolutionary or reactionary violence. According to the F.B.I.'s definition, terrorism is violence directed against civilians. Its aim is either to secure or discourage citizen support for a government or for an antigovernment force. As such, terrorism can be used by the state or by "sub-national" or "clandestine" organizations. According to Noam Chomsky and Edward Herman, state terrorism is far more common and devastating than the sub-national or clandestine variety. Chomsky and Herman, then, refer to state terrorism as "wholesale," and is non-state counterpart (like the 9/11 attacks) as "retail" (Chomsky and Herman 83).

is almost never even named as such. This is so despite the fact that structural violence is the most pervasive and deadly kind. It is simply accepted as the way the world is. Augustine's 4th century invention about "original sin," the all-pervasive corruption of human nature, and of the physical world itself, is central to acceptance of this deceit. So is Luther's elaboration that humans can in no way avoid sinning. All of this normalizes structural sin, even making it part of God's plan. It closes believers' eyes to the proposition that another world is possible. On the contrary, Christians have been led to believe that no other world is possible; this one has in fact been divinized.

Violence the Son

The trinity's second "person" is revolutionary violence—the rebellious offspring of structural violence. As was the case with Jesus himself, this is the only manifestation of God that the prevailing system is willing to condemn as such. Still, this "God the Son" comes closest to being justified. Traditional just war theory recognizes it as expressing the legitimate right to self defense. Even the U.S. Declaration of Independence endorses "revolutionary violence" not only as a right, but as a duty, when governments fail to live up to their obligation to insure citizens' claims to life, liberty and the pursuit of happiness. Both Dom Helder Camara and Oscar Romero found themselves in sympathy with revolutionary violence as well. Of the three levels they named, second level violence alone, they said, could be theoretically justified, as peasants and workers sought to defend their families from aggressions of the rich represented in the first and third levels.

Even the practice of Jesus shows sympathy for the goals of second level violence. It is clear that his words and deeds led his contemporaries to associate him with the Zealots of the first century—the insurgents against Roman occupation. Mark, whose gospel was written at the height of Zealot rebellion, lists one of them among Jesus' inner circle, Simon the Zealot (Mk. 3:18). Luke and Matthew follow suit (Lk. 6:15; Mt. 10:4). There is also suspicion that others in Jesus' band were associated with *sicarii*, knife-carriers or assassins dedicated to wearing down the Roman occupying forces by killing them one by one. The name "Iscariot" and its similarity to *sicarii* perhaps associates Judas with the knife carriers. There is even stronger reason for believing that Peter might have been one. Why, after all, was he (and according to Luke, others in Jesus' band) armed with a "sword" when Jesus was arrested in his Gethsemane hideout just before his death (Mt. 26:51-52; Lk 22:49-51; Jn. 18:10-11)? Had Jesus been so ineffective in convincing his closest followers of the futility of armed resistance?

Above all, the title Jesus is portrayed as most associating with himself reveals his sympathies with insurgents. "Son of Man," of course was taken from the Book of Daniel, a virulent anti-imperial tract penned during the occupation of Palestine by the Seleucid forces of Antiochus IV Epiphanes, in the middle of the second century B.C.E. There "a figure like a Son of Man" is identified as the judge of all of history's empires, not only of the Greek Seleucids, but of all the bestial powers that came before and that will arise in the future (Dn. 7:13-14). That the gospels so consistently associate this title with Jesus of Nazareth gives nearly unmistakable indication that his public life had a strongly anti-imperial character. The over-all conclusion is that there exists ample evidence to support belief that Jesus was sympathetic to the Jewish revolutionary movement and its antiimperial tendencies.

Yet Jesus was clearly not himself a Zealot, nor in any way approving of violence. His sympathies may have been with that group, but his tactics were not. In fact, as Walter Wink indicates, though Jesus' appropriation of the title "Son of Man" clearly made him anti-imperialist and anti-Rome, it associated him with a non-violent strain of opposition to empire (45). That is, the apocalyptic tradition represented by the book of Daniel believed empire would be defeated, not by armed rebellion, but by waiting for God's intervention. Additionally, of course, Jesus' teachings on loving enemies contradicted the assassination tactics of the Zealots. So did his words on turning the other cheek, and on living and dying by the sword. Add to this Jesus' example of non-resistance in the face of his own arrest and execution, and one finds the profile of one who like many Pharisees in his day, advocated non-violent resistance to empire and other forms of oppression (45). Finally, associating Jesus with Zealot resistance ignores the fact that Zealots were not nearly as prominent during Jesus' public life as they became, for instance, in the revolutionary period providing the background of Mark's gospel.

No, Jesus distanced himself from second-level violence, as well as from the first as represented by the Roman Empire. His parable about the absentee landlord and his tenants (Mk. 12:1-12) explains why. The story tells of a man who planted a vineyard and built a winepress, protecting both with surveillance devices (a wall and watchtower), then leaving it in the hands of sharecroppers. Harvest time comes, and the landlord sends one of his servants to collect the owner's share. The resentful sharecroppers beat the slave, and send him back to his master without anything to show for his efforts. Undeterred, the landlord sends another slave who suffers the same fate, this time with insults added to injury. Yet another servant is sent. The sharecroppers kill him. Finally, the owner sends his son, mistakenly thinking his son's family status would protect him. Instead the tenant farmers kill the son as well. At story's end, Jesus answers his own question with the words, "What then will the owner of the vineyard do? He will come and destroy the tenants and give the vineyard to others" (v. 9).

This story was told to peasants familiar with first level structural violence under the Roman colonial arrangement. As such, they were victims a landlord system that had them working for absentee owners – many of whom were linked to the temple leadership under the chief priests and scribes. As a matter of course, these landlords had increased their holdings by buying up the property of small farmers who had fallen hopelessly into debt. The bankrupt farmers would have been forced to sell their lands at undervalued prices. To add insult to injury, the dispossessed farmers ended up having to work as tenants for the same landed gentry that had displaced them, sometimes on the very land that used to be their own. As a final straw, the new owners typically transformed the purpose of their newly acquired holdings. They changed it from subsistence to cash crop production, such as wine, for export to Rome. All of this left Palestinian sharecroppers in utter destitution, with a large reserve of anger. Consequently, Jesus' parable must have at first delighted them as they recognized in the revenge of its tenant farmers the very acts they would have liked to perform. As William Herzog writes,

> The parable provided its hearers with a vicarious experience of striking back: first, the hearers vicariously beat, brutalized, and killed the hated retainers; then, they attacked the son who would inherit what was once their land (Quoted in Nelson-Pallmeyer, *Is Religion* . . . 44).

Violence, the Evil Spirit

Yet Jesus does not completely share his listeners' delight. Instead he sobers them by indicating the consequences of their second level response to first level, structural violence. He says starkly that the owner ". . . will come and kill those tenants and give the vineyard to others." That is, the sharecroppers second level violence will itself inevitably invoke a (third level) response, and nothing will have been changed as a result. The landowner will simply exploit other peasants now taking the place of the ones he has killed. The parable's intent, then, was to indicate the counter-productivity of revolt in a Palestine tightly controlled by the Roman Empire. No wonder Jack Nelson-Pallmeyer joins William Herzog in calling this story "Peasant Revolt and the Spiral of Violence" (*Is Religion* . . . 44).

It was reasoning similar to that found in Jesus' parable that led both Dom Helder Camara and Oscar Romero to recognize the idolatrous character of even second level violence. It too reflects the worship of

Marduk, of a divinized Violence, and ultimately of Satan precisely as the author and patron of empire. To begin with, second level violence is unacceptable, because it is simply no match for the overwhelming (third level) violence of the system against which it rebels. It is obvious that the state can respond to it with all the resources that a half a trillion dollar annual "defense" budget can afford. Blackhawk helicopters, U2 and AWACS planes, spent uranium shells, strategic and tactical nuclear weapons, cluster bombs, "daisy cutters," Humvees, Abrams tanks, high speed troop transport vehicles, and armor that renders imperial soldiers far less vulnerable than their opponents, are then pitted against peasants, workers, shopkeepers, students, and ordinary citizens who finish by being completely vulnerable by comparison – their only effective weapons, the roadside bomb and suicide "martyrs." One thousand to one casualty ratios are often the result. Think of the millions slaughtered by empire in the Vietnam conflict, the 200,000 in Guatemala, the 80,000 in El Salvador, the 70,000 in Nicaragua, the more than one million so far in Iraq. And for what? El Salvador is still run by the infamous 14 families. The Somocistas were restored to power in Nicaragua for more than fifteen years. Guatemalan indigenous are little better off than before the start of the forty year conflict that ended in the early '90s. Vietnam has returned to its traditional colonial function of privileged locale for foreign capital accumulation thanks to the cheap labor it provides to multinational factories like Nike, who thrive by underpaying the coolie labor there.

But that's not the half of it. Second level violence also ends up stimulating and feeding the same satanic military industrial complex it proposes to defeat. This is because those rebelling against the system need to arm themselves to carry on their project of rebellion. That's good news to the military-industrial complex, which happily supplies its deadly products to both sides in any conflict. Even more, insurgencies provide the rationale for increased military spending on the part of the empire itself. In sum, the whole cycle only strengthens the imperial economy, its military, and the politicians who can use rebellion to keep their populations ready and willing to pay for unending wars. Second level violence inevitably leads to the response of the third "person" of the Violent Trinity, Violence the Evil Spirit.

Conclusion

Essential to understanding American idolatry is calling its actual God by his own name. Wink, Nelson-Pallmeyer and others have come close in identifying that deity as "Violence." Hinkelammert suggests "the God of

Unlimited Progress." The preferred title throughout the present study has been "Satan." It is chosen because that designation more clearly links America's supreme idol with empire, and uses a familiar theological category to more explicitly challenge the pretensions of a Christianity which in most of its forms has been completely co-opted by the imperial state. Still, however, as this chapter has shown, violence is such an inherent part of empire that identifying the Three Persons in its infernal Trinity is not only useful but necessary for thinking more carefully and articulately about a highly complex category. The truth is, structural violence most often goes unnoticed and unaddressed. Meanwhile, common practice identifies and vilifies second level violence ("revolutionary") alone as violence and to be rejected out of hand. The reality is, however, that violence at this level is the most understandable and even the most justifiable, at least from the viewpoint of American history, Just War theory, and perhaps even in the light of Jesus' own sympathies.

The practice of Jesus is another matter. It clearly challenges Christians to implement the practice of non-violent resistance, both as a matter of practicality and spiritual conviction. Nonetheless, it seems inappropriate for First World Christians to insist that Third World resisters adopt strategies and tactics of non-violent resistance in situations where they must actually defend the "least of the brethren" in contexts shaped by extremely violent structures financed by U.S. tax dollars. In any case, Christians living comfortably in the U.S.A. must overcome the impulse to condemn second level violence while excusing systematic aggression in service to U.S. corporate interests. Perhaps Philip Berryman says it best, "I would assert that people who have not actively opposed the violence of the powerful against the poor, at some cost to themselves have no moral authority to question the violence used by the poor." (Quoted in Nelson Pallmeyer, *The Politics of Compassion* 87.)

Misunderstanding Nineteen:

Activism and Spirituality Are Incompatible

> I could not be leading a religious life unless I identified myself with the whole of humanity, and that I could not do unless I took part in politics. (Gandhi 75.)

In the light of the foregoing chapters, it might be concluded that Christian churches have been completely co-opted by Empire ever since Constantine. Today most U.S. Christians go along quite easily with the imperial program in the same way German Christians in the '30s and '40s went along with Adolph Hitler. The Gospel has been tamed and domesticated by misunderstandings taught to congregations whose worship is actually directed towards the author of empire whom Jesus expressly repudiated. Each of the chapters of this book has addressed one of those misunderstandings.

The question is what can be done about all that? How can believers respond to Bonhoeffer's call for Christian faith without the religious trappings that have made it, on the whole, a force for evil, division, violence, and hatred in the world – one that (along with other fundamentalisms) is killing us all?

The answer, I believe, is by adopting the strengths of fundamentalism, and by avoiding its weaknesses and those of liberation theology, while at the same time, centralizing liberation theology's strengths. Let me explain, eventually returning to my own personal experience.

It seems to me that the strength of fundamentalism is that it takes personal relationships between God, Jesus and individual believers seriously. The fundamentalist students I've taught are nothing if not serious about prayer, offering praise to God, and attending church regularly. They read their Bibles, commit verses to memory, and discuss them in Sunday school and in their Christian university settings. They are dedicated to living upright personal lives free from addictions to drink, drugs, smoking, gambling, sex, and bad language. There is no question that many, many evangelical Christians live those commitments faithfully and admirably. Accepting Jesus as one's personal savior does in fact change lives. Addictions fall away, self-esteem rises, and families are restored. All of that cannot be questioned.

Nonetheless, it is also true to say that the weakness of fundamentalism is that it takes personal relationships between God, Jesus and individual believers seriously. As a result, the undeniable political dimensions of Jesus' life and words are all but ignored. So are his critique of empire in general and his implied criticism of U.S. Empire in particular.

It's easy to get the impression from evangelicals that the whole purpose of Jesus' life was to make believers feel good about themselves, to help them overcome the addictions just listed, along with negative self-images. In some versions, a promised side-benefit of accepting Jesus is that the believer will become wealthy. All of this renders the Gospel politically powerless except as ally of empire.

Liberation theology corrects the weaknesses of fundamentalism. It is concerned about this world, taking the material universe and human bodies with absolute seriousness. In fact, for liberation theologians, the human body is the starting point of all theology. Providing rationale and incentive for keeping human bodies alive as human subjects living together in dignity (not as objects manipulated by others) is the purpose of theological reflection. Liberation theologians are fond of quoting St. Anselm. "*Gloria Dei homo vivens est.*" (The glory of God is found in living human beings.) In line with that aphorism, theologians of liberation also take delight in turning upside-down over-spiritualized understandings of key elements of accepted doctrine. For instance, Hinkelammert describes the essence of the Eucharist not as the transformation of bread into the body of Jesus, but as the body of Jesus becoming bread. In some real sense, for liberation theologians, God is Bread.

Nonetheless, it must also be admitted that the weakness of liberation theology is that it takes the material world and human bodies seriously. As a result, prayer and spirituality become marginalized considerations. None of the attempts at correcting this lacuna has ever helped me pray in any sustained way—though that might well be due to my own obtuseness and lack of perception.

Spiritual Hunger

My complaint about spiritual hunger is reflected in my own personal journey from Catholic fundamentalism and the rich interior life it fostered, to the insights and commitments provided by liberation theology along with a disturbing and unrequited spiritual longing. Having been raised (from the age of 14) in the Roman Catholic seminary, my "fundamentalist" understanding of faith was completely personalized. The purpose of life was to avoid hell and to get to heaven. That was it. The world was not important to me, except insofar as I had to deal with it defensively in terms of resisting "the world, the flesh and the devil." As noted earlier, I was completely lacking in critical political consciousness until the years of my graduate study, around the age of 27. On the other hand, morning prayer, meditation, attendance at daily Mass (twice on Sundays and important "feast days"), visits to the Blessed Sacrament, rosaries, spiritual reading, daily "holy hours," benediction, night prayer, retreats, days of recollection, and eventually (after ordination) praying the Divine Office, all represented the center of my life. And all of that helped me a great deal. I am convinced that over a period of about 16 years (before I began calling my inherited spirituality in question), I had built up a considerable fund of spiritual capital that not only helped me be a good seminarian and a dedicated and effective young priest, but that carried over into the early years of my marriage.

But eventually, I must admit, the capital dissipated, largely because I stopped really praying – stopped meditating. At that time I would have said that I was still a person of faith, even a "man of prayer." Along with my wife and young family, I continued to attend Mass on Sundays, and we were all active in church affairs (especially those connected with social justice). I convinced myself that my reading of liberation theologians represented my "spiritual reading," and that my reflections on those readings for purposes of my own teaching and writing somehow constituted the "prayer life" I had found so essential in my early years. The fact was, however, that I found myself more and more uncomfortable in praying – especially out loud in public. True, in the early years of our marriage, my wife, Peggy, and I had tried to pray together. But I found myself uneasy with her use of guided imagery, and eastern prayer forms. So unfortunately (I see now in retrospect), I made a serious error of breaking off our commitment to meditate and pray together.

And my life (our life) showed it. We had become pretty much like everyone else, apart from our political commitments. Those were considerable. At the beginning of the '80s, we had worked with others in our town to found the Berea Interfaith Taskforce for Peace. We worked locally and with regional and national groups mostly on issues of the nuclear arms race, and the wars in Central America. For the next 25 years there were regular and frequent meetings, potlucks, demonstrations, rallies and speeches. In 1984, we went to Brazil for six months. Peggy studied with the great Brazilian educator, Paulo Freire; I studied liberation theology in Sao Paulo. From 1985 on, I traveled repeatedly to Nicaragua, doing what I could, both there, and especially back home to "fight the Contras" (as I told my 5 year old son). Meanwhile, Peggy worked in El Salvador, and with the Mexican community in our town, Berea, Kentucky. Both of us studied liberation theology in Costa Rica throughout the 1990s, where we worked with the Departamento Ecuménico de Investigaciones in San Jose. Our entire family of five traveled to Africa for a year, when Peggy received a Fulbright Grant to teach in the University of Harare. Then came several solidarity and scholarship trips by each of us to Cuba, and my teaching with the Latin American Studies program, mentioned in Chapter 1.

As for our spiritual life, we tried to be prayerful in all of that. After all, our group did call itself "Interfaith." Meals and potlucks always began with prayer. And we observed regular prayer vigils at the local army base, and on more than one occasion, in our Congressional Representative's office (which we occupied in protest). In fact, one of our group's strengths was that it could always call on the symbols and stories of Christian faith to frame the political projects we had embarked on. Several "Peacemaker" groups even formed from the Interfaith Taskforce. Following guidance from Washington, D.C.'s Church of the Savior, we all recognized that effective peacemaking had to embrace both one's "inner journey" and "outer journey." The latter, of course, we were doing with great energy. Pursuing the inner journey, our weekly Peacemaker gatherings had us begin each meeting with twenty minutes of silent prayer, and with subsequent reports about the progress of our inner journeys. We were trying hard. Yet I personally never knew the inner commitment and focus I had experienced in the seminary and early years of my priesthood.

Spirituality Rediscovered

Then about 130 months ago (I'm still counting as though I were in Alcoholics Anonymous), everything changed. I rediscovered spirituality that connects deeply with fundamentalism's insistence on the centrality of the life of prayer, and with liberation theology's emphasis on body and world. For Christmas at the end of 1997, Peggy gave me four books, all by the same author, Eknath Easwaran. They were *Meditation*, *Conquest of Mind*, *Dialog with Death*, and *Journey into a Far Country*.

I remember reading the introduction to *Meditation*, and being decidedly alienated by it all. It seemed so traditional. For instance, Easwaran spoke of the three basic discoveries revealed in sincere, systematic and sustained commitment to meditation. The first is that I am not my body. The second is that I am not my mind either. The third is that instead of body and mind, my fundamental identity is experienced as unity with the Spirit of God that inhabits every human being, that is found at the heart of every created thing, and that at the same time transcends all of creation. The purpose of meditation, I read, was to establish conscious contact with that basic reality, to remain connected with it throughout the day, and to bring it to practical expression in world-changing service of others. "I've been there and done that before," I remember thinking. It's that old Augustinian spirituality, negative about the body, and probably world-denying.

I read on, however, and found that Easwaran did not understand either the spiritual life or Augustine in that way. Rather, he saw at least certain parts of Augustine as "mystical," and Christianity itself as offering a rich mystical tradition that finds itself in perfect harmony with similar convictions found in each of the world's great religions, including Judaism, Hinduism, Buddhism and Islam. Earlier in this book, those mystical certainties were summarized under five points, viz. that (1) there is a spark of the divine found within every human being; (2) such divine presence can be realized in the sense of making it real, in the processes of decisionmaking and of life in general; (3) it is the purpose of life to come to such realization; (4) spiritual disciplines are found in all the world's Great Religions to assist in that purpose, and (5) once one realizes the divine spark within, she or he becomes capable of recognizing that same spark in every other human being and in all of creation.

To me those points sounded very like the simple Gnostic tradition that Elaine Pagels and others had explained so well as characterizing broad sections of the early church, before the emergence of uniform creeds in the 4th century of our era. The tradition flourished before the formulation of the complex set of beliefs that have since characterized Christianity, which has become, as a result, a cause of division rather than of unification. As expressed, for example, in the Gospel of Thomas, Gnostics believed that Jesus was God's son, but not uniquely so. Instead, he demonstrated in his person the God-potential within every human being (Pagels, *Beyond Belief* 55). As Pagels puts it, the Gospel of Thomas was written for seekers, rather than for believers. Pagels contrasts the Gospel of Thomas with the Gospel of John, which may have been written as a direct attack on the former (41). John agrees with Thomas that Jesus was God's son, but in a unique sense which cannot be experienced by ordinary human beings (40).

In 367, Athanasius, the powerful bishop of Alexandria, issued an order calling for the destruction of all Gospel versions not in tune with John's conviction. Athanasius was worried about the just-mentioned wide variety of theologies and understandings of Jesus of Nazareth that had characterized the Christian community from the beginning. He wanted standardization in church belief and practice, and thought he could impose uniformity by way of book burning. He could do so, he thought, because the books in question were housed in the monastery library of Egyptian monks who fell under his jurisdiction. His order was instrumental in establishing the canon of the New Testament as we know it. Had not disobedient monks hidden copies of the forbidden books in earthen jars and buried them in a hillside near their monastery in Nag Hammadi, we would still be ignorant of the widespread nature of early Christian mystical thought, and of the deep Christian connection with the mysticism centralized in the work of Eknath Easwaran and other classic and contemporary spiritual teachers. The Nag Hammadi discoveries studied intensely by scholars for the past 60 years are finally coming to light for the general public, thanks to the work of scholars such as Pagels.

Whether or not he was personally aware of those discoveries, Easwaran did his part to bring the ancient mystical traditions of Christianity into practice. He validated them by establishing connections the writings and practices of mystics such as Theresa of Avila, John of the Cross, John Wolman, and Meister Eckhart, Anthony de Mello and Hildegard of Bingen.

However, he also did his work of teaching meditation in ways clearly connected with commitment to justice and social change. Easwaran was a disciple and admirer of Gandhi and of Afghanistan's Badshah Kahn, the so-called "frontier Gandhi." Kahn was converted to non-violence by Gandhi himself, and succeeded in turning some of the fiercest Pathan tribes of Afghanistan from their traditional ethic of violent revenge to the nonviolent ways championed by Gandhi.

Easwaran also had high consciousness of the evils of British colonialism in India, of the tremendous waste of the nuclear arms race, of environmental destruction at the hands of western civilization, and of the scandal of global poverty in the face of conspicuous over-consumption in the so-called developed world. He recommended meditation as the basis for dealing with all those problems in ways modeled on Gandhi's methods.

Painfully recalling the brutality of British colonialism, Easwaran writes:

> Every part of the country could tell of events that, if collected, would give a very damning picture of British rule. . . Probably we will never have a full history of those times, constructed from the microhistories of the seven hundred thousand villages whose economies the English so systematically destroyed. We are left with documentation only of the large-scale horrors recorded in the files of the British administrations: famines like those in Orissa and Bengal, where millions of people died after their croplands were taken over by English landlords; slaughters like those of 1857, when in retaliation for Indian revolt, villages throughout India were burned and the wholesale massacre of not only men but women and children was officially allowed for a solid month. (To Love . . . 275-76)

Easwaran's gentle anger over such atrocities, as well as his grasp of the reasons for imperialism, surfaces in the following anecdote:

One of my English friends of those days once asked me, "Tell me frankly, what is it about our being here that bothers you most?" We knew each other well, so we could exchange these views without losing affection or respect. I replied, "Your overbearing sense of superiority. Instead of all this talk about the 'white man's burden' and 'bringing the light of civilization to benighted heathens,' why don't you just say you are here to exploit us and be done with it?" This is not an Indian's idea of politeness, but one curious thing about the British is that they rather like this kind of strong talk. He actually respected me more after that. "Very good!" he said. "That's true; that is why we are here." (279)

I am tempted to review the eight-point program Easwaran recommends for pursuing the spiritual life and for combating social injustices like colonialism from the inside out. I'll name them instead. They include meditation, choice and frequent repetition of a mantram, spiritual reading from the great mystics of all religions, maintaining one-pointed attention, slowing down, training the senses, associating with others on the same spiritual path, and putting the needs of other first. It's that last point that results in Easwaran's insistence on service towards remedying problems in the areas already mentioned. Elaboration of all these points is easily available in the two dozen or so books Easwaran has authored.

The point here is not to say that Eknath Easwaran is a guru that everyone must follow. He is not. In fact, there are many teachers, methods and programs of meditation and the spiritual life that are equally valid and adaptable to the needs of individuals, who, after all, find themselves at different places in their spiritual development. Rather, the point is to indicate that the recuperation of the mystical tradition of Christianity on the one hand and the recovery of the liberation thrust of the biblical tradition on the other represent two of the most important spiritual developments of the last half century. They should not be understood as antithetical or in tension. They are clearly complementary. Neglecting the liberation thrust domesticates the teaching and person of Jesus as we have seen in fundamentalist movements both Catholic and Protestant. But neglecting the mystical thrust leads to activism that can easily lead to burnout, discouragement and cynicism as hoped-for results fail to materialize again and again.

There are strong indications that the basis for this same spirituality is presenting itself to important liberation theologians like Franz Hinkelammert. In 2003 he wrote of the "heavenly nucleus" found within everyone and everything on earth. He compares it to the Tao of Lao-Tse, and to the Nirvana of Buddha. It is a reality that transcends cultural and religious differences, and which unites all of reality from within. (*El asalto* . . . 263).

Meditation and the Battle of the Gods

Connecting experientially with the mystical tradition—with the spark of the divine within—brings to light the real nature of the Battle of the Gods centralized in these reflections. It makes it clear that my students are correct when they object to the concept of the Battle of the Gods, claiming correctly that God loves everyone without distinction. The truth in their claim is that the Transcendent Presence is indeed found within every creature without distinction, and, of course, within every human being, simply in virtue of their being alive. All of life both inner and outer is a revelation then of the single most important spiritual truth, viz. that everything is connected at the deepest level; that everything is one—that the other is our very self. Another way of describing this universal presence of the divine within all peoples is to affirm that God loves everyone and all of creation.

However this clarification in no way negates the fact that there does exist a God of the Rich and a God of the Poor. The latter emerged as the basis of the three great monotheistic faiths, Judaism, Christianity and Islam. It was originally a slave spirituality expressing the conviction that God was concerned about people at the bottom of the social ladder —that they too were people of God. This claim was made in the face of counter-claims by the Egyptian pharaohs that the slaves were nobodies, created to serve the direct royal representatives of the Sun God, Ra. So the Hebrew slave religion represented insistence on the part of the poor that God is universal, and that consequently the Egyptian exclusivist, manipulative and enslaving God of Empire and of the rich, was a false idea of God— an idol.

This is not to say, however, that as an idol, the God of the Rich and Empire had no real existence then or none today. The rich God turns out to be an extremely powerful spirit that informs people, nations, and the entire world as "the domination system" described in Walter Wink's *Engaging the Powers*. As such it is the spirit of the "World" warned against in the Gospel of John. This spirit possesses power to destroy entire nations and even (with today's nuclear capabilities), the entire planet. It has intellectual power too—the power to change minds through propaganda, to make them subservient, and to cause the world to be perceived falsely. In fact, most of the time, the power represented by the phrases "God of the Rich," "God of Empire," "God of the Domination System" seems infinitely more potent than any claimed by the "God of the Poor."

The ancients, of course, recognized all of this. So they gave a name to the power of the Rich and of Empire. They called it Satan. As we have seen, they accorded him a place in the divine Council presided over by Yahweh. They said that Satan was the founder of empire, the one to whom empire's power was given to bestow as he wished. Again, as we have seen, this spirit was elevated to the divine level, when in the 4th century, the Catholic Church accepted the temptation refused by Jesus, to do what was necessary to attain imperial authority. In effect, it fell down in worship before Satan, as Jesus had refused to do. But it obscured its Satanism by changing the name "Satan" to "God." Since then anyone who has accepted empire as God's will, i.e. most Christians, have really been satanists.

Mysticism and Violence

The mystical tradition fortified by its practice of intense meditation and its allied disciplines rejects the ruinous superstition at the basis of Satan's empire, viz. that violence somehow saves. With immense compassion, mystics suggest the genesis of that belief and its vision of a punishing God by referencing the universal law of karma, also recognized by the Jesus tradition. Karma, of course, refers to the insight, as Jesus put it, that sowing and reaping are intimately connected. Put negatively, people are inevitably punished not for the sins, but by their sins. One merely has to wait for the wheel to turn to verify the law that what goes around comes around.

It is a short step from that belief to the poor imagining with great relish what it will be like on that Great Day when the rich oppressors get what is coming to them. From such imaginings spring the apocalyptic poetry of Daniel and the Book of Revelation. However, one must hasten to add that these are actually non-violent books (Wink 45). They are not meant to encourage the poor to rise up violently against their oppressors, but to await certain activation of the law of karma. Seen from the karmic viewpoint, then, Apocalypse is not so much a description of what the God of Violence will do to the rich. Rather it is a poetic representation of what the rich are actually doing to the poor – and eventually to themselves. It message is that by inflicting first and third level violences and terrorism, the rich are actually invoking such horrors on themselves. Their own acts of violence, described so richly in apocalyptic image, will inevitably come back to haunt them.

The problem is that historically not all teachers, and spiritual guides, and certainly not all their pupils or followers, have understood either karma or its double-edged, apocalyptic description. As a result, the God of the Bible has been turned into a war God on the one hand and into a revolu- tionary God on the other. Ultimately he becomes the Great Torturer in the sky. He threatens sinners with confinement in an eternal fiery pit, where unimaginable punishments are inflicted on sinners with no possibility of reprieve. In other words, the belief has prevailed that this God punishes oppression and sin, rather than oppression and sin punishing their perpetrators. God, then, has been transformed into the quintessential embodiment of the Domination System. He has been transformed into Satan.

Conclusion

In his book, *Is Religion Killing Us?* Jack Nelson-Pallmeyer levels a withering criticism at the Violence of God strains in both the Judeo-Christian tradition and the Holy Quran. In both forms, he says, the cult of violence threatens to destroy human civilization, and possibly the entire planet itself. It must therefore be rejected.

At the same time, Nelson-Pallmeyer suggests that believers might still use the Violence of God traditions by spiritualizing them the way that Gandhi spiritualized the Bhagavad-Gita. Nelson-Pallmeyer writes,

> Although the Gita encouraged war, Gandhi reinterpreted it to be a spiritual message requiring human beings to struggle against the violence within in order nonviolently to transform the world without. He also pointed out that the whole of the Mahabharata (the Gita was part of this larger work) revealed the futility of violence (*Is Religion. . .* 139)

The interpretation of Apocalypse offered immediately above (in karmic perspective) offers an example of how an apparently blood-soaked book might be interpreted to eliminate its Violence of God overtones.

Following that example, and Gandhi's relative to the *Gita*, might possibly do the same for the many other biblical passages that celebrate an incredibly brutal and patriarchal idea of God.

As Nelson-Pallmeyer adds, however, there is a much easier way to approach the Bible and its threatening, patriarchal, blood-thirsty God who holds in thrall fundamentalist literalists with such devastating effect. That way is not dependent on interpretational acrobatics performed by high-wire biblical experts who are able to nuance and contextualize interpretations in ways not available to ordinary Bible readers. It is simply to admit that the Bible (and Quran) was authored by human beings, not by God.

Those human beings had political, economic and class agendas that made them present God in ways ultimately out of tune with the culminating revelation of the compassionate God as understood by Jesus. Even some Gospel portrayals of Jesus are infected with the violence of God tradition— as when Jesus is presented in terms of final judgment, condemnation and eternal punishment. As the work of the Jesus Seminar has shown, the authenticity of those portrayals is highly questionable. They are the product of authors so steeped in violence of God thinking that they found it impossible not to squeeze Jesus into its confining categories.

Fundamentalists might well object that admitting the human authorship of "sacred" texts will prove fatal for faith, and will deprive the human community of ethical certainty provided only by documents believed to be the very word of God. Nevertheless, as Nelson-Pallmeyer indicates, these fears are ill founded. To begin with, even texts considered to be the word of God are susceptible to multiple interpretations. Such variety has been illustrated in the early chapters of this book—in the case of the first woman and first man, Cain and Abel, Abraham and Isaac, Moses and David, and ultimately in the book of Revelation and the gospels themselves.

Moreover, faith would not disappear, even if the biblical texts were jettisoned altogether. Personal experience and attention to history, especially where attempts have been made to eradicate religion, show how impossible it is to extinguish the religious drive within human beings. Human beings in every culture, whether they've been exposed to the Bible or not, have always searched for meaning. They have attempted to describe and respond to the intersection between human experience and what all cultures perceive as transcendent reality. This phenomenon is in perfect accord with the central conviction of the mystical tradition, that the very purpose of life is to discover and realize (i.e. make real) the "spark of the divine" within each human being and all of creation.

As for ethics, morality is only tangentially connected to the Bible. As this study has attempted to show, the Bible has, on the one hand, been used to justify the most immoral acts in the history of the world including the Crusades and Inquisition, slavery and racism, oppression of women, cruelty to children, homophobic behavior, genocidal wars, use of nuclear weapons, torture, and cruel and unusual punishments of all kinds. On the other hand, so many who have rejected the Christianity and the sacredness of its texts have exemplified behavior of the highest moral character. For instance, the number of communists who have dedicated their lives to relieving the poverty of those they considered comrades, brothers and sisters, and who have given their lives for others, has been legion.

Nothing is lost, then, if one recognizes as a primary biblical revelation the fact that the Bible itself represents contested terrain. Its challenge lies in its description of the God of the Rich and the God of the Poor, and call to discern between the two. Defining such a challenge has been the main task of this book. Another has been to blend the strengths of fundamentalism and its concern for the spiritual with those of liberation theology with its focus on "idology" (the study of idols), and on bringing about the "other world" that liberation theologians, the prophets and Jesus were convinced is possible. It is a world devoid of the "domination system," and characterized by a "partnership system" marked in turn by justice, equity and sharing. Finally, this book has tried to combine the contextual approach to Bible reading with one that makes clear the "sacred" text's human authorship and conflicting purposes. The contention here has been that the God of the Poor most closely reflects the universal love and compassion of Ultimate Reality. The rich have repeatedly tried to rob the poor of God's favor, and to turn revelation into a tool of empire and one more weapon in an arsenal intended to justify the wealth of the few and the poverty of the many.

Let's say it clearly once again: This project of the rich, developed most often with the complete support from Christian churches, is Satanic.

APPENDIX

Clarifying Concepts: Economic Systems

Author and social critic, Gore Vidal, tells the story of a revealing exchange with an audience member following one of his speeches. A woman came up to him and said, "Mr. Vidal, I am grateful for your marvelous presentation. However, I have two questions for you."

"Thank you," Vidal answered. "And what might your questions be?"

"The first question," the woman said, "is what can I as an ordinary housewife do to stop the advance of godless communism?"

"Yes," Vidal answered." And what's your second question?"

"My second question," the woman answered, "is what is communism?"

The exchange depicts the confusion typical of most Americans when facing questions of communism and capitalism – and Marxism and liberalism as well. Most simply do not know the difference. They are convinced, of course, that communism is bad, and that capitalism is good. Beyond that, ideas remain confused. Most are even unaware that all the terms mentioned describe positions adopted towards the free market economic system.

It is the modest, yet ambitious, purpose of this appendix to clear up confusion. The point is to address questions of definition that may have arisen in connection with assertions already made in previous chapters. What follows will therefore attempt, first of all, to compare and contrast the notions of "capitalism" in Marxist and liberal thought – all in relation to the free market. Secondly this chapter will similarly treat the explanations of "the way the world works" as they emerge from these opposed understandings of capitalism. The focus in both sets of comparisons will be the contrasting notions of political freedom belonging to each of the understandings in question.

To begin with, it is extremely important to define our terms. What, then, do we mean by capitalism? And what is meant by "Marxism," as well as by the "socialism" and "communism" that Marx espoused? Oversimplifying tremendously, for purposes of discussion and clarity, it is possible to summarize each in three points.

Capitalism

Capitalism is an economic system based on (1) private ownership of the means of production (2) free and open markets (places where goods are bought and sold), and (3) unlimited earnings. Private ownership of the means of production dictates that individuals should be empowered to own fields, forests, farms, factories and other sources of products for sale and exchange. Communal ownership is thus excluded. Free and open markets means that private ownership should permit those in question to produce what they choose to produce, where and when they choose to do so, employing whom they choose, without any power outside of market forces of supply and demand dictating that production. Here government interference in the market by way, for instance, of outlawing or controlling some productions (such as liquor or cigarettes) and mandating others (such as beans and rice) is rejected. Moreover, anyone at all should be able to enter an open market regardless of personal attributes such as race, age, gender, nationality, or religion. In all this emphasis on "freedom," we find expressed the "liberal" nature of "liberal capitalism." Finally, liberal capitalism calls for unlimited earnings. That is, the producer's talent and the quality of her or his product alone should limit the income goals attainable. Limits on earnings such as taxes should be kept to the minimum necessary to provide public protection of private property (police, military, prisons, the judicial system) and to supply the infrastructure necessary for commerce (roads, bridges, etc.) Income ceilings, of course, are out of the question.

Marxism

For its part, Marxism represents the Western tradition's most trenchant critique of capitalism. In a phrase, Marxism is *the philosophy of Karl Marx*. Traditionally, how to interpret that philosophy has been a matter of lively controversy. At one point, the debate reportedly moved even Marx himself to pound the table and say, "I am not a Marxist." At the risk of evoking the same response from the grave, the present summary understands Marxism under the following three points. First of all, Marxism's critique of capitalism holds that the system *necessarily* exploits workers (and by extension, as we shall see, the environment). The adverb "necessarily" is emphasized here to show that, on Marx's analysis, the destructive nature of capitalism is not dependent on the personal qualities of individual capitalists. Regardless of their personal virtue or lack thereof, capitalists are forced by the free market mechanism itself to exploit workers (and the environment). This is because, for one thing, workers are forced to enter a labor market whose wage level is set by competition with similar workers seeking the same job. As a result, each prospective employee will bid his competitors down until what David Ricardo called the "natural" wage level is attained. Ricardo described this wage as follows,

> The market price of labour is the price which is really paid for it, from the natural operation of the proportion of the supply to the demand; labour is dear when it is scarce and cheap when it is plentiful. However much the market price of labour may deviate from its natural price, it has, like commodities, a tendency to conform to it. (50)

Marx found this "natural" level below what workers and their families need to sustain themselves. Marx and Engels comment,

> The average price of wage-labor is the minimum wage, i.e., that quantum of the means of subsistence, which is absolutely requisite to keep the laborer in bare existence as a laborer. What, therefore, the wage-laborer appropriates by means of his labor, merely suffices to prolong and reproduce a bare existence. . . (All that we want to do away with is the miserable character of this appropriation, under which the laborer lives merely to increase capital, and is allowed to live only in so far as the interest of the ruling class requires it). (97)

For Marxists, the capitalist system does not merely exploit workers of necessity. It also *necessarily* exploits the environment. That is, the market's supply and demand guidance dynamic punishes the presence of environmental conscience on the part of producers. Thus, for example, a conscientious entrepreneur might be moved to put scrubbers on the smokestacks of his factory and filters to purify liquid effluents from his plant entering a nearby river. In doing so, he will, of course, raise his costs of production. Meanwhile, his competitors who lack environmental conscience will continue spewing unmitigated smoke into the atmosphere and pouring toxins into the river. Their lowered costs will enable them to undersell the conscientious producer, and eventually drive him out of business. In this way, the market rewards absence of environmental conscience.

Marx's second point is that the exploitation which the capitalist system necessarily fosters will cause rebellion on the part of workers. They will rise up against their employers and overthrow the capitalist system. They will replace capitalism with socialism (explained immediately below). Finally, Marx's third point is that socialism will eventually evolve into communism (also explained below).

Socialism

For Marx capitalism's replacement at the hands of workers is socialism. This economic system is capitalism's opposite on each of the three points indicated earlier. First of all, whereas capitalism espouses private ownership of the means of production, socialism advocates public ownership. According to this theory, the workers themselves take over the factories and administer them, not for the profit of the few, but for the benefit of workers and their families. Secondly, whereas capitalism demands free and open markets, socialism mandates controlled markets. Since socialism has the interests of the working majority at center, its pure theory will not allow, for instance, production of luxury crops (such as roses or coffee) if that production deprives workers of the food they need for subsistence. Thirdly, whereas capitalism idealizes unlimited income, socialism calls for redistribution of income – for instance, through a progressive income tax. Socialism might also limit income by establishing ceilings beyond which personal incomes are not permitted to rise. Taxes and surplus earnings are then used for the common good, for example to fund schools, clinics, food subsidies, affordable housing, rents and health care.

Communism

For its part, communism is a "vision of the future" which some, though not by any means all, socialists entertain as history's end point. That is, while all communists are socialists, not all socialists are communists. This is because some socialists (along with all capitalists, of course) consider the communist vision of the future as unrealistic and unattainable. That vision, overly idealistic or not, is of a future where there will be (1) abundance for all, (2) no classes, as a result of such plenty, and (3) no need for a state.

To begin with, the vision of virtually unlimited abundance marks communists such as Marx and Engels as convinced industrialists. They were highly impressed by the unprecedented output of the factory system of the late nineteenth and early twentieth centuries. Shirts, for example, that would take a skilled seamstress or tailor days to produce, were turned out in minutes, once an assembly line based on "division of labor" was set in motion. Soon, communists theorized, the world would be filled with consumer goods. And in a context of such abundance "yours" and "mine" would cease to have meaning. Neither would it make sense for some to horde goods to themselves at the expense of others. The result would be the disappearance of classes. There would be no rich and no poor. Everyone would have more than enough of what they need.

With the disappearance of classes would come the gradual "withering away" of the state. This is because "the state," by communist definition is simply the armed administrator of the affairs of society's dominant class. In the words of Marx and Engels, "Political power, properly so called, is merely the organized power of one class for oppressing another" (105).

Thus the state's job is to impose the will of a ruling class on others. Under capitalism, the state's function is to oblige the working class to accept conditions profitable to the bourgeoisie. In other words, under capitalism, the state imposes the "dictatorship of the bourgeoisie." Meanwhile, under socialism, the function of the state is to impose the will of the working class on the bourgeoisie. It enforces the "dictatorship of the proletariat." By way of contrast, under communism, in the absence of classes (eliminated by a condition of abundance) there remains no group whose will needs to be imposed on others. The state's function thus ceases. It gradually disappears.

Capitalist Theory

In contrast to the vision of Marx and Engels, Adam Smith and the other theoreticians of liberal capitalism see the system of capitalist economic organization as wonderful and nearly magical. When the free choice of private producers is left to itself, they hold, it results in the best of all possible worlds. Goods are produced at the lowest possible cost. This keeps consumer prices low. Moreover, both wages and profits find those "natural" levels described earlier. Put otherwise, goods are produced and distributed with the greatest possible efficiency. The miraculous part of all this is that the end state of maximum efficiency or of benefiting consumers is not even intended – at least, not necessarily. It is instead an unintentional side effect of unbridled (i.e. free or liberal) self-seeking. As Smith puts it, the individual producer . . .

> intends only his own gain; and he is in this, as in many other cases, led by an invisible hand to promote the end which was no part of his intention. Nor is it always the worse for society that it was no part of it. By pursuing his own interest, he frequently promotes that of society more effectively than when he really intends to promote it. . . . (Vol. II, 242)

That is, in producing shoes, the private shoemaker, for instance, intends nothing other than her or his own welfare and profit. But, wonderful to say, that very self-seeking produces benefits for the entire community. This is because competition with other shoemakers leads every producer of shoes to manufacture a better and/or cheaper product. Consumers thus turn out to be the real, though unintended beneficiaries. Meanwhile, the good producer of shoes gets rich. What could be simpler? No wonder free market advocate, Ronald Reagan, was fond of referring to "the magic of the market."

In view of such "magic," the worst action a government can perform is to interfere in the market—to rob entrepreneurs of their freedom. Such interference by way of public ownership or controlling markets and/or income, however well-intentioned, interposes government bureaucracy between producers and consumers. It thus nullifies the most direct expression of consumer will expressed in their daily, hourly and even minute-by-minute "votes" expressed in the choices they make at the vegetable stand, the supermarket or the mall. Such bureaucratic interposition creates huge inefficiencies. For example, it leads a central body to "command" that toothbrushes or shoes be produced in quantities disproportionate to consumer need. Thus the creativity of producers is stymied, consumer choice is limited and incentive diminished. Smith says,

> It is thus that every system which endeavors, either by extraordinary encouragements, to draw towards a particular species of industry a greater share of the capital of the society than what would naturally go to it, or, by extraordinary restraints, to force from a particular species of industry some share of the capital, which would otherwise be employed in it, is, in reality, subversive of the great purpose which it means to promote. It retards, instead of accelerating, the progress of the society towards real wealth and greatness; and diminishes, instead of increasing, the real value of the annual produce of its land and labor. (Vol. III, 66)

Similarly, for market liberals, government attempts to redistribute income by creating "make-work" jobs, by welfare programs and by "confiscatory" taxes, are all counterproductive. Despite the intentions of such programs to help the working class, they actually create misery for those they are meant to help, as well as deprive capitalists of their just rewards. The programs in question, first of all, diminish employment opportunities. This is because government controls deprive capitalists of incentive to invest. In this way, fewer factories, for example, are built, and fewer workers are employed. For their part, welfare programs deprive workers of the incentive, drive, hard work and competition they need to fully realize their dignified status as human beings. Welfare programs are paternal in relation to workers who are adults, after all, and who should be able to make their way in a competitive world without the help of some "nanny state." In other words, programs of income redistribution are negative, not only for those whose money is taken, but for the recipients as well, whose very human nature is diminished by such "handouts." Referring to what in his day were called "poor laws," Ricardo blamed such welfare for what he determined to be the main cause of poverty in his own day, viz. overpopulation. He wrote,

> Like all other contracts, wages should be left to the fair and free competition of the market, and should never be controlled by the interference of the legislature.
>
> The clear and direct tendency of the poor laws is in direct opposition to these obvious principles. . . . It is a truth which admits not a doubt that the comforts and well-being of the poor cannot be permanently secured without some regard on their part, or some effort on the part of the legislature, to regulate the increase of their numbers, and to render less frequent among them early and improvident marriages. The operation of the poor laws has been directly contrary to this. They have rendered restraint superfluous, and have invited imprudence by offering of the wages of prudence and industry. (57)

Marxist Critique of Capitalism

The Marxist understanding of the way the world works has a contrasting understanding of market freedom in relation to both "efficiency" and the causes of misery for the working classes. For Marxists, economic "efficiency" is not to be measured principally in low production costs, or in the achievement of "natural" levels of wages, prices and incomes. Instead, Marxism emphasizes human welfare as the measure of economic success. Are the basic needs of workers met? Do they have rewarding jobs? Are they eating well? Are their clothing and housing adequate? Can their children avail themselves of good education? When they are sick, do workers (and those unable to work) have access to adequate medical care?

As already indicated, Marxists see capitalism itself as responsible for the misery of the working class. Its wage system enables the owners of the means of production not only to keep wages to an inhuman subsistence level through labor market competition. It also explains profit itself. For Marxists, profit comes from money earned by workers, but not paid to them. That is, in the industrial process, workers add value to the raw materials they work with. That value exceeds the wages paid the workers.

In the system of private ownership, the excess in question is pocketed by the owners of the means of production. In other words, the profit system, for Marxists, is based on robbery.

With such analysis in mind, poverty's solution for Marxists is not free competition. As already indicated, it involves, first of all, elimination of private property. Secondly, it entails temporarily replacing the "dictatorship of the bourgeoisie" with the "dictatorship of the working class" (Marx, Engles, "Manifesto,"105). This arrangement expropriates the former property owners. The state structures that had formerly favored the bourgeoisie are then restructured to favor the majority working class through direct government intervention in the market place. Private profit is replaced by community profit which is used to pay each worker according to his or her effort, to set up social services such as public health, education, and housing, to reinvest in industry's productive base, to pay for administrative expenses and to care for those unable to work.

Competing Understandings of Political Freedom

At the heart of the discord between the theorists of capitalism on the one hand, and the critics of that system on the other, is disagreement about the meaning of political freedom. Economic liberalism's concept of political freedom should be clear from what has already been said. In terms exposed by the eminent British historian and philosopher, Sir Isaiah Berlin, economic liberals espouse "negative freedom," not only in the market place, but in civil society as well. As described in Berlin's classic, *Four Essays on Liberty*, negative freedom refers to restrictions put on the state to prevent its interference with the freedom of individual citizens.

Negative Freedom

John Locke perhaps best expressed the meaning of negative freedom.
It was set by what he called "nature's law of liberty" which provided each man with freedom . . .

> to be under no other legislative power, but that established, by consent, in the commonwealth; nor

under the dominion of any will or restraint of any to the trust put in it. Freedom, then, is . . . to have a standing rule to live by, common to everyone of that society, and made by the legislative power erected in it; a liberty to follow my own will in all things, where the rule prescribes not; and not to be subject to the inconstant, uncertain, unknown, arbitrary will or another man; as freedom of nature is, to be under no other restraint but the law of nature. (BK. II, Ch. 4, Par. 22)

Negative freedom thus resembles ideas espoused by laissez-faire capitalists whose most prestigious contemporary spokesman might be identified as Milton Friedman. Friedman's words echo Locke. However instead of emphasizing Locke's "free will," Friedman emphasizes the political freedom to benefit from one's talents.

No arbitrary obstacles should prevent people from achieving those positions for which their talents fit them and which their values lead them to seek. Not birth, nationality, color, religion, sex, nor any other irrelevant characteristic should determine the opportunities that are open to a person – only his abilities. (123)

As already indicated, this type of approach sees the economic world controlled by nature. Supply and demand govern the exchange of goods and services as inevitably and inexorably as the law of gravity operates in the realm of physics. Thus government has no role in establishing freedom and justice. Freedom is a given and is fostered by a government which simply remains "off the backs" of entrepreneurs. Similarly, justice is the natural result of the outworking of free market mechanisms. As a result, unrestrained self-interest leads to the greatest possible social good. In other words, negative freedom for laissez-faire capitalists necessarily involves political freedom from government interference in the marketplace, but also in private life. Freedom in this sense is the freedom of capitalists from government interference to earn as much profit as possible, and to live life as one chooses. Politically speaking, negative freedom finds expression in the U.S. Constitution's Bill of Rights guaranteeing among other freedoms, citizens' freedom of speech, religion, and assembly.

Positive Freedom

Socialists, Marxists, communists and political liberals champion what Berlin calls "positive freedom." Here "political liberals" (as opposed to economic liberals) are those who, while not embracing complete socialism, recognize that the government must at least in limited ways interfere in the marketplace and in civil society to insure that individuals outside the ruling class will able to control their own destinies. In other words, liberals hold that government has a strong role to play in promoting freedom and justice. Without such government intervention, individuals without money, position or friends in high places will almost inevitably be overwhelmed by economic laws of supply and demand and by political alliances which otherwise exercise what amounts to "the law of the strongest." Here, then, "positive freedom" is understood to mean the freedom of individuals from the power of the capitalist ruling class to ensure that everyone has a decent standard of living.

Mixed Economy

According to Berlin, it was the idea of "positive freedom" that led to the establishment of the modern "welfare state." This state represents neither pure capitalism nor pure socialism, but a combination of the two that is typically described as a "mixed economy." As the phrase implies, this involves (1) some private ownership of the means of production and some public ownership, (2) some free and open markets and some controlled markets, and (3) earnings typically limited by a progressive income tax.

As one might imagine this liberal position has evoked criticism from both capitalists and socialists. Conservative (or neo-liberal) capitalists criticize political liberalism for interfering excessively in the economy. For their parts, socialists and communists lament government intervention that they see as too timid, and which consequently allows the injustices inherent in the capitalist system to survive virtually unchecked.

Human Rights

As for human rights relative to economic systems. . . . no system of political-economy has shown consistent respect for all human rights. Instead all systems prioritize them according to what they consider the most basic (Hinkelammert, *Democracia y* . . . 137). Capitalism puts the rights to private property, the right to enter binding contracts, and to maximize earnings at the top of its list. These are the rights that belong specifically to corporations. On the other hand, capitalism's tendency is to deny the legitimacy of specifically human rights as recognized, for example, by the U.N. Declaration. For this reason, the U.S. has never ratified conventions implementing the Declaration or other key documents asserting rights beyond the civil and corporate (Hinkelammert, "*La economia. . .*" 242). Moreover, if capitalism's prioritized rights are threatened, all others are subject to disregard, including the rights to free elections, speech, press, assembly, religion, and freedom from torture. Historical references already made in this essay support that observation.[46] Similarly, socialism heads its own list with the rights to food, shelter, clothing, healthcare and education. In the name of those rights, socialism relativizes rights to private ownership and the rights to enter binding contracts, and to maximize earnings. If the rights socialism considers basic are threatened, history has shown that it too, like capitalism, will disregard all others.

Conclusion

So how should Vidal have answered his questioner? Certainly not in a sentence or two. He could have said, "Communism, dear lady, is a vision of the future shared by some socialists." That, however, would probably have confused his interrogator even more. The truth is that the questions implied by Vidal's appreciative listener cannot be answered much more briefly than indicated in the foregoing pages. There we have seen that capitalism is both a simple and complicated system. It has spawned trenchant criticism from Marx and Engels and vigorous defense from the likes of Milton Friedman. Capitalism implies as well an entire approach to politics. This sees the market as a central factor in producing just outcomes without government intervention. That vision has led political liberals like Isaiah Berlin to espouse tinkering with the economic systems to incorporate the best of capitalism and of its antithesis, socialism. Thus our own political positions and those of most of our contemporaries find definition.

---

[46] Under what Hinkelammert terms "market totalitarianism," economic structural adjustment policies are imposed by means of state terrorism, which includes summary arrests, detention without charges, torture, and nullification of elections, disappearances and assassination. This has been especially true in the United States since 9/11/01 and in Latin America since the 1960s, in countries like Brazil, Chile, Argentina and Uruguay (Hinkelammert, "La economia. . ." 240). Contemporary Colombia suffers especially under such measures. There opposition to free market policies has been treated as subversion and terrorism. The concept of "insurgency" has been widened not only to include guerrillas in arms, but also membership in and activity led by human rights organizations (Gutierrez 103-4).

WORKS CITED

Batalla, Guillermo. *Mexico Profundo*. Austin: university of Texas Press, 1996.
Berlin, Isaiah. *Four Essays on Liberty*. London: Oxford University Press, 1969.
Borg, Marcus. *Meeting Jesus Again for the First Time*. San Francisco: Harper Collins, 1995.
Calvin, Jean. Calvin: *Institutes of the Christian Religion*, edited by John T. McNeill and translated by Ford Battles, vol. 20 and 21: The Library of Christian Classics. Philadelphia: The Westminster Press, 1960.
Chomsky, Noam. *The Real Terror Network*. Boston: South End Press, 1982.
Crossan, John Dominic. *God and Empire*. San Francisco: Harpers, 2007.
Drake, Stillman. *Discoveries and Opinions of Galileo*. Translated with introduction and notes by Stillman Drake. Garden City, New York: Doubleday Anchor Books, 1957 Duchrow Ulrich, et al. *Confidential Documents of the 17th Conference of The American Armies*. Mar del Plata, Argentina, 1987.
Easwaran, Eknath. *Like A Thousand Suns: the Bhagavad-Gita for Daily Living*, Vol. 2. Tomales, California: Nilgiri Press, 1979.
_____ *Original Goodness*. Tomales, California: Nilgiri Press, 1989
_____ "Sharing the Wealth of the World." *Blue Mountain, A Journal for Spiritual Living*. May/June, 1999: 1-5.
_____. *To Love Is To Know Me: The Bhagavad Gita for Daily Living*, Vol. 3. Tomales, California: Nilgiri Press, 1984.
Friedman, Milton and Rose. *Free To Choose*. New York: Avon Books, 1979
Galeano, Eduardo. *Las Venas Abiertas de America Latina*. Mexico: Siglo Veintiuno, 1980.
Gandhi, Mohandas K. *Essentail Writings*. John Dear, editor. Maryknoll, New York: Orbis Books, 2005
Griffin, David Ray. *Christian Faith and the Truth Behind 9/11: A Call to Reflection*. Westminster:John Knox Press, 2000.
Gutierrez, German. "Colombia: la estrategia de la sin razon." El *Huracan de la Globalizacion*. Ed. Franz J. Hinkelammert. San Jose, Costa Rica: DEI, 1999. 175-207.
Hinkelammert, Franz J. "*El Apocalipsis Como Visión de La Historia Occidental*." Pasos. Enero/Febrero, 2004: 3-12.
_____. *El asalto al poder mundial y la violencia sagrada del imperio*. San José, Costa Rica: Editorial DEI, 2003.
_____. *El grito del sujeto: del teatro-mundo del evangelico de Juan al perro-mundo de la globalización*. San José, Costa Rica: Editorial DEI, 1998.

_____. *El Huracan de la Globalizacion*. San Jose, Costa Rica: DEI, 1999.
_____. *El sujeto y la ley*. Heredia, Costa Rica: EUNA, 2003.
Johnson, Paul. *A History of Christianity*. New York: Atheneum, 1977.
Kamil, Jill. *Christianity in the Land of the Pharaohs*. New York: Routledge, 2005.
Kendrick, M. Gregory. *Documents of Western Civilization. Vol.II,1150* Loretta O'Hanlon, *to Present*. Cincinnati: West/Wadsworth, 1999 Janice Archer.
Lernoux, Penny. *Cry of the People: The Struggle for Human Rights in Latin America—The Catholic Church in Conflict with U.S. Policy*. New York: Penguin Books, 1982.
Locke, John. *Two Treatises of Government*. New York: New American Library, 1960.
Luther, Martin. "An Appeal to the Ruling Class of German Nationality as to the Amelioration of the State of Christendom." *Reformation Writings of Martin Luther*, Vol. 1, Bertram Lee Woolf, ed. New York: Philosophical Library, 1953.
_____. "Preface to the Epistle of St. Paul to the Romans." *Martin Luther: Selections from His Writings*. John Dillenberger, ed. Garden City, N.Y.: Anchor Books, 1961.
Marx, Karl. *Capital*. Trans. By Samuel Moore. New York: Modern Library, 1906.
Marx, Karl and Friedrich Engels. *The Communist Manifesto*. New York: Penguin Books, 1967.
McMurtry, John. "Understanding 9/11 and the 9/11 Wars." http://scienceforpeace.sa./utoronto.ca/Essays_Briefs/McMurtry/McMurtry-911_Wars-04.html
Mesters, Carlos. *Flor Sem Defesa*. Petropo´lis: Vozes, 1984.
Miranda, Jose. *Marx and the Bible*. Maryknoll, New York: Orbis Books, 1974.
Myers, Ched. *Binding the Strong Man*. Maryknoll, New York: Orbis books, 1988.
Nelson-Pallmeyer, Jack. *Is Religion Killing Us? Violence in the Bible and the Quran*. New York: Trinity Press International, 2003.
_____. *The Politics of Compassion*. Maryknoll, New York: Orbis Books, 1987.
_____. *Saving Christianity from Empire*. New York: Continuum, 2005.
Pagels, Elaine. *Adam, Eve and the Serpent*. New York: Random House, 1988.
_____. *Beyond Belief: The Secret Gospel of Thomas*. New York: Random House, 2003.

_____. *The Origin of Satan.* New York: Random House, 1995.
Policy Planning Study (Feb. 24, 1948, FRUS 1948), I (part 2). (PPS), 23 Quoted in Noam Chomsky, *Turning the Tide.* Boston: South End Press, 1985, 48.
Ricardo, David. *The Works of David Ricardo.* J.R. McCulloch, Ed. London, 1853.
Richard, Pablo. *Apocalipsis: reconstrucción de la esperanza.* San José, Costa Rica: Departamento Ecuménico de Investigaciones, 1994.
_____. *La lucha de los dioses: los ídolos de la opresión y la búsqueda del Dios liberador.* San José, Costa Rica: Editorial DEI, 1989.
Ratzinger, Joseph. "The Ecclesiology of Vatican II." Presentation to the Pastoral Congress of the Diocese of Aversa. 15 September, 2001 http://www.ewtn.com/library/CURIA/CDFECCV2.HTM.
Rivage-Seul, D. Michael, and Marguerite K Rivage-Seul. *A Kinder and Gentler Tyranny: Illusions of a New World Order.* Westport, Connecticut: Praeger, 1995.
Smith, Adam. *An Inquiry into the Nature and Causes of the Wealth of Nations.* Edinburgh: 1806.
Spielvogel, Jackson, J. *Western Civilization*, Vol. 2. 4th ed. Connecticut: Wadsworth Thomas Learning, 1999. 3 Vols.
Tamez, Elsa. *Contra Toda Condena.* San José, Costa Rica: Editorial DEI, 1991.
Tolle, Eckart *The Power of Now.* Novato, California: New World Library, 1999.
Weaver, Mary Jo, with David Brakke. *Introduction to Christianity.* Third Edition. Cincinnati: Wadsworth Publishing, 1998.
Jason Bivins Willard, Dallas *The Divine Conspiracy: Rediscovering Our Hidden Life in God.* New York: HarperCollins, 1998.
Wink, Walter *Engaging the Powers: Discernment and Resistance in a World of Domination.* Minneapolis: Fortress Press, 1992.
Zinn, Howard *A People's History of the United States.* New York: Harper Collins Publishers, 1995.

INDEX

A
Abel 63, 65, 66, 67, 187
Abortion i, viii, ix, 7, 8, 32, 33, 114, 149, 150, 151, 152, 153, 154, 155, 156, 157
Abraham 7, 41, 48, 53, 55, 61, 62, 63, 64, 69, 70, 71, 72, 97, 102, 169, 187
Acts of the Apostles 73, 162
Adam and Eve 39, 60, 61, 62, 63, 65, 66, 87, 91, 102
Afterlife 8, 25, 44, 114, 115
Aggiornamento x
Alexandria 84, 181
American i, ii, vii, viii, 3, 7, 10, 21, 22, 23, 24, 29, 31, 34, 35, 38, 86, 105, 111, 114, 116, 118, 131, 133, 134, 157, 160, 169, 174, 175, 180, 201, 202
    Empire 34, 116
    history 21, 175
    politics 31
    way of life 22, 24, 114, 160
Amos 37, 48, 49, 108
Antiochus IV Epiphanes 49, 88, 172
Apocalypse ix, 4, 14, 49, 85, 87, 88, 185, 186
    Apocalyptic writers 44, 53
Aquinas, Thomas 12, 13, 38, 57, 144
Archangel Michael 56, 92
Arians vi, vii
Armageddon 39, 85, 86
Athanasius 84, 181
Atlacan platoon 169
Augustine 12, 13, 38, 40, 41, 42, 55, 57, 61, 63, 65, 75, 97, 98, 171, 181
    Augustinian spirituality 180

B
Baal 53, 55, 62, 70, 102
Babylon 41, 48, 88, 93
Babylonians 48, 66, 77
Barth 12, 14
Base Communities 129
Batalla 133, 201
Battle of the Virgins 131, 169
Benedict XVI x, 117, 169
Berea College v, 7, 18, 30
Berea Interfaith Taskforce for Peace 179
Berrigan, Dan 5, 12, 15
Berrigan, Phil 26
Bible iii, viii, ix, 3, 4, 5, 8, 14, 16, 17, 18, 19, 21, 25, 27, 28, 30, 32, 35, 36, 37, 38, 39, 44, 51, 53, 54, 55, 58, 62, 67, 69, 70, 83, 86, 90, 108, 109, 111, 117, 128, 134, 139, 141, 143, 145, 147, 159, 160, 169, 186, 187, 188, 202
    Biblical mythology 59
    Biblical Study 12
    Biblical texts 20, 32, 33, 38, 43, 108, 118, 187
Bonhoeffer, Dietrich 7, 8, 12, 14, 15, 156, 177
Book of Revelation viii, 12, 25, 27, 28, 37, 39, 56, 57, 85, 86, 87, 88, 92, 93, 94, 185, 187
Borg, Marcus 74, 201
Bultmann, Rudolf 12, 14
Cain 55, 63, 65, 66, 67, 69, 87, 102, 103, 169, 187
Calvin, Jean 3, 12, 13, 19, 99, 100, 201
Camara, Dom Helder 169, 170, 171, 173
Capitalism 3, 16, 18, 20, 23, 24,

25, 26, 29, 32, 34, 102, 105, 115, 116, 142, 162, 189, 190, 191, 192, 193, 195, 196, 198, 199
Champagne glass 147, 170
Chardin, Teihard de 12, 15, 16
Chiapas 32, 33
Child sacrifice ix, 54, 62, 69, 70, 71, 72, 103
Chomsky, Noam 5, 107, 170, 201, 203
CIA 7, 106
Communism ix, 4, 18, 20, 23, 24, 27, 30, 31, 42, 83, 102, 112, 113, 127, 162, 189, 191, 192, 193, 199
Conservatives 18, 19, 20, 22, 23, 87, 115, 155, 156
Constantine 9, 10, 55, 60, 73, 74, 75, 76, 79, 80, 81, 84, 87, 97, 108, 177
Copernicus, Nicolaus 143
Council of Christian Colleges and Universities 105
Council of Nicea vi, 74
Cox, Harvey 14
Criswell, W.A. 26

D
Darwin, Charles 7, 139, 140, 141, 143, 147
Darwinian capitalism 16
Davidic Covenant 46, 47
Devil iii, iv, 53, 54, 55, 57, 58, 62, 63, 65, 78, 86, 90, 91, 92, 159, 178
Divino Aflante Spiritu 14
Duchrow, Ulrich 35, 201

E
Easwaran, Eknath 64, 75, 180, 181, 182, 183, 201
Edict of Milan 9, 60, 79
Empire i, ii, vii, viii, ix, 7, 8, 9, 10, 16, 17, 18, 24, 26, 29, 34, 37, 40, 43, 49, 53, 54, 55, 57, 58, 60, 61, 62, 63, 65, 66, 67, 69, 71, 72, 73, 74, 75, 76, 77, 78, 79, 80, 85, 86, 87, 88, 91, 92, 93, 94, 97, 98, 103, 108, 116, 117, 149, 168, 172, 173, 174, 175, 177, 178, 184, 185, 188, 202
  imperial law 61, 63, 74, 75, 76, 97, 98
  imperial powers 115
  imperial Rome 116
  imperial wars 69, 97
Imperialism viii, 15, 20, 21, 130, 182
Evolution i, viii, ix, 7, 8, 15, 21, 139, 140, 143, 145, 146, 148
  evolutionary theory 36, 139, 143, 145
  evolutionists 14

F
Fee, John G. 30
Feminists 135
First Great Awakening 29
Fourth Century 85
Freire, Paulo 179
Freud, Sigmund 163
Friedman, Milton 146, 197, 199, 201
Fundamentalism i, ii, viii, ix, 1, 4, 10, 18, 19, 26, 29, 30, 31, 34, 67, 85, 86, 113, 177, 178, 180, 188
  fundamentalist theology 39
  fundamentalists viii, 3, 7, 9, 10, 11, 17, 18, 19, 20, 21, 23, 24, 25, 30, 32, 33, 34, 35, 38, 39, 54, 58, 86, 87, 90, 94, 117, 139, 143, 145, 146, 160, 162, 187

G
Galeano, Eduardo 5, 201
Galilei, Galileo 143
Gandhi, Mohandas K, 177, 182, 186, 201
Gaudium et Spes 14

Genesis viii, 21, 37, 39, 42, 53, 59, 60, 61, 63, 64, 65, 66, 69, 86, 87, 89, 90, 92, 102, 114, 139, 141, 146, 147, 161, 185
Gnostics vi, 75, 83, 181
Goddess 63, 64, 65, 88, 89, 90, 94, 131, 135
    goddess tradition 64
Great Awakening 19, 29, 30, 31, 33, 34
Gutierrez, Gustavo 5, 199, 201

H

Hinkelammert, Franz 5, 12, 16, 53, 55, 56, 63, 64, 65, 71, 74, 75, 87, 89, 91, 92, 93, 94, 174, 178, 183, 198, 199, 201
Hitler, Adolf 6, 7, 15, 16, 66, 109, 111, 177
Human sacrifice 43, 50, 69, 70, 71

I

Idolatry 9, 11, 56, 93, 109, 116, 128, 161, 174
Inerrancy 3, 17, 19, 25, 33
Intelligent design 21
Introduction to Christianity viii, 9, 18, 203
Invisible Hand 83, 101, 163, 193

J

Jesus of Nazareth i, viii, 8, 10, 50, 80, 147, 172, 181
Jesus Seminar 82, 187
Jesus-Lucifer 57, 58
Job, Book of 4, 32, 56, 80, 107, 190, 193

K

Kennan, George 6, 7, 24
Kingdom of God 11, 33, 42, 74, 105, 160

L

Lady of Guadalupe 131, 135
Latin American Studies Program (LASP) 3, 105, 180

Liberation theology viii, ix, 3, 5, 16, 25, 26, 27, 28, 29, 31, 33, 34, 43, 82, 106, 111, 116, 127, 128, 168, 169, 177, 178, 179, 180, 188
Lucifer 53, 55, 56, 57, 58, 86

M

Market 18, 23, 32, 33, 69, 102, 115, 129, 140, 142, 189, 190, 191, 194, 195, 196, 197, 199
Marxism 20, 31, 189, 190, 195
Meditation 134, 179, 180, 182, 183, 184, 185
Mixed economy 20, 198
Moral relativism 21
Mosaic Law 44, 45, 46, 47, 49, 70, 108
Mystical traditions 182
    Mystics 64, 75, 133, 134, 182, 183, 185
Myth 4, 14, 37, 38, 42, 56, 59, 60, 61, 62, 65, 88, 139, 140, 145, 146, 152

N

Nag Hammadi vi, 181, 182
Nazi 15, 109
    Nazi imperialists 15
    Nazism 7
Nelson-Pallmeyer 37, 173, 174, 186, 187, 202
Nicea, Council of vi, 74
North American Free Trade Agreement (NAFTA) 131

O

Old time religion ix, 33, 34
Origen 57
Original sin viii, 38, 39, 42, 60, 63, 66, 67, 87, 90, 169, 171

P

Parables 74, 114
Patriarchal God 37, 65, 103
Peace Movement 12
Pilgrim People of God 11, 16

Q
Qumran v, vi
R
Reformation viii, 7, 12, 18, 19, 98, 99, 164, 202
Reign of God 15, 82, 124, 125, 159
Resurrection 5, 19, 20, 81, 162, 168
Revelation, Book of viii, 12, 25, 27, 28, 37, 39, 56, 57, 85, 86, 87, 88, 92, 93, 94, 185, 187
Richard, Pablo 55, 87, 112
Roe v Wade 149, 150, 152, 154, 155, 156
Roman Catholic Church ix, 18, 143, 153
S
Santa Fe Document 31
Satan iii, iv, 37, 50, 53, 55, 56, 57, 58, 61, 62, 67, 69, 72, 78, 82, 86, 90, 91, 92, 93, 94, 98, 101, 102, 103, 117, 147, 159, 174, 175, 185, 186, 203
    Satan's imperial order 56
    Satanic dragon 57
    Satanism 102, 148, 185
Second Great Awakening 29, 30
Serpent 63, 64, 65, 90, 141, 202
Sicarii 171
Simon the Zealot 171
Smith, Adam 24, 30, 101, 163, 193
Social Darwinism 18, 139, 140, 148
Social Gospel 28, 33, 105, 116
Socialism ix, 18, 20, 29, 32, 34, 189, 191, 192, 193, 198, 199
Society of St. Columban 4
Society of St. James 127
Sociology of knowledge 17
Solentiname 168
Solomon 37, 41, 47, 48, 63, 87, 90, 103
Son of Man 49, 77, 172
Spencer, Herbert 140, 141, 142, 143
Spielvogel, Jackson 9, 142, 203
Spiral of violence 169, 173
Structural adjustment 157, 199
Survival of the fittest 139, 140
Syllabus of Errors ix
T
Theodosius 61, 76
Theology of Liberation 16, 112, 117
Third Great Awakening 29, 30, 31, 33, 34
Third Reich 7
U
Understandings of Christianity v, vi, vii, viii, 9, 18, 109, 115
V
Vatican II 4, 9, 12, 14, 16, 203
Virgin birth 75
W
Wink, Walter 38, 56, 85, 100, 169, 170, 172, 174, 184, 185, 203
Women's Movement 12, 15
Y
Yahweh 38, 41, 44, 45, 46, 47, 50, 53, 55, 56, 57, 61, 62, 70, 71, 72, 82, 86, 88, 91, 97, 101, 111, 133, 169, 185
Z
Zealots 171, 172
Zeus 39, 40
Zinn, Howard 5, 203
Zwingli, Ulrich 19

www.ingramcontent.com/pod-product-compliance
Lightning Source LLC
Chambersburg PA
CBHW041629220426
43665CB00001B/1